RETHINKING THE CONCEPT OF WORLD

RETHINKING THE CONCEPT OF WORLD

TOWARDS TRANSCENDENTAL MULTIPLICITY

Rok Benčin

EDINBURGH
University Press

Edinburgh University Press is one of the leading university presses in the UK. We publish academic books and journals in our selected subject areas across the humanities and social sciences, combining cutting-edge scholarship with high editorial and production values to produce academic works of lasting importance. For more information visit our website: edinburghuniversitypress.com

We are committed to making research available to a wide audience and are pleased to be publishing an Open Access ebook edition of this title.

© Rok Benčin, 2024 under a Creative Commons Attribution-NonCommercial licence

Edinburgh University Press Ltd
13 Infirmary Street
Edinburgh EH1 1LT

First published in hardback by Edinburgh University Press 2024

Typeset in 10/13 Warnock Pro by
IDSUK (DataConnection) Ltd

A CIP record for this book is available from the British Library

ISBN 978 1 3995 0289 4 (hardback)
ISBN 978 1 3995 0290 0 (paperback)
ISBN 978 1 3995 0291 7 (webready PDF)
ISBN 978 1 3995 0292 4 (epub)

The right of Rok Benčin to be identified as the author of this work has been asserted in accordance with the Copyright, Designs and Patents Act 1988, and the Copyright and Related Rights Regulations 2003 (SI No. 2498).

Contents

	Acknowledgements	vi
	INTRODUCTION: THE PROSE OF WORLDS	1
1.	WORLD ACCORDING TO CONTEMPORARY PHILOSOPHY: OBSOLETE, LOST OR MULTIPLIED?	16
2.	THE LEIBNIZIAN TURN	50
3.	BETWEEN ONTOLOGICAL AND TRANSCENDENTAL MULTIPLICITY	69
4.	FROM COSMOPOLITANISM TO THE CONFLICT OF WORLDS	104
5.	WORLDS AS FICTIONS, ARTWORKS AS MONADIC OBJECTS	137
6.	PROUST'S WORLDS: FROM LOGIC TO PROSE	163
	CONCLUSION: THE MULTIPLICITY OF WORLDS AND INTER-WORLDLY PHENOMENA	195
	Bibliography	208
	Index	221

Acknowledgements

I owe immense gratitude to Jelica Šumič and Rado Riha for the opportunities and guidance from the early stages of my path as a researcher in philosophy. I would also like to thank my other former and current colleagues at the Institute of Philosophy of the Research Centre of the Slovenian Academy of Sciences and Arts for their tips and comments while planning this book project: Matej Ažman, Aleš Bunta, Aleš Erjavec, Marina Gržinić, Peter Klepec, Lea Kuhar, Boštjan Nedoh, Samo Tomšič, Tadej Troha, Matjaž Vesel, Alenka Zupančič.

I am grateful to Jean-Jacques Lecercle, Antonia Birnbaum, Dimitris Vardoulakis and Jernej Habjan, whose generosity and encouragement have helped this book come to life. I am also indebted to the conversations I have had with many other friends and colleagues about my research, including Natalija Majsova, Magdalena Germek, Jan Völker, Frank Ruda, Steven Corcoran, Cindy Zeiher, Helmut Draxler, Jacques Rancière, Ivana Momčilović, Leonardo Kovačević, Amelia Kraigher, Anna Montebugnoli, Anna Longo, Zdravko Kobe, Arthur Bradley, Ruth Ronen, Roland Végső, Marko Jenko, Amanda Holmes, Alexi Kukuljevic. I would also like to thank the students who discussed with me the ideas presented here at the Postgraduate School ZRC SAZU and during the seminars I held at Université Paris 8 and Universität für angewandte Kunst Wien.

I sincerely appreciate the support, patience and effort shown by Carol Macdonald, Sarah Foyle and others who have worked on the book at Edinburgh University Press.

This book would not exist without the loving support of my wife Darja, my son Vid, my parents Jožica and Branko and my in-laws Živa and Zoran.

This book is a result of the research programme P6-0014 'Conditions and Problems of Contemporary Philosophy', the research project J6-4623 'Conceptualizing the End: Its Temporality, Dialectics, and Affective Dimension' and the research project J6-3139 'Reconfiguring Borders in Philosophy, Politics, and Psychoanalysis', which are funded by the Slovenian Research and Innovation Agency, and the support of the ZRC SAZU development fund. It was written at the Research Centre of the Slovenian Academy of Sciences and Arts (ZRC SAZU), which has provided me with a great working environment over the years.

Earlier versions of some ideas for this book have appeared in my articles 'Rethinking Representation in Ontology and Aesthetics via Badiou and Rancière', *Theory, Culture & Society* 36, no. 5 (2019): 95–112; 'Worlds as Transcendental and Political Fictions', in 'The Concept of World in Contemporary Philosophy', ed. Rok Benčin, special issue, *Filozofski vestnik* 42, no. 2 (2021): 221–43; 'World at the Border: The Cosmopolitan Ideal between Loss and Multiplication', *Filozofski vestnik* 43, no. 3 (2023): 29–42; and my book *Okna brez monad: estetika od Heideggerja do Rancièra* (Ljubljana: ZRC Publishing House, 2015).

Introduction: The Prose of Worlds

WORLD IS A CONCEPT at once most evident and most evasive. While we often spontaneously refer to everything that surrounds us in external reality as constituting 'the world', when world is grasped as a philosophical concept, the existence of an object that would correspond to it becomes highly uncertain. This has nothing to do with doubting the existence of external reality, for in modern European philosophy world is not an ontological category. In the *Critique of Pure Reason*, Immanuel Kant relegated it to the sphere of transcendental illusions inscribed into reason by default. Defined as 'the sum total of all appearances', world is for Kant one of the ideas of pure reason to which nothing in experience can ever correspond.[1] It does not refer to appearances (nor the thing-in-itself), but to their totality, which cannot be empirically given. The problem is that reason cannot but rely on such ideas, even though they make it prone to the errors of metaphysics. Kant's treatment is emblematic of the way the concept of world emerged in modern philosophy as a problematic concept that seems in equal measure obsolete and indispensable. Its obsoleteness was perhaps best described by Alexandre Koyré in *From the Closed World to the Infinite Universe*, his canonic study of the modern scientific and philosophical revolution. He argued that this sixteenth- and seventeenth-century intellectual revolution, of which Kant is an heir, 'can be described roughly as bringing forth the destruction of the Cosmos, that is, the disappearance, from philosophically and scientifically valid concepts, of the conception of the world as a finite, closed, and hierarchically ordered whole'.[2] The infinite universe, theorised by modern science, ultimately prevailed over metaphysical cosmologies. In modern philosophy, however, the end of the concept of world is also its beginning. It is precisely when it can no longer be simply equated with external reality or a metaphysical totality that the concept of world becomes an intriguing philosophical problem.

The need to reconceptualise some sort of worldliness – not as an ontological category but as that which frames our grasp or experience of reality – persisted and resurfaced strongly in twentieth-century philosophy. Various strains of philosophy have reconceived the concept of world either as the horizon of existential experience (the phenomenological concept of world from Edmund Husserl and Martin Heidegger onwards) or as the totality of facts (as in Ludwig Wittgenstein).[3] Alongside such revitalisations of the concept, however, its problematic nature returned in new forms as well. On the one hand, the phenomenological concept of world soon came to be associated with loss. Being-in-the-world as what forms the authentic horizon of human existence is considered to be in a perpetual crisis, endangered by modern science and technology as well as social and political developments (the 'darkening' of the world in Heidegger, its 'alienation' in Hannah Arendt).[4] On the other hand, the concepts of world that still held to the idea of totality in a more factual way have again been subjected to the criticism that they are prolonging an obsolete metaphysical fantasy that is no longer relevant in the age of modern science (as pointed out by Jacques Lacan and, more recently in another context, Markus Gabriel).[5] Recent literature on the concept of world remains within this horizon: it seeks to further deconstruct the concept of world in order to declare the loss of world or the obsoleteness of the concept.[6]

In this book, however, I aim to challenge this well-established narrative by tracing another genealogy of the modern concept of world. Instead of clinging to the loss or obsoleteness of world as a totality, I explore its multiplication into many singular worlds. But before we come to a clearer picture of what this entails, we must first clarify what it does not. As with the concept of world itself, the multiplicity of worlds can mean several things. I will not be dealing here with the long and well-studied history of what could be called the cosmological multiplicity of worlds, which assumes the existence of other worlds or universes beside our own. This idea can be tracked from its origins in the atomist philosophies of ancient Greece via the decentralisation of the universe during the modern Scientific Revolution to present-day physical theories of the multiverse.[7] I will also (apart from brief excursuses) not be interested in the logical multiplicity of worlds, which has been theorised in great detail in analytic philosophy as the multiplicity of possible worlds.[8] This is again a perspective that assumes the logical possibility (or sometimes even parallel reality) of other worlds to ours. What I set out to explore in this book are not other worlds, but rather the multiplicity of our own world(s). The idea is that what we perceive as reality is structured as a multiplicity of divergent, yet coexisting worlds. I call this third figure of multiplicity of worlds transcendental. In this sense, worlds are singular transcendental frameworks that define the coordinates of the experience and understanding of ontological reality and thereby the parameters of sense, thought and action.

The assumption of the existence of a divergent multiplicity of worlds implies that there can be no common fundamental structure of existential experience, such as Husserl presumes with his notion of the life-world as that which is always-already given and intersubjective, or as Heidegger does with his notion of being-in-the-world as the fundamental structure of Dasein. For this reason, I look beyond the phenomenological approach to the concept of world. The transcendentalist approach I am suggesting also goes against the grain of the new realist trends in contemporary philosophy. Rather than doing away with Kantian 'correlationism',[9] this book embraces a 'hypercorrelationist' perspective that explores a divergent and overlapping multiplicity of transcendental frameworks. In this sense, it is based on post-Kantian and poststructuralist pluralisations and historicisations of the transcendental. Nevertheless, these multiple transcendentals are understood as framings of the same ontological multiplicity – the real groundless ground that can never be totally enframed within a world. Each world frames ontological multiplicity in a singular way, but can also be unframed and dissolved back into this multiplicity. The relation between ontological and transcendental multiplicity is thus characterised by both the excess of worlds over being (the overlapping multiplicity of transcendentals) and the excess of being over world(s) (there is no world as totality).

Genealogically, uncovering such a concept of world entails a return to G. W. Leibniz, for whom worlds are different possible configurations of an ontological multiplicity of substances (monads). I argue that Leibniz's multiplicity of possible worlds introduces a radically new perspective on the concept of world itself.[10] According to Leibniz, a world is not simply a totality, but rather a particular construction of a multitude of substances that is just one among many of its kind. The multiplicity of monads can be arranged in different ways so that it constitutes an infinite number of possible worlds. With Leibniz, we no longer speak of *the* world but of *a* world, this world or that world, thereby shifting focus from totality to multiplicity and singularity.

While Leibniz claimed that only the best of all possible worlds was ultimately created, some contemporary philosophers have argued instead that reality is actually constituted as a multiplicity of worlds. In the works of Alain Badiou, Gilles Deleuze, Jean-Luc Nancy, Jacques Rancière and others, we find different versions of the idea that the multiplicity of worlds is no longer merely possible but has become actual.[11] Such arguments are often made with explicit reference to Leibniz. The return to a Leibnizian concept of world as a transcendental arrangement of ontological multiplicity is accompanied by the claim that the divergences that Leibniz distributed among separate possible worlds now emerge in actuality as coexisting simultaneously. Throughout this book, I analyse different philosophical formulations of this hypothesis along with their political and aesthetical implications.

How does this undertaking relate to the contemporary experience of being-in-the-world? Towards the end of the twentieth century, the accelerated process of globalisation and the development of media technology anticipated an increasingly connected and cohesive experience of the world. The so-called end of history and of grand narratives suggested an image of the convergence and stabilisation of historical trajectories. The new millennium, however, brought about a series of global political, economic, environmental and health crises, which have shattered this image and drawn new lines of division across the globe. It now seems that the anticipated unified world has been both realised and lost. While such crises keep reminding us that the reality we live in is global, the growing political and ideological polarisation, coupled with increasing socio-economic inequalities, have dispelled any impression of a post-historical convergence.

On the one hand, as many philosophers and theorists have noted, the current global reality seems worldless, since it does not provide a shared sense of belonging to or orientation in a common world.[12] On the other hand, the erection of new walls and the rise of 'alternative facts' point to the realisation that we are not merely faced with differences between worldviews, but rather with the more radical phenomenon of people living in different worlds. What can the shared phenomenological life-world or world as the totality of facts possibly mean today, when the foundations of shared experience are no longer evident and the elementary framework of modern rationality is regularly contested? The world thus seems both lost and multiplied. While the idea of (re)constructing a unified world seems implausible from both perspectives, the urgency of producing a common frame of reference becomes all the more evident, since action in the face of global crises seems impossible without it.

In political thought, the concept of world is mostly associated with the tradition of cosmopolitanism, which grants the world the status of a political ideal. Yet, can there be a cosmopolitanism after the modern destruction of the cosmos? What happens to the cosmopolitan ideal when it is observed from the perspective of loss and multiplication of world? Even political thinkers such as Arendt, Nancy and Badiou, who are sceptical towards the notion of cosmopolitanism, suggest that politics is only possible if it constructs a new kind of common world against the impositions of capitalist globalisation.[13] The concept of world thus somehow finds a way to transform itself in order to regain its status as a political ideal.

The alternative to this can be found in Rancière's conception of politics as a conflict of worlds. Rancière understands worlds as shared structures determining the coordinates of perception and intelligibility that define a common reality and the way various subjects can take part therein. He sees political subjectivation primarily as a dissensual evocation of another world (of equality) within a given one (of inequality). For Rancière, worlds are irreconcilable framings of the common and therefore constitute an agonistic multiplicity rather than a common horizon of politics.[14] Following the transcendentalist approach to the concept of world, this book builds on the insight that instead of consolidating a perception of a natural or social totality, the series of economic, political and ecological crises that have occurred over the last decade have contributed to the impression that people live in different worlds, worlds divided by ideological polarisation and socioeconomic inequality. I argue that the role of the concept of world in emancipatory politics is not to remind us of a shared totality, but to help us grasp worlds in terms of their dissensual singularisation.

The multiplicity of worlds explored in this book also has an aesthetic dimension. Deleuze, for example, developed his thoughts on the bifurcation of worlds through constant reference to literature. On several occasions, Leibniz himself referred to works of fiction in order to give an indication of the structure of other possible worlds. It is thus no wonder that literary theory, especially narratology, found great use for the Leibnizian concept of possible worlds as a way of explaining the composition of fictional worlds in literature. In this book, however, I go in the opposite direction to understand how the philosophical understanding of the concept of world has ultimately come to be decisively shaped by the category of fiction. Instead of proposing a new realism, the book aims to show how fictional structures participate in the transcendental constitution of actual worlds. Again taking cue from Rancière and his notion of the distribution of the sensible, I understand fiction not as the invention of imaginary worlds but as the construction of spatio-temporal frameworks within which subjects, things and situations are perceived as belonging to a shared world – frameworks that not only exist in works of fiction, but also shape social and political realities.

I will also be interested in artworks as objects in which interferences between worlds can be detected, that is, the ways in which artworks enable us to trace another world within a given one. The Leibnizian conceptual framework will again come to the fore in this context when we will turn our attention to Theodor W. Adorno's description of artworks as monads.[15] For Adorno, artworks are like monads because in their aesthetic separation from the world, they express the social disharmony of their world, but also hint at the harmony of a world in which antagonisms would be resolved. By reassessing Adorno's aesthetics through the one proposed by Rancière, I will show how artworks reframe the transcendental coordinates of experience and understanding.

Such political and aesthetical considerations bring us back to the philosophical problems related to the notion of multiple actual worlds. The book closely examines contemporary philosophical conceptualisations of the multiple worlds paradigm – especially Deleuze's conception of the 'chaosmos', Badiou's notion of multiple transcendentals as objective logical structures and Rancière's understanding of worlds as fictional framings of sensible multiplicity – while also pointing to the problems and questions that they give rise to so as to outline new perspectives.

The first major problem is the relation between the fictional and the real. If world is not an ontological category and worlds as transcendental frameworks are structured as fictions, in what way does the real interfere in this divergent realm of multiplicity? I aim to show that the real does not necessarily have to be thought of only in terms of worldlessness but that it can also be approached through interruptions of the transcendental logic of a world, emergence of conflicts between worlds, the sudden presence of one world within another, points of incommensurability between different worlds and so on. The discontinuities in worldly experience of reality should not only be understood as signs of an underlying worldlessness, but also as points of bifurcation out of which new singular, yet shareable, worlds can emerge.

This brings me to the second major problem, namely, the relation between the singular and the universal. If the multiplicity of singular worlds presupposes no reference to a common universe that unites them, how can anything universal come to be? In other words, is there anything that makes a difference in the seemingly indifferent proliferation of worlds? Acknowledging that the world as a totality of facts or a horizon of commonly shared experience cannot be restored, but also recognising that the divergent proliferation of worlds may only amount to an indifferent multiplicity, I inquire whether the transcendentalist approach to the concept of world can nevertheless account for the emergence of singular worlds that are universal in the sense of being potentially addressed to anyone in an egalitarian way.

The existing approaches to the multiplicity of worlds either affirm its plurality (Nancy) and radical divergence (Deleuze) or else oppose it to trans-worldly universalities (truth procedures in Badiou). My approach is perhaps closest to Badiou's, but with an important shift. Universalities cannot be produced through a restoration of a single common world nor as trans-worldly (valid in all worlds), but as a construction of a new, singular transcendental. This book seeks to show how such new worlds can emerge at the points of political conflict and aesthetic interference between worlds.[16] To articulate universality with the multiplicity of worlds, it is thus necessary to examine divergent inter-worldly phenomena instead of jumping straight to trans-worldly truths.

In summary, I do not seek here to restore an ideal of worldliness, but to conceptually outline the prose of worlds, which consists of bifurcations of worlds, the conflicts and interferences between them, their beginnings and ends.

*

This book has two main goals. First, to provide a comparative overview of contemporary conceptualisations of the notion of world, and second, to provide a comprehensive examination of the idea that multiple actual worlds exist. Despite the fact that there is a significant number of studies on the concept of world in the work of individual authors and in particular philosophical traditions, systematic examinations and comparative readings of different approaches in contemporary philosophy are rare. Existing literature that provides such an overview mostly focuses on loss or obsoleteness of world, leaving the multiple-worlds perspective on the sidelines.[17] On the other hand, studies on the multiplicity of worlds most often focus on cosmological or logical multiplicity of worlds.[18] Compared to this, what I call the transcendental multiplicity of worlds is understudied.

My attempt at a comparative study of contemporary approaches to the concept of world is presented in Chapter 1. The chapter gives a mapping of various conceptualisations of the notion of world in contemporary (mostly 'continental') philosophy. Instead of studying different concepts of world within various predefined theoretical brackets (such as phenomenology, poststructuralism, deconstruction and so on), I propose a categorisation of the different ways in which contemporary philosophy reacts to the modern destruction of the cosmos. I thus identify three tendencies of defining the destiny of the concept of world within modernity.

1. The first tendency rejects the world as an obsolete metaphysical category that is no longer viable in the age of modern science. I analyse two versions of this hypothesis. The first is the psychoanalytical one, formulated by Lacan, according to which the concept of world is a philosophical fantasy. Lacan of course remains influential for a number of contemporary philosophers such as Slavoj Žižek and Badiou. The other version is found in the new realist trends in philosophy. I focus on Gabriel's thesis that the world does not exist.
2. The second tendency diagnoses the loss of world as a horizon of common existential (and often also political) experience. Here, I

mostly analyse the concept of world as developed in phenomenology. I discuss Husserl, Heidegger, Nancy and Jacques Derrida. I also take into account the versions of this hypothesis in Arendt, Badiou and Deleuze.
3. The third tendency detects a multiplication of coexisting actual worlds. I examine a phenomenological version of this hypothesis in Nancy before focusing on Badiou, Deleuze and Rancière.

Through a comparative analysis, I clarify what defines the concept of world as it appears within each of these three tendencies. It should be noted, however, that several tendencies can often be found to coexist within the work of one and the same philosopher (for instance, Deleuze, Badiou, Nancy and Derrida all declare the loss of world, its obsoleteness and its divergent proliferation at some point). I conclude by laying out the rationale behind choosing the third tendency as the primary subject of this book.

In Chapter 2, I focus on the origins of what I call the transcendental multiplicity of worlds in Leibniz. I argue that the vast scholarly interest in Leibniz's presentation of God's choice to create the best possible world somewhat overshadowed Leibniz's revolutionary way of thinking the concept of world in terms of singularity and multiplicity. Leibniz was not interested in the contemporary debate on multiple worlds in the cosmological sense, since other planets or universes merely add to the sum of creation, without truly producing another world altogether. Leibniz rather introduces the question of world as a question of the relation between an ontological multiplicity (substances or monads) and the singular way in which it is arranged so as to form a world (the pre-established harmony, specific to a particular world). The various possible worlds existing in God's mind are unique infinite sets of substances and harmonic arrangements of these sets that fill the times and spaces of the universes they construct in completely different manners. Apart from the modal multiplicity of possible worlds, Leibniz also presents a double perspectivist multiplicity. He often claims that the unique ways in which individual monads as 'worlds apart' reflect or express the world they are part of entail a multiplication of the world itself. A similar multiplication also takes place in relation to material reality, depending on the level at which it is observed: in the smallest portion of matter, Leibniz claims, whole worlds of creatures lurk.

I conclude the chapter by discussing the role Leibniz has in contemporary conceptualisations of world on the examples of Deleuze and Badiou. Both contemporary philosophers take Leibniz as a point of departure for their own endeavours to think the multiplicity of worlds in relation to ontological and transcendental multiplicity. Adopting a Leibnizian concept of world seems crucial for developing a transcendentalist approach to the multiplicity of worlds. For both philosophers, however, returning to Leibniz also entails subverting his distinction between the multiplicity of possible worlds and the one and only actual world. For both thinkers, modernity marks the passage of multiple worlds from possibility to actuality.

In Chapter 3, I examine in detail the transcendental multiplicity of worlds as it is theorised by Deleuze and Badiou in relation to their understandings of ontological multiplicity. Despite their common Leibnizian framing of the problem, their solutions differ greatly. First, we take a closer look at their respective conceptions of multiplicity at the ontological level and how they both relate it to a figure of oneness (the univocity of being in Deleuze and the count-as-one in Badiou) and to events. We will see that in Deleuze the one does not exist outside of its production of multiplicity (events), while for Badiou multiplicity does not exist outside of the production of oneness (which is occasionally interrupted by events).

The second issue is their understandings of the relation between ontological and transcendental multiplicity. In the case of Deleuze, ontological multiplicity is itself a virtual transcendental field in which worlds are formed as actualisations of series of singularities. I propose to call this process transcendental folding. In the case of Badiou, however, both levels are more clearly separated. Worlds are formed by transcendental structures imposed upon ontological multiplicity. I propose to call this process transcendental framing.

Clearly, this also entails major differences in how the multiplicity of worlds itself is envisioned by both thinkers. According to Deleuze, Leibniz's error was not only to reduce the multiplicity of worlds to the realm of possibility but also to impose clear boundaries between different worlds. With the coexistence of 'incompossibilities', which for Leibniz could never be parts of the same world, the universe can be described as a 'chaosmos', uniting the cosmic element of world-making with the chaotic element of unbound ontological singularities. For Badiou, on the contrary, any unification of worlds, even in a chaosmos, would amount to another figure of the one, which philosophy should leave behind. Badiou conceives the multiplicity of worlds as strictly distinct, although overlapping, in the sense that different transcendentals can share the same ontological multiples. As we will see, however, this nevertheless introduces a chaotic element in Badiou, since it opens the door for a multiple to coexist in a 'virtually unlimited number of worlds'.[19] I argue that Badiou fails to take this surplus of worlds into serious consideration in his elaboration of truth procedures.

Chapter 4 examines the role the concept of world has had in modern political thought. Can the multiplicity of worlds as transcendental fictions describe political realities in any significant way? The chapter begins with Kant's struggle with the metaphysical assumptions of cosmopolitanism. Kant defines cosmopolitanism as a perspective upon history that presupposes humanity's gradual progress towards a cosmopolitan condition in which the peoples of the earth enter a global federation, which henceforth guarantees peace and prosperity. This perspective, however, requires a faith in natural providence, which cannot be easily reconciled with critical philosophy. Kant admits that the world as a political ideal projected upon history might be nothing more than a fiction in the head of a philosopher wishing to rewrite history as a story inevitably moving toward a reasonable end. Yet, as we will see, this fiction has a particular rationality that Kant struggles with throughout his political writings.

We then take the opposite road, one that sees cosmopolitan unification of the world not as an ideal, but as an undesirable reality. The globalised social reality brought about by modern science, technology and the global capitalist market actually brought about the loss of world as a common horizon of intersubjective coexistence and thereby the basic condition of political life in any meaningful sense. I analyse Arendt's and Nancy's respective versions of this view, which distances the world as a political ideal from cosmopolitan unification.

Finally, I analyse Rancière's description of politics as a conflict of worlds. His conception of shared frameworks of perception and intelligibility as social fictions that connect subjects, objects and events by producing a sense of a common reality situates the transcendental multiplicity of worlds in the political realm. Any construction of a common world entails a division, which leaves no space for worldliness as a political ideal. For Rancière, the political question is not how to reconstruct a common sense of worldliness, but how reconfigurations of what is considered to be common emerge in spatial and temporal intervals between worlds. Political subjectivation makes apparent the presence of several worlds in one, not to revel in their plurality, but to expose and oppose the inegalitarian structures that govern the distribution of social bodies and capacities. Following Rancière, my wager is that there is little political use in trying to reconstruct a consensual common world, either through cosmopolitan unity or through a worldly plurality. The task of emancipatory politics is rather to open up singular worlds that dissensually reframe what is perceived as common. The hypothesis I pursue is that the shared world required by emancipatory politics should itself be considered as a collective construction of a singular, yet universally addressed world.

In Chapter 5, I discuss the aesthetic dimension of the multiplicity of worlds. I first address the use of the concept of possible worlds in literary theory and the differences between the constructions of possible worlds in logics and fictional worlds in literature. I argue that this distinction sheds additional light on Deleuze's and Badiou's different understandings of multiple actual worlds: while the former's worlds are structured as possible worlds, the latter's are structured as fictional worlds. I discuss the implications of this fictional structure for Badiou's insistence on the objectivity of transcendental structures and for the transcendental account of the multiplicity of worlds more generally.

I then go on to discuss the aesthetic interference between worlds through artworks. Based on the monadological aspects of Adorno's aesthetic theory and Rancière's notion of the aesthetic regime of art, I develop an understanding of artworks as monadic objects, which seem separated from the surrounding world because what is inscribed behind their closure is the transcendental of another world. Their windowless monadic nature paradoxically enables artworks to become windows to other worlds, thereby reconfiguring the limits of possible experience.

The final chapter presents a reading of Marcel Proust's *In Search of Lost Time* as a model for thinking the transcendental multiplicity of worlds – a prose work with which to demonstrate the prose of worlds. Reading Proust's novel through the prism of interferences between multiple worlds rather than through temporal discontinuities, I show how Proust's own conception of artistic cosmogony can help us resolve some of the problems of the transcendental conception of the multiplicity of worlds developed throughout the book. I thereby concretise the claims made in Chapter 5 on aesthetics (I demonstrate the functioning of monadic objects in Proust's narrative), but also return to Chapter 3 and the problems of Badiou's understanding of the multiplicity of worlds. Even though Badiou is not a reader of Proust in any significant way, I show how Proust's 'prose of worlds' not only illustrates but supplements Badiou's 'logics of worlds'. I first explore how the main concepts of Badiou's logics (the transcendental, object, relation) can be used to describe the structure of Proustian worlds (the transcendental of the salon, the constitution of the love object, the relations between sensible impressions). Then, I show how the novel itself functions as a truth procedure precisely in the sense of developing a supplementary world based on the encountered 'monadic' objectivations of interferences between multiple worlds.

The Conclusion ties together some loose threads from the individual chapters. I present in more detail the notion of inter-worldly phenomena in which the conflicts and interferences between worlds are objectivised. When the existence of ontological multiples as an object within one world becomes incompossible with their existence as an object in another, a conflict of worlds may arise. I call such objects contested objects. In other instances, objects appear within one world as though they would be moulded according to an alien transcendental, setting off an interference between worlds. I call such objects monadic objects. This lets me return once again to the philosophical, political and aesthetical stakes of the book in order to show more comprehensively what it means to live in a multiplicity of worlds.

Notes

1. Immanuel Kant, *Critique of Pure Reason*, trans. Paul Guyer (Cambridge: Cambridge University Press, 1998), 406 (A 334/B 391).
2. Alexandre Koyré, *From the Closed World to the Infinite Universe* (Baltimore: Johns Hopkins University Press, 1957), 2.
3. I return to Husserl and Heidegger in more detail in the second section of Chapter 1. As for Wittgenstein, I am referring here to the proposition 1.1 of the *Tractatus*: 'The world is the totality of facts, not of things.' *Tractatus Logico-Philosophicus*, trans. D. F. Pears and B. F. McGuinness (London: Routledge, 2002), 5.
4. Martin Heidegger, *Introduction to Metaphysics*, trans. Gregory Fried and Richard Polt (New Haven: Yale University Press, 2014), 29; Hannah Arendt, *The Human Condition* (Chicago: University of Chicago Press, 1958), 248–57.

5. I discuss Lacan's and Gabriel's views in the first section of Chapter 1.
6. Among the monographic studies closest to my efforts in this book due to their genealogical and comparative approaches, Sean Gaston's *The Concept of World from Kant to Derrida* (London: Rowman & Littlefield, 2013) and Roland Végső's *Worldlessness After Heidegger* (Edinburgh: Edinburgh University Press, 2020) stand out. Gaston's detailed study on the concept of world in Kant, Hegel, Husserl, Heidegger and Derrida is a remarkable effort, yet his focus on the dissolution of the world as a totality through phenomenology and deconstruction leaves aside the problem of the multiplicity of worlds. Neither Leibniz nor Deleuze, Badiou or Rancière feature in the book in any meaningful capacity. My project thus presents a significantly different genealogy of the modern concept of world and emphasises other contemporary lines of thought. Végső's book provides a detailed reading of the concept of world in Heidegger, Arendt, Derrida, Freudian and Lacanian psychoanalysis and Badiou from the perspective of worldlessness. Végső offers an affirmative account of worldlessness and thus strongly aligns with the tendency to renounce the concept of world. By emphasising the multiplicity of worlds, my own attempt provides different readings of the authors also assessed by Végső.
7. See Steven J. Dick, *Plurality of Worlds: The Origins of the Extraterrestrial Life Debate from Democritus to Kant* (Cambridge: Cambridge University Press, 1982), and Mary-Jane Rubenstein, *Worlds Without End: The Many Lives of the Multiverse* (New York: Columbia University Press, 2014).
8. For an overview, see John Divers, *Possible Worlds* (London: Routledge, 2002).
9. 'Correlationism' is a term coined by Quentin Meillassoux to describe post-Kantian philosophy, which is dominated by the idea that we cannot access objectivity outside of its correlation to subjectivity. All we can ever hope to know is the correlation between thinking and being and never being on its own. The critique of correlationism became hugely influential for the new realist currents in philosophy. See Quentin Meillassoux, *After Finitude: An Essay on the Necessity of Contingency*, trans. Ray Brassier (London: Continuum, 2008).
10. I return to Leibniz in detail in Chapter 2.
11. I discuss all these authors in detail throughout the book. Although I predominantly deal here with the so-called continental philosophy, this hypothesis can also be found in analytic philosophy, especially in the work of Nelson Goodman. See in particular Goodman's *Ways of Worldmaking* (Indianapolis: Hackett, 1978).
12. I return to this hypothesis in Chapters 1 and 4.
13. See Chapter 4.
14. I discuss Rancière's concept of world in Chapters 1 and 4.
15. I return to Adorno's aesthetics in Chapter 5.

16. Apart from political transformations and artistic transfigurations, scientific breakthroughs and technological innovations could also be studied in this regard but fall out of the scope of the present book. The modern Scientific Revolution itself discarded one concept of world (the closed world) and replaced it with another (the infinite universe, to use Koyré's phrase), therefore replacing the totality of the cosmos with a particular singularisation of world on the basis of the mathematisation of nature.
17. See in particular Gaston's and Végső's books that I briefly described in note 6 above. Other recent comparative monographs on the concept of world include Paul Clavier, *Le concept du monde* (Paris: PUF, 2000), Jean-Clet Martin, *Plurivers. Essai sur la fin du monde* (Paris: PUF, 2010), and Julien Rabachou, *Qu'est-ce qu'un monde?* (Paris: Vrin, 2016). I would also like to draw the reader's attention to 'The Concept of World in Contemporary Philosophy', a special international issue of the journal *Filozofski vestnik* that I recently edited, which includes several significant contributions that have influenced my writing in this book. See 'The Concept of World in Contemporary Philosophy', ed. Rok Benčin, special issue, *Filozofski vestnik* 42, no. 2 (2021), https://ojs.zrc-sazu.si/filozofski-vestnik/issue/view/849.
18. See notes 7 and 8 in this chapter.
19. Alain Badiou, *Logics of Worlds: Being and Event, 2*, trans. Alberto Toscano (London: Continuum, 2009), 114.

| 1   World According to Contemporary Philosophy: Obsolete, Lost or Multiplied?

A BROAD COMPARATIVE SURVEY of different conceptualisations of the notion of world in contemporary philosophy looks like a daunting task. The problem is not only in the sheer number of approaches and authors to be considered but primarily in finding a perspective that allows for a comparison. Philosophical terminology is not fixed but dependent on conceptual innovation that makes comparisons problematic. What a phenomenological philosopher calls 'world' might be a completely different matter than what goes under that word in the work of an analytic philosopher. Finding conceptual common ground between different approaches and individual authors might be impossible.

Instead of examining different definitions of the concept of world as they appear in different philosophical traditions and theoretical orientations in the hope that they turn out to be comparable, my approach in this chapter is to first find a common topic of discussion in which the concept of world plays a crucial role. The common topic I focus on is the discussion on what happens to 'world' (whatever its definition might be) in modernity. For many philosophers, modernity seems to introduce a radical break that transforms what is to be thought of as world. As we have seen in the Introduction, this modern event was most succinctly described by Alexandre Koyré as the destruction of the cosmos.[1] What destiny, so to speak, befalls what various philosophers call world after it can no longer be thought of as a cosmic totality? Therefore, instead of directly observing how the concept of world is defined in phenomenology, poststructuralism, analytic philosophy, postcolonial studies and so forth, I propose a comparison based on different destinies of the concept of world in modernity. Renouncing the ambition of being exhaustive in my survey, I prefer to focus on a limited number of thinkers that are representative of the various destinies I have identified. I leave out those conceptualisations of world in which the question I am focusing on does not feature as a relevant topic of discussion.

In what follows, I propose a categorisation of three tendencies according to which contemporary philosophy has reacted to the modern destruction of the cosmos:

1. The first tendency generalises Koyré's assertion by rejecting the concept of world as an obsolete metaphysical category that is no longer viable in the modern age. It argues that the concept of world should be simply abandoned, since it does not accurately describe the nature of reality.
2. The second tendency claims that the modern dissolution of the cosmos also brought forth the loss of world as a horizon of commonly shared experience and reflects on the possibility of rebuilding it. World is something that we are on the verge of losing and it is the task of philosophy to reflect on how to renew it.
3. The third tendency argues that the dissolution of the cosmic totality resulted in the multiplication of worlds. The modern condition is one of navigating a divergent multiplicity of coexisting worlds, which we are simultaneously inhabiting.

It should be noted that the distinction between these tendencies can only be made analytically. In reality, they are deeply intertwined and often coexist within the work of one and the same philosopher. Some philosophers, as we shall see, feature under all three categories.

World as Obsolete

From the point of view of the first tendency, world should no longer be considered a valid philosophical concept. It belongs to the metaphysical arsenal of classical philosophy and has no place in modern thought. Retaining the concept of world thus amounts to an outdated form of thinking. Renouncing the concept of world, however, does not entail an anti-realist position. The obsoleteness of the concept of world does not mean that we should question the existence of reality surrounding us. In fact, the necessity to dispose of the concept of world is dictated by a realist imperative. It is modern science that shows us that the concept of world does not adequately describe the nature of reality. The concept of world is thus made obsolete by a certain understanding of what is more real than the world. Different versions of this thesis are distinguished by how they understand the real in question and, most importantly for us, what kind of concept of world this real makes obsolete. We will take a closer look at two versions of this tendency, one articulated in psychoanalytic theory and the other in the new realist currents of philosophy.

In direct reference to the modern Scientific Revolution, the French psychoanalyst Jacques Lacan influentially argued that the concept of world is nothing but a philosophical fantasy. Modern science, according to Lacan, shows that the nature of physical reality does not constitute what philosophers have called world: 'If we leave behind philosophical discourse, nothing is less certain than the existence of a world.'[2] Lacan specifically mentions the discovery of subatomic particles ('quarks') as evidence of the fundamental insufficiency of the philosophical concept of world.[3]

In his critique of philosophy, Lacan follows Sigmund Freud's critical remarks on the worldview (*Weltanschauung*). For Freud, the worldview is 'an intellectual construction which solves all the problems of our existence uniformly on the basis of one overriding hypothesis'.[4] Freud considers philosophy to be very close to such constructions 'by clinging to the illusion of being able to present a picture of the universe which is without gaps and is coherent'.[5] In *Seminar XX*, Lacan takes a step further and identifies the worldview of philosophy with ontology itself.[6] Philosophy tends to construct its ontological theories so as to present reality as a complete whole without gaps. The concept of world that we should now recognise as obsolete is thus clearly defined:

> For quite some time it seemed natural for a world to be constituted whose correlate, beyond it, was being itself, being taken as eternal. This world conceived of as the whole (*tout*), with what this word implies by way of limitation, regardless of the openness we grant it, remains a conception – a serendipitous term here – a view, gaze, or imaginary hold.[7]

The term 'conception' corresponds here to worldview, which in French translates to *'conception du monde'*. The world as a whole, supported by eternal being, is thus the primary referent of philosophical ontology. This image of the world as a whole presupposes an observer, a human subject that can grasp this totality.

But what exactly is it in modern science for Lacan that takes us away from the worldview of philosophy? In *Seminar XX*, Lacan focuses on how the modern Scientific Revolution questioned the position of the centre, which was essential to pre-modern cosmologies. Lacan claims that the main turning point in this regard was wrongly attributed to Copernic, who replaced the body in the centre (the earth for the sun) but kept the position of the centre occupied. It was Kepler who emptied the centre by showing that the planets move in ellipses and paved the way for the discovery of the gravitational law, which replaced the image of turning around the centre with the idea of falling through space.[8]

But there is something even more essential behind all of this, namely the mathematisation of nature, which destabilises the relation between the signifier and the signified. The prevalence of the mathematical letter and the signifier as such is what alienates scientific knowledge from lived experience and therefore from what makes sense to human observers. The primacy of the signifier is what makes psychoanalysis – but also modern literature with Joyce – aligned with modern science.[9] Samo Tomšič comments that through 'the combination of formalisation and experimentation', modern science succeeded 'in actualising the symbolic in the real'.[10] The symbolic operations of modern science dismiss cosmic imaginaries by demonstrating that 'the real resists totalisation'.[11]

Through science and of course the psychoanalytic experience itself, the concept of the real assumes a central role in Lacan's later thought. In 1974, Lacan addressed the École freudienne de Paris with a paper that reiterated the positions developed in *Seminar XX*, which had concluded a year earlier, but added some interesting details. Again, Lacan references physics, both quantum and wave-particle theories, to underline his main point: 'The real is not the world.'[12] Lacan mentions set theory as further evidence against the notion of worldly totality (as Alain Badiou also will): 'There is no such thing as *all elements*, there are only sets to be determined in each case.'[13] Even more interestingly for us, Lacan presents here his standard definitions of the real as the impossible, which he contrasts with Leibniz's understanding of compossibility.[14] That the world is composed only of things that can be possible together – through what Leibniz called a pre-established harmony – is a cornerstone of philosophical idealism, which precisely misses the real as the impossible. For Lacan, the formalisation operated by modern science is aimed precisely at this real at the expense of any harmonious wholeness implied by the notion of world. Even if the full formalisation of the real is ultimately impossible, it is through the impasses of formalisation itself that science establishes its relation to the real.

Philosophers influenced by Lacan have taken up his critique of philosophy in order to develop new approaches to ontology starting from the concept of the real. Most notably, Slavoj Žižek stated that 'the only consistent materialist position is that the world does not exist – in the Kantian sense of the term, as a self-enclosed whole'.[15] The nonexistence of the world in this case is not an expression of a radically scepticist or solipsistic position, but an ontological claim based on the assumption that the real is itself incomplete and not reducible to any image of a cosmic whole. If the world does not exist, it is because of 'the ontological incompleteness of reality' itself.[16] Or, as Adrian Johnston summarised Žižek's position, 'the ultimate *Grund* hypothesized at the level of ontology should be envisioned as a lone inconsistent immanence riddled with gaps and deprived of [. . .] wholeness'.[17]

Before developing his own conception of an infinite multiplicity of worlds, even Badiou subscribed to a Lacanian negation of the concept of world. Ten years before *Logics of Worlds*, Badiou asserted that

> philosophy begins by destroying the very concept of the world; it knows, as does Lacan, that there only is a fantasy of the world, and that it is only in its defection, or its defeat, that one can subtractively think some real.[18]

For Badiou, as well as for Lacan, the problem with the concept of world at that time was that it implies an ontological wholeness (to which Badiou's set-theoretical ontology objects, as we will see in Chapter 3), which prohibits an encounter with the impossible (the real for Lacan, an event for Badiou).

Another kind of rejecting the concept of world as obsolete has more recently emerged within the so-called new (or speculative) realist movement in philosophy, most notably in the work of Levi R. Bryant, Markus Gabriel and Roland Végső. We will take a closer look at Gabriel, who attempts to develop a new philosophy explicitly based on the fact that the world does not exist.[19] The world in question here is 'any kind of unrestricted or overall totality, be it the totality of existence, the totality of what there is, the totality of objects, the whole of beings, or the totality of facts or states of affairs'.[20] The non-existence of such a totality does not imply that everything we see is just an illusion; on the contrary, Gabriel is developing a realist philosophy in which the existence of all sorts of objects as independent of our consciousness is in no doubt. If the world does not exist, it is because there is no total domain in which all existence can be placed and no universal principle that would ultimately explain the existence of everything.[21]

The reasoning Gabriel gives in support of this hypothesis loosely draws on the problems of 'the combination of totality and self-containment' developed in set theory and mathematics, according to which the very idea of a set of all sets is paradoxical.[22] The main argument, however, is based on the ontology Gabriel himself develops. He equates existence with appearance, whereby the question is where, on what background, or in what framework, do objects appear. According to Gabriel, something exists if it appears in a 'field of sense'.[23] Fields of sense are objective structures (like magnetic or electric fields) that give a certain appearance to things. For example, unicorns do not exist in the field of sense defined by the natural environment of the planet Earth, but do exist in stories, comic books, colouring books, children's imagination and so on. Clearly, the same thing can appear in several fields: 'Depending on the field of sense, the same thing is a hand, a whirl of atoms, a work of art, or a tool.'[24]

Fields of sense are essentially plural. There is no ultimate, universal field of sense that would include all others and which we could call the world. This does not, however, lead to relativism regarding truth: the truth regarding the existence or non-existence of unicorns can be objectively determined, providing that the field of sense that frames the question is specified. Given that existence equals appearance, unicorns are no less real than horses, but relative to the field of sense in which they appear. A hand is no less real as a tool for a writer than as a whirl of atoms for a physicist, again depending on the given field of sense. Nevertheless, Gabriel insists that fields of sense are not dependent on subjective perspectives or constructions, but exist as objective structures, which determine what things really are in themselves: 'Fields are not horizons or perspectives; they are not epistemological entities or objects introduced to explain how we can know how things are. They are an essential part of how things are in that without fields, nothing could exist.'[25] This is what grounds Gabriel's peculiar realism, in which all appearances are real in some (field of) sense.

Depending on the kind of objects we want to focus on, we can quickly imagine an indefinite number of fields to which these objects could belong. According to Gabriel, a field of sense only exists if it itself appears within another field of sense, which makes the proliferation of fields impossible to contain within a total world.[26] As we have seen, Gabriel insists that the non-existence of the world does not imply an epistemological relativism since it is in principle objectively determinable what does or does not belong to a particular field. It does, however, imply a multiplication of worlds. Gabriel states that his ontology 'boils down to the claim that, although the world does not exist, there do exist infinitely many worlds, which in part overlap but are also partly independent of one another'.[27] Gabriel even admits that his concept of a field of sense is very close to Badiou's concept of world from *Logics of Worlds*.[28] The reason why the term 'field of sense' is nevertheless given advantage over 'world' is that 'the term "world" is deceptive, as it always suggests some kind of closed totality'.[29] Since it is too closely tied to its obsolete meaning, Gabriel thus opts to introduce a new concept rather than to reconceptualise the notion of world.

Although Gabriel defends a strictly realist perspective, his arguments for the non-existence of the world are less dependent on modern science than Lacan's. For Gabriel, in fact, natural sciences only establish one particular field of sense among many others. His version of realism is based precisely on not allowing any notion of the real that would be distinct from appearances. There is no need to think the real as opposed to the reality of appearances, since any appearance is already a part of (the non-totalisable) reality. For Lacanian psychoanalysis, on the other hand, the real is not only what prevents the totalisation of world but also what can potentially disturb any field of sense. Gabriel's position does not seem to allow for something like the Lacanian analytical distinction between the real, the symbolic and the imaginary.

Despite very different attitudes towards the real that makes the concept of world obsolete, both strands of thought, the Lacanian and the new realist one, share the basic definition of world as a unified, all-encompassing totality. It is primarily in this sense, they claim, that the concept of world should be abandoned. In this book, I will not disagree with this. I will not attempt to reinstate the notion of world as totality; I will, however, claim that the disintegration of metaphysical frameworks of totality does not entail the renunciation of the notion of world *tout court*, but rather the need for its thoroughgoing reconceptualisation. While acknowledging that the world as a proper totality cannot be restored, I will examine – on a trail leading from Leibniz to Badiou – a concept of world as singular rather than total.

As we will see later on, a renewed concept of world in this sense can only be thought in the plural. Curiously, not only Gabriel but also Bryant and Végső see in Badiou's understanding of multiple worlds a good approximation to their own understandings of a worldless ontological landscape.[30] We might ask ourselves why we need to think in terms of worldlessness or invent new terms for something that can be perfectly well described as a world. This indicates the point of proximity between the first (world as obsolete) and the third (world as multiplied) tendencies in thinking world in contemporary philosophy and shows that they are not entirely mutually exclusive. The question I consider crucial in this regard, however, is not only whether a concept of world can be thought that would no longer be based on totality, but whether it is possible to 'think some real' – to use Badiou's phrase – within the realm of the multiplicity of worlds. The point is not only to spread existence over a plurality of worlds, but to see in what way this plurality is riddled by instances of the real (a consideration that is often, paradoxically, missing from new realist philosophies).

World as Lost

The concept of world as a totality may not be a suitable means of describing the nature of reality, but this is precisely why some have considered it urgent to develop the concept anew on different grounds and use it for something that eludes the scientific grasp, namely the nature of human experience. It could be argued that this is the reason for the concept's key role in phenomenology. From Edmund Husserl's surrounding world and Martin Heidegger's being-in-the-world onwards, the concept of world has been used in phenomenology to describe an essential structure of primarily individual experience that precedes the constitution of scientific knowledge and cannot be adequately grasped by it. On the contrary, it is on the basis of the world constituted by this primary experience that the meaning of the scientific attitude towards natural reality can be understood and evaluated. Yet, the scientific destruction of the cosmos still haunts this reconceptualised notion of world. The advancement of modern science and technology threatens the world-building capacity of human beings and thereby their authentic relation to what surrounds them.

Husserl develops his idea of the surrounding world in relation to the distinction between the naturalistic and the personalistic attitudes. Within the naturalistic attitude, we perceive the world as 'the totality of "Objective" physical nature', which determines our perception of particular things as natural objects – our bodies, psyches and social interactions included.[31] Husserl's question here is not – as it is for Lacan or Gabriel – whether objective reality constitutes a totality. Rather, he seeks to contrast the naturalistic attitude to a phenomenologically more original one, which the naturalistic attitude presupposes but ultimately obscures. The world that we actually live in and experience is not the objective world of natural objects but a 'surrounding world' of each individual person, which forms the 'horizon of his existence'.[32] The surrounding world is a world of lived experience in which things are intuitively given to us through action, use, thought, value and affection. It 'is not a world "in itself" but is rather a world "for me"'.[33]

For Husserl, the surrounding world is not a fixed totality but a constantly evolving horizon open to change and expansion. It is the framework within which we engage with objects and encounter other persons. We immediately recognise other people as subjects in their own right and centres of their own surrounding worlds. Through such mutual comprehension, individual worlds merge within a common, intersubjective one: 'We could not be persons for others if a common surrounding world did not stand there for us in a community, in an intentional linkage of our lives.'[34] Within this intersubjective sphere, linked together by communication, social objects like marriage or states arise. The common surrounding world of intersubjective interaction and social objects constitutes the shared world of spirit.

In his late work, the earlier opposition Husserl identified between the naturalistic attitude and the surrounding world of lived experience will take on an even more fundamental and urgent proportion. The prevalence of the naturalistic attitude, Husserl argues, has brought European society to a state of crisis. In the mid-1930s, Husserl called for a renewal of proper philosophical rationalism against its naturalistic degradation that contributed to the European descent into barbarity.[35] The general cultural crisis is thus also a crisis of science and its role within society:

> The exclusiveness with which the total world-view of modern man, in the second half of the nineteenth century, let itself be determined by the positive sciences and be blinded by the 'prosperity' they produced, meant an indifferent turning-away from the questions which are decisive for a genuine humanity. [. . .] In our vital need – so we are told – this science has nothing to say to us. It excludes in principle precisely the questions which man, given over in our unhappy times to the most portentous upheavals, finds the most burning: questions of the meaning or meaninglessness of the whole of this human existence.[36]

The concept that paves the way towards establishing an alternative to the prevalent naturalistic attitude and thus to the solution for the pending crisis is the concept of world. What Husserl previously elaborated as the surrounding world is now reworked as the life-world. The life-world is the pre-scientific world of actual concrete experience of everyday life. It is the world of original self-evidence of our surroundings that is always assuredly given: 'To live is always to live-in-certainty-of-the-world.'[37] This stands in stark contrast to the objective world of science, governed by mathematical constructions, which cannot be experienced in this way.

However, it would be wrong to think Husserl's aim is to doubt the validity or the significance of natural sciences. On the contrary, he understands his phenomenological project as laying the foundations of science. The aim is to show that science itself has its roots in the primary experience of the life-world: 'The knowledge of the objective-scientific world is "grounded" in the self-evidence of the life-world.'[38] Husserl thus argues not against science *per se* but against a certain scientific worldview in which the life-world is obscured. The crisis is a result of the loss of the life-world caused by the naturalistic attitude in which science has lost its meaningfulness to human existence.

For Husserl, therefore, the life-world as the ultimate horizon of genuine human experience is pre-given and self-evident; however, it is also endangered, constantly under threat by developments connected to modern science. This double attitude towards the concept of world as what most evidently frames human experience but is at the same time always on the verge of loss will be retained by most phenomenologists that followed in Husserl's path – most notably, of course, by Heidegger.

In Heidegger's version of phenomenology, world again takes the role of a primary place of dwelling in contrast to the objective totality of objects as understood by science. It is through world that being can be understood and beings encountered. The 'existential analytic' Heidegger undertakes in *Being and Time* starts by identifying 'being-in-the-world' as 'a fundamental structure of Dasein'.[39] Dasein does not find itself in the world as a dress would find itself in a closet; rather, being-in is a structure of its existential constitution, an expression of Dasein as being-there: '"World" is ontologically not a determination of those beings which Dasein essentially is not, but rather a characteristic of Dasein itself.'[40] Being-in-the-world precedes the formation of the subject-object relation and the opposition between subjective interiority and objective exteriority. Any such relation or opposition is secondary and only possible on the basis of Dasein always-already being in the world and encountering beings as they appear alongside it within this world. Heidegger thus shares Husserl's view that the possibility of knowledge is conditioned by our being-in-the-world. Scientific cognition, however, overlooks the worldly aspect of phenomena due to its exclusive focus on natural objects:

> Dasein can discover beings as nature in this sense only in a definite mode of its being-in-the-world. This kind of knowledge has the character of a certain 'de-worlding' of the world. As the categorial content of structures of being of a definite being encountered in the world, 'nature' can never render worldliness intelligible.[41]

Worldliness, however, does not provide an easily accessible refuge of authentic experience in opposition to the de-worlding of knowledge. In fact, inauthentic attitudes of Dasein towards its own worldliness are the most natural modes of its everyday being-in-the-world. Heidegger insists that the existential analytic must start with everyday modes of being in which Dasein deals with innerworldly things it handles and uses while missing out on the phenomenon of worldliness itself.[42] In its inauthentic attitude towards the world, Dasein is so fully absorbed in the world that it does not see the world as world. Worldliness as such only reveals itself when this immersion of Dasein into the 'handiness' of things is disturbed by something not being at hand. When something we need is broken, unsuitable or missing, it appears in its raw presence in which worldliness makes itself felt in absence as the 'condition of the possibility of discovering innerworldly beings in general'.[43] Yet, even these inauthentic modes of experience are still part of being-in-the-world: 'Inauthenticity does not mean anything like no-longer-being-in-the-world, but rather it constitutes precisely a distinctive kind of being-in-the-world which is completely taken in by the world.'[44] As Végső observes, Heidegger's being-in-the-world entails a complex interplay of worldliness and worldlessness: 'Once the world emerges, useful things cease to appear as worldly beings and become mere objectively present (worldless) objects. Once the world disappears, useful things become worldly again.'[45]

While Husserl relied on the certainty of the life-world despite the preponderance of the naturalistic attitude, for Heidegger the world itself is withdrawn from the innerworldly things that it gives rise to. Only in the experience of an uncanny presence do we get a glimpse of its conditioning function. Worldliness is thus only fully revealed by anxiety: 'Being anxious discloses, primordially and directly, the world as world.'[46] Dasein attempts to flee this uncanniness and lets itself be immersed in handiness in which its own being and with it its authentic existential possibilities are concealed. Yet, it is anxiety that can get 'Dasein back from its falling prey and reveals to it authenticity and inauthenticity as possibilities of its being'.[47] A certain loss of world is thus inscribed into the being-in-the-world itself, which makes Végső claim that there is a structural worldlessness at work in the way Heidegger and the whole subsequent phenomenological tradition define worldliness.[48] World is a place of experiential self-evidence, but in this self-evidence, it is concealed as world. If Dasein wants to step into the world as world, it has to experience the anxiety of seeing its everyday inauthentic innerworldly experience dissolve.

In the 1929–30 lectures *The Fundamental Concepts of Metaphysics*, Heidegger returns to the problem of world through an examination of how different types of beings establish (or not) their relation to world.

He introduces the following typology: '(1.) the stone (material object) is *worldless*; (2.) the animal is *poor in world*; (3.) man is *world-forming*.'[49] The stone cannot in any way be considered as having a world, since it can form no relation to its surroundings. It simply lies where it finds itself. Only animals and humans can be said to not only be in the world but also in a certain sense to have a world. Animals, however, despite enjoying a specific access to their environment, are partially deprived of world.

The question of what forms the specificity of human relation to world will thus hinge on a comparison of animals and humans. Heidegger admits that the assumption that humans have a far richer relation to world in comparison to the animal's poverty and deprivation is problematic, since such a comparison can only be made from a human perspective.[50] Furthermore, as we have already seen, world is more often than not withdrawn from human experience as well. These considerations, however, did not stop Heidegger from ultimately drawing a clear distinction. Only humans – as Dasein – are in a proper relation to world as world. The animal, Heidegger claims, remains captivated by its environment, where it is completely absorbed in itself.[51] A lizard may form a relation to the rock it rests on and yet is not aware of the rock as a rock.[52] A human being, in contrast, is capable of moving beyond themselves and therefore being in the midst of other beings in their manifestness. Through their access to beings *as* beings, humans can at the same time be detached from the immediacy of their environment and truly be among beings as beings. This 'as' will define the specific way beings are accessible to humans as world:

> The manifestness of beings as such, of beings *as* beings, belongs to world. This implies that bound up with world is this enigmatic 'as', beings *as* such, or formulated in a formal way: 'something *as* something', a possibility which is quite fundamentally closed to the animal.[53]

When Dasein experiences beings as beings, it is no longer engaged with this being or that being, but encounters beings as a whole – or, what is called world. At this point, Heidegger identifies world with 'the manifestness of beings as such as a whole', which resonates with his initial characterisation of world in *Being and Time* as 'a structure which is primordially and constantly whole'.[54] This wholeness, however, is not identical to the natural conception of totality. The wholeness of the world does not refer to the sum total of beings, but to their grounding in being. When beings are manifested as beings, Heidegger claims, 'the unveiling of the being of beings' occurs for Dasein.[55] The phenomenon of worldliness thus ultimately reveals the ontological difference between being and beings. It awakens humans to their world-forming Dasein and thereby to the ontological truth of being. In later writings, Heidegger often returns to describing world as the openness of being.[56]

Heidegger's famous definition of truth as unconcealment implies that being and world are concealed in everyday modes of being. As we have seen already in *Being and Time*, the concealment of world is part and parcel of the way world occurs for Dasein (what Végső calls structural worldlessness). In *Fundamental Concepts*, however, Heidegger presents the discrepancy between Dasein and the human being in more dramatic terms when he talks about *'the liberation of the Dasein in man'*, which has to launch an *'attack upon man'* in order to get 'back into the ground of things'.[57] This is necessary because of a historical threat of worldlessness that endangers humanity and its capacity of world-formation. In his writings from the mid to late 1930s, Heidegger detects a 'darkening of the world' as part of a general 'spiritual decline' of humanity that also involves 'the flight of the gods, the destruction of the earth, the reduction of human beings to a mass' and so forth.[58] Beings are reduced to objects at a subject's disposal, making up a sphere of production, calculation and regulation 'within which no world is worlding anymore'.[59] World as a whole is now no longer accessible as the openness of being but is reduced to a 'world picture' within worldviews in which beings are not only represented but also measured and produced.[60] The forgetting of the question concerning the meaning of being in Western metaphysics paved the way for the de-worlding domination of science and technology that governs modernity. Geopolitically, the culmination of this development coincides with the global domination of America and Russia, who catch Europe and especially Germany from each side in the 'pincers' of their 'same hopeless frenzy of unchained technology and of the rootless organization of the average man' – a diagnosis that goes hand in hand with Heidegger's notorious involvement with the National Socialist movement.[61]

Many subsequent authors, inspired by phenomenology, described the ethical and political dimensions of the modern loss of world in similar terms, despite diverging radically from Heidegger's political affinities from that era. Hannah Arendt thus claimed that the modern age brought about 'world alienation' of humanity as a consequence not only of modern science and technology, but also of capitalist dispossession.[62] Even though her concept of world is of a more materialist kind (world as the artificial environment humanity makes for itself), her understanding of world alienation as undermining the conditions of public political life shows that politics proper is dependent on the phenomenological experience of a common world. In the work of Jean-Luc Nancy we find another elaboration of the loss of world not only as an existential problem, but also as a political one. In his understanding of being-in-the-world, Nancy emphasises 'being-with' as an essential characteristic of Dasein as 'being-there'.[63] Making a world thus entails a sharing of being, a circulation of sense that is produced in the mutual exposure of beings to each other.[64] This world-making capacity, however, is threatened by the process of globalisation, which brings about

> an indefinite growth of techno-science, of a correlative exponential growth of populations, of a worsening of inequalities of all sorts within these populations – economic, biological, and cultural – and of a dissipation of the certainties, images, and identities of what the world was with its parts and humanity with its characteristics.[65]

Globalisation unites the world but alienates any genuine experience of worldliness: 'there is no longer any world' in which 'one might find a place, a dwelling, and the elements of an orientation'.[66] The struggle to renew a sense of worldliness thus becomes an ethical and political commitment.[67] We will take a closer look at Arendt's and Nancy's respective understanding of the loss of world in political terms in Chapter 4.

Among contemporary thinkers, it was Jacques Derrida who pushed the phenomenological thought on world and its loss to its limits, where it becomes almost undistinguishable from the other two tendencies – namely that there is not actually any world, or that there is a multiplicity of worlds. In his early critical readings of Husserl and Heidegger, Derrida deconstructed some of the central pillars of phenomenology, including, to an extent, the phenomenological concept of world.[68] Here, however, we will focus on Derrida's intricate reflections on the concept of world in his final seminar, which is to a large extent dedicated to a reading of Heidegger's *The Fundamental Concepts of Metaphysics*.[69]

Derrida follows Heidegger in posing the question of world in relation to the difference between humans and animals. He does so not by proposing a different concept of world but by bringing into play alongside and against each other the different senses in which this concept can be defined. In the introductory session of the seminar, Derrida proposes three possible hypotheses that rely on different senses of 'world':

> 1. Incontestably, animals and humans inhabit the same world, the same objective world even if they do not have the same experience of the objectivity of the object. 2. Incontestably, animals and humans do not inhabit the same world, for the human world will never be purely and simply identical to the world of animals. 3. In spite of this identity and this difference, neither animals of different species, nor humans of different cultures, nor any animal or human individual inhabit the same world as another, however close and similar these living individuals may be (be they humans or animals), and the difference between one world and another will remain always unbridgeable.[70]

The second hypothesis in this series is the one Heidegger developed in his seminar. As we have seen above, it was based on a fundamental difference between humans and animals regarding the accessibility to the world as such and as a whole, which also provides access to the ontological difference between being and beings. Emphasising Heidegger's own hesitation regarding the worldly status of animals (the animal as what does and does not have a world), Derrida puts this distinction into doubt via the first hypothesis, not only because humans and animals share the same world objectively, but also because their senses of inhabiting this world may not be all that different. Animals and humans share the same habitat, which they co-inhabit and in which both find their deaths: 'The common world is the world in which one-lives-one-dies, whether one be a beast or a human sovereign, a world in which both suffer, suffer death, even a thousand deaths.'[71] As Sean Gaston remarks, the co-habitation of animals and humans in the same world – in continuity with Derrida's earlier deconstruction of phenomenology – 'should make us rethink the idealization of the concept of world in the history of philosophy'.[72]

While the first hypothesis questions Heidegger's distinction from above by claiming that animals and humans share the same world, the third one undermines it from below by implying that there might not actually be a common world even for humans. Derrida does not stop at animals of different species or humans of different cultures; he suggests that no animal or human individual inhabits the same world as another. There is thus a multiplicity of worlds – a 'my world' for any individual animal or human being – separated from each other by 'an infinite difference'.[73] If each world is inhabited by one sole individual and is thus not shared at all, the question arises whether it still makes sense to call it a world. Derrida does not shy away from this implication as he states: 'There is no world, there are only islands.'[74] It is thus no wonder that another text Derrida analyses extensively in this seminar alongside Heidegger's lectures is Daniel Defoe's *Robinson Crusoe*.

The third hypothesis thus questions the very possibility of shareable experience and stretches out between the non-existence of world ('there is no world') and its multiplication ('there are only islands'). If there is no common world, it is

> because the community of the world is always constructed, simulated by a set of stabilizing apparatuses, more or less stable, then, and never natural, language in the broad sense, codes of traces being designed, among all living beings, to construct a unity of the world that is always deconstructible, nowhere and never given in nature.[75]

Any supposedly common world is a constructed unity that can just as well be deconstructed. Even the argument that the incommensurable multiplicity of worlds must be sustained within 'a certain presumed, anticipated unity of the world' is but a mask designed to 'protect us against the infantile but infinite anxiety of the fact that there is not the world, that nothing is less certain than the world itself, that there is perhaps no longer a world and no doubt there never was one as totality of anything at all'.[76]

Even though these statements might seem apocalyptic, Derrida argues, they stem from everyday experience of 'the absolutely unshareable' that makes us feel like even those closest to us live in a completely different world.[77] There is thus nothing like an intersubjective life-world which we could fall back on. Even though Derrida claims that this experience tells us that there might never have been any common world, he still presents this insight as a loss. The lack of world condemns all living beings to 'irredeemable solitude'.[78]

Nevertheless, the individual islands of living beings still constitute worlds – and here Derrida comes closer to Heidegger again – through their relation to death. Derrida even claims that the death of a living being is not only an end of a world – the island-world of that individual being – but an end of the world as a whole:

> Death puts an end neither to someone in the world nor to one world among others. Death marks each time, each time in defiance of arithmetic, the absolute end of the one and only world, of that which each opens as a one and only world, the end of the unique world, the end of the totality of what is or can be presented as the origin of the world for any unique living being, be it human or not.[79]

There is no common world, apart from the world that ends each time in a unique way with the death of a living being.

A fourth hypothesis is thus implied, one that presents the world as lost. This is suggested by another text Derrida keeps returning to throughout his seminar, namely the last line of Paul Celan's poem 'Vast, Glowing Vault': 'The world is gone, I must carry you.'[80] According to Derrida, the poem tells us that 'the world has gone, the world has gone away, the world is far off, the world is lost, there is no world any more'.[81] Even if it turns out that there has never been any world, *'die Welt ist fort'* designates that this fact is experienced as a loss of world corresponding to a general 'desire for a world'.[82] But if there really is no world, what does this desire leave us with?

Derrida's conclusion hinges on the meaning given to the second part of Celan's verse, the commitment suggested by 'I must carry you'. Again, Derrida proposes two hypotheses. According to the first, the carrying takes place with no world in sight, 'where we share at least this knowledge without phantasm that there is no longer a world'.[83] Despite suggesting this option, as Végső sharply notices, 'the possibilities of inhabiting and, more importantly, co-inhabiting worldlessness are simply discarded by Derrida' in favour of an 'ethical duty [. . .] to live life *as if* the world existed'.[84] Indeed, the second option, which Derrida seems to accept since it is the one elaborated in more detail in the last session of his seminar, is that the duty of carrying is to 'make it that there be precisely a world, just a world, if not a just world, or to do things so as to make *as if* there were just a world'.[85] The logic of the 'as if' brings Derrida to Kant and his notion of world as a regulative idea. In Kant (as we will see in more detail in Chapter 5), the world in this sense is a morally useful fiction. In the conclusion of his seminar, Derrida finds in the Kantian 'as if' an alternative to the Heideggerian 'as such'. The 'as if' functions as an ethical fiction which replaces Dasein's privileged access to world. Faced with the loss of world, the human desire for world leaves us with the task of sustaining a fiction of worldliness. The carrying thus takes place following a disappearing trace of a world being lost.

From Husserl to Derrida via Heidegger, the phenomenological experience of worldliness becomes less and less evident. While for Husserl, the life-world was a pre-given certainty, Heidegger's Dasein already has to wrestle with the everyday inauthentic attitudes of the human being in order to gain access to world as a source of authentic existential possibilities. While for both Husserl and Heidegger, the loss of world was a dramatic unfolding threat, for Derrida it has become a completed certainty. Everyday experience now testifies not to the existence of a pre-given life-world, but to the abyss of worldlessness. Even for Derrida, however, world is still something that should be regained. It seems that whenever philosophy diagnoses a loss of world, it commits to the task of reclaiming the possibility of restoring it. This is what distinguishes this position from the first tendency, which rejects the very ideal of worldliness.

We can now see that in phenomenology and in some other philosophies, world is not merely a descriptive notion, but constitutes an endangered ideal of an authentic existential and/or political mode of being that is significantly threatened by modern ways of life and thought dominated by science, technology, globalisation, capitalism and/or totalitarian ideologies. The task of philosophy is to avert this threat by renewing the thinking of world and through it reawaken a more authentic relation to being. In *Worldlessness After Heidegger*, Végső shows how the spectre of worldlessness haunted those contemporary philosophies that tried to redeem and reconceptualise the notion of world. His book thus identifies and examines worldlessness as 'the continuous undercurrent' and even 'the disavowed center of contemporary thought'.[86] According to Végső, the historical loss of world announced by phenomenology is in fact secondary to a structural worldlessness that precedes any constitution of a world both ontologically and phenomenologically. The supposed historical threat of worldlessness, Végső argues, prevented Heidegger and his followers from exploring worldlessness affirmatively – which might bring them close to admitting that the concept of world is obsolete. Instead, it made them reactively cling to an ideal of worldliness as an ethical and political task.

Similar diagnoses of loss can also be found outside phenomenology. For Badiou, as we will see later on, worlds are defined by their transcendental logics, which make ontological multiples appear in a certain way. However, in today's world dominated by 'capitalo-parliamentarianism', large numbers of people are deprived of any historical appearance and quite literally count for nothing.[87] We live in a time, Badiou claims, in which *'there is not any world'*.[88] Badiou then formulates the slogan 'there is only one world' as a horizon of all emancipatory politics.[89] It is only if we understand the existence of all human beings as belonging to the same world that we can resist the capitalo-parliamentarianist order, which uses the processes of globalisation to impose divisions based on exclusion and inequality. Yet another version of this thesis can be found in Gilles Deleuze, who claims that the link between human beings and the world has been broken and that at a certain point in modern history, we have stopped believing in the world around us.[90] We will examine Badiou and Deleuze more closely in relation to the third destiny of world, namely its multiplication. Their inclusion here, however, goes to show that all three tendencies in thinking the notion of world today are closely intertwined.

World as Multiplied

The third tendency sees the modern destiny of world as one of multiplication. From this perspective, the multiplicity of worlds is not merely a consequence of the fragmentation that occurred with the demise of the cosmos, but is understood as forming a multifaceted realm in its own right. Genealogically – as we will observe in more detail in Chapter 2 – this perspective entails a return to Leibniz, for whom worlds are different possible configurations of ontological multiplicity (the multiplicity of monads). Monads can be arranged in different ways so as to constitute an infinite number of possible worlds. For Leibniz, the principle of world-making was convergence: only monads that are 'compossible' – whose coexistence does not imply a contradiction – can belong to the same world. Since Leibniz, however, the multiplicity of possible worlds has become actual and divergent. This tendency in contemporary philosophy therefore claims that the modern experience of reality is marked by the actual coexistence of divergent, yet overlapping, worlds. These worlds do not constitute parallel realities in some distant, inaccessible place, on which we can only theoretically speculate. On the contrary, they overlap in the sense that ontological entities can coexist in several worlds at once, each time within a different transcendental framework.

Before we can go into any more detail – which I will do in the rest of the chapters of this book – we should first acknowledge that this tendency exists in various guises in the works of different philosophers. The different conceptual forms these views take cannot always be reduced to the same common denominator, which makes such schematic summaries not entirely accurate. It is thus necessary to first briefly introduce some of the versions of the multiple-world hypothesis found among the leading figures of contemporary philosophy.

Within the phenomenological tradition, this hypothesis was brought furthest by Nancy with his emphasis on being-with as a crucial element of being-in-the-world. Nancy displaces Heidegger's notion of world from the existential analytic of *Dasein* to the 'coexistential analytic' of *mitsein*: being-there is originally being-with.[91] Contrary to what we have seen in Derrida, Nancy's multiplicity of worlds is not a multiplicity of isolated islands surrounding particular Daseins. Singular beings do not come to existence on their own and then share or not share a world; instead, their very existence is one of mutual exposure in which a common world is formed. Nancy defines a world as 'a differential articulation of singularities that make sense in articulating themselves'.[92] He connects this articulation to the Leibnizian multiplicity of singular monads, although – contrary to what Leibniz held – such singularities can only form a 'nontotalisable totality', 'a constellation whose compossibility is identical with its fragmentation'.[93] Due to the fundamental character of being-with, each being forms a singular origin of a common world. Because of 'the originary plurality of origins and the creation of the world in each singularity', the unity of the world is equivalent to a multiplicity of worlds.[94] For Nancy (as for Arendt, as we will see in Chapter 5), therefore, 'the world is always the plurality of worlds'.[95]

In what relation, then, is this plurality of worlds to the loss of world Nancy also declares, as we have seen above? The first chapter of his book *The Sense of the World* starts with what seems like a definitive assertion: 'There is no longer any world.'[96] Yet, as the chapter progresses, we see that this loss or lack can also be understood as a transformation of world. The very fact that there is something available to our senses, Nancy argues, seems to contradict the initial assertion. The mutual presentation of existing beings to each other indicates at least a certain 'being-*toward*-the-world' that produces sense.[97] For Nancy, this is crucial, since the question of world is coextensive to the question of sense: '*world* is not merely a correlative of *sense*, it is structured as *sense*, and reciprocally, *sense* is structured as *world*'.[98] Sense is produced by the mutual exposure and articulation of singular beings through an originary 'we' that gives rise to a world.[99] Where there is existence, there is sense, and where there is sense, there is also world.

Nancy can now present loss and transformation of world as two modes of the relation between world and sense:

> for as long as the world was essentially in relation to some other (that is, another world or an author of the world), it could *have* a sense. But the end of the world is that there is no longer this essential relation, and that there is no longer essentially (that is, existentially) anything but the world 'itself'. Thus, the world *no longer has* a sense, but it *is* sense.[100]

The loss of world was a loss of something transcendent to the world, something that could impose a totality on the world and assign a sense to it from the outside. Now, the world can only produce sense in its *being* world and in the absence of *having* sense. The end of the world (as a totality that has sense) thus actually opens the world as a praxis of sense-making: '*the end of the world of sense opens the praxis of the sense of the world*'.[101]

In Nancy, we thus encounter a complicated version of what Végső calls the tension between structural and historical worldlessness. The end of the world is a historical occurrence that coincides with the beginning of modernity, yet also constitutes a structural worldlessness that opens the practice of sense-making as world-making. However, worldlessness also persists as a historical threat of globalisation that is tearing sense to shreds.[102] The plural world is thus far from a self-evident certainty or an immediate given. It is an ethical and political imperative in the face of its impending loss.[103]

While phenomenology is arguably the main source of a renewed philosophical interest in the concept of world in the twentieth century, it is not the only one. One alternative has been presented by Badiou. In a commentary on Nancy, he rejects the phenomenological understanding of world as 'a category of the sense of being'.[104] As we will see in much more detail in Chapter 3, Badiou proposes a 'subtractive ontology' based on mathematical set theory, in which no sense can be ascribed to being. Badiou sees this move as a radical break from phenomenology and its 'poetic ontology':

> Heidegger still remains enslaved, even in the doctrine of the withdrawal and the un-veiling, to what I consider, for my part, to be the essence of metaphysics; that is, the figure of being as endowment and gift, as presence and opening, and the figure of ontology as the offering of a trajectory of proximity. I will call this type of ontology poetic; ontology haunted by the dissipation of Presence and the loss of the origin.[105]

Dispensing with being as the bearer of sense and truth also entails for Badiou a break from the obsession with loss. Badiou thus proposes a move from being as a source of ontological truth to a being that presents itself as an indifferent and inconsistent multiplicity. The question of world, then, is the question of the way this 'essential unbinding of multiple-being give[s] itself as a local binding and, in the end, as the stability of worlds'.[106] This relation between the ontological level of multiplicities and the level of worlds in which these multiplicities appear according to a certain transcendental logic defines Badiou's approach to the concept of world.

Badiou claims that ever since Plato, there have been two meanings of the concept of world in philosophy: while one pertains to the sense of being (the rejected phenomenological option), the other (the one adhered to by Badiou) refers to the logic of appearance.[107] According to Badiou, the logic of appearance is a matter of both plurality and contingency. There is 'a plurality of worlds due to a plurality of possible logics' and none of them defines the true sense of being – not even their plurality itself.[108] Badiou attributes the origins of the logical approach to the concept of world to Leibniz, but argues that the multiplicity of worlds should now be regarded as actual.[109] In *Logics of Worlds*, Badiou claims that human beings are capable of actually inhabiting a 'virtually unlimited number of worlds'.[110] This hypothesis is not formulated in the same manner as it is in Derrida or Nancy, since it rests on a different, non-phenomenological concept of world. In Badiou's understanding, worlds are not centred on isolated Daseins, nor are they a result of the mutual exposure to the *mitsein*. For Badiou, world is not a category of existential experience, but a category of objective appearance. In this setting, human beings (like any other subject or object) are ontologically reducible to multiples that can appear in many worlds according to different transcendental logics: 'Not only is there a plurality of worlds, but the same multiple – the "same" ontologically – in general co-belongs to different worlds.'[111] Since no mode of appearing is inscribed in being as such, the way a certain ontological multiple will appear in a certain world is contingently dependent on transcendental frameworks. For Badiou, a world is shaped by an objectively given transcendental that determines which multiples will appear in this world and with what intensity, how they will compose objects, and how the relations between them will be established.

Moving from the sense of being to the logic of appearance, the concept of world no longer constitutes an ethical ideal or an authentic mode of existence. For Badiou, being-in-multiple-worlds is nothing but an indifferent factuality, the way the appearance of being is structured. The truth that his philosophy is interested in is not – as it is in Nancy – related to uncovering the plurality of world(s) as the singular-plural praxis of sense-making, but to events as radical breaks from the logic of a particular world. Badiou defines truths as subjective procedures of fidelity to events that occur in the fields of science, politics, art and love.[112] The subjectivity that forms in relation to these events strives to transform the transcendental coordinates of the world in question. Badiou characterises the truths that are established as results of this collective subjective endeavour as 'trans-worldly'.[113] Even though they originate within a particular world, they are accessible from other worlds as well. In Chapter 3, we will take a closer look at the problems of Badiou's understanding of truth in relation to the multiplicity of worlds.

The multiplication of world in relation to ontological multiplicity is also essential to Deleuze's philosophy. As we will closely examine in Chapters 3 and 5, Deleuze's multiplicity of worlds is of a different kind compared to Badiou's. First of all, for Deleuze the many worlds are not completely discrete. Rather, the bifurcation of worlds blurs the boundaries between them. Second, in Deleuze we find no clear distinction between the ontological and transcendental multiplicity that is crucial to Badiou. Instead, the multiplicity of pre-individual singularities is itself the transcendental field in which ontological singularities are actualised and distributed to form worlds. Third, while Badiou constructs worlds according to what appears within a certain transcendental frame, Deleuze's worlds are produced as bifurcations concerning different possible outcomes of events.

To understand all this, we need to take into account the Leibnizian origins of the concept of world Deleuze operates with. As in Leibniz, worlds are systems of singularities. Yet, while for Leibniz, such systems can only be formed on the basis of convergence (the compossibility of monads), Deleuze emphasises the coexistence of divergences. He claims that since Leibniz, the 'play of the world' has changed: now, incompossible divergences coexist and can no longer be separated into different, merely possible worlds.[114] This can be understood as incompossibilities becoming parts of the same world or forming different coexisting worlds. No strict boundaries between worlds are possible because nomadic singularities, split between worlds, are continuously distributed and redistributed to form worlds anew. The bifurcation of worlds also implies the simultaneous actualisation of different possibilities. With the 'unfurling of divergent series in the same world comes the irruption of incompossibilities on the same stage, where Sextus will rape *and* not rape Lucretia, where Caesar crosses *and* does not cross the Rubicon'.[115]

The coexistence of incompossibilities also gets a psychoanalytic treatment by Lacan in his seminar on anxiety. Commenting on Claude Lévi-Strauss's distinction between analytic and dialectical reason, Lacan toys with the idea of a psychoanalytic reason and the cosmology it might imply.[116] He uses the Shakespearean metaphor of the world as a stage to introduce the basic distinction between the cosmic and the historical world. When we make the world climb up on to the stage, Lacan says, we introduce to it historical time and the laws of the signifier.[117] What comes on to the stage of history, he adds, must eventually also fall back off it. These remains of fallen worlds form a sort of natural history in which partial leftovers of past worlds persistently inform our contradictory cultural realm:

> Everything that throughout the course of history we have called *the world* has left behind superimposed residues that accumulate without the faintest care for contradiction. What culture transports to us in the guise of the world is a stack, a shop crammed full of the flotsam and jetsam of worlds that have followed one after the other, and which, for all their incompatibility, don't get on any the worse with each other within every single one of us.[118]

For Lacan, worlds are phantasmatic – but this does not imply that there is a natural cosmos accessible to us beyond the stage.[119] What interests him is rather the moment of the fall, not as loss of world, but as the subject's identification with the object of desire (the object *a*) which falls out of the phantasmatic transcendental framing of a world.[120] The identification with the object *a* as 'this remainder, this residue' of what falls from the stage is an identification with something that 'escapes the status of the object derived from the specular image, that is, the laws of transcendental aesthetics'.[121] The status of object *a* entails a reframing of the transcendental aesthetics in a way that fits the psychoanalytic experience.[122] This suggests a move away from the concept of world, consistent with what we have discussed in the first section of this chapter, but also indicates that Lacan might leave the door open for a transcendental concept of world in its multiplicity.

The move away from the phenomenological concept of world entails not only ontological but also political consequences. When the ideal of worldliness is cast aside, the divergence between worlds reveals its conflictual side. In Chapter 4, we will take a closer look at Jacques Rancière's understanding of politics as a conflict of worlds. According to Rancière, worlds are formed by structures of perception and intelligibility that define the coordinates of a common reality and the way people can take part in it.[123] The formation of a common world, however, also produces a division between what can and cannot be perceived as part of the common world, who can and cannot take part in it. It always entails a hierarchical distribution of bodies and capacities that enforces a logic of inequality. For Rancière, the crucial political task is therefore not to renew a lost sense of worldliness, but to reconfigure the coordinates of experience that constitute a common world in order to reverse the wrongs done by this constitution. Whenever a political subject forms to state such a wrong, there appears a contradiction of two worlds in one: the world fought for by the political subject and the world in which the subject counts for nothing.[124]

*

In the rest of this book, I follow the third tendency in examining the ontological, political and aesthetical problems that open up when the world is seen as multiplied. I argue that the multiple-worlds perspective can account for both of the other tendencies. If world is seen as obsolete or lost, we can always ask which world or which concept of world is obsolete or lost. When the concept of world is rendered as obsolete, as the first tendency claims, it is always a particular concept of world that is made redundant. As we have seen above, the criticism is usually aimed at the concept of world as a unified, closed and well-ordered totality, in either a cosmological (made obsolete by modern science) or an ideological (the 'worldview') sense. When the world is said to be lost, as the second tendency claims, we are again talking about a specific world that is lost, usually the world as what grounds a meaningful existential experience or a political sense of community.

Many of those who proclaim that the world as totality does not exist end up affirming a kind of multiplicity of domains or structures through which the worldless ontological reality is accessible. We have already seen that Gabriel, Bryant and Végső as philosophers of worldlessness declare a certain affinity to the multiple-worlds perspective, especially the one elaborated by Badiou. Gabriel gives a nod to Badiou, but prefers the term 'field of sense' since the concept of world deceptively suggests a closed totality. Yet, this is again a particular understanding of the concept of world that does not reflect how this notion is conceptualised by the philosophers of the third tendency. Végső similarly admits that Badiou's worlds as systems of transcendental indexing could be treated as 'the real immanent organisational structures of worldlessness' or 'an effective description of worldlessness itself', but claims that we have nothing to gain by describing such structures as worlds.[125] I propose to turn the tables and ask the following question: what is there to gain from dropping the concept of world entirely, if the only aim is to challenge a particular concept of world that no longer has anything to do with what is conceptualised as world by Badiou? For what I have described here as the third tendency, the concept of world criticised by the first tendency no longer bears any relevance. I will show in the following chapters, starting from Leibniz, how a radical turn in conceptualising the concept of world has indeed taken place.

Another objection of the first tendency against the concept of world is that it establishes a phantasmatic whole whose only function is to exclude any encounter with the real. This objection, while very valid in relation to what is pejoratively called a worldview, is again misplaced when directed to the multiple worlds conceptualised by the third tendency. In the case of Badiou, there is no contradiction between his rejection of the concept of world as totality, influenced by Lacan, and his return to the concept of world in *Logics of Worlds*. For Badiou, the multiple worlds are objective transcendental fictions that regulate the logics of appearance, not an essential plurality in which the sense of being would be revealed. The real, for Badiou, can only be said to take place where the transcendental logic is ruptured by an event and where the collective subject makes an effort to transform a world through a truth procedure. In the case of Deleuze, the multiplicity of worlds is constituted not by worlds as closed totalities but precisely by bifurcations that occur around coexisting incompossibilities. The multiplication of worlds implies the end of the world as a totality and does away with the neat separation of divergences into possible worlds. In the case of Rancière, what matters politically is not the multiplicity of worlds itself, but a conflict of worlds instigated by a political subjectivation. In the transcendentalist conceptualisation, therefore, the multiplicity of worlds is not a restoration of the phantasmatic world as either totality or plurality, but an instable realm of often conflictual coexistence that proliferates around points of real incompossibility.

It has to be noted that this last point introduces a split within the third tendency since it does not fully apply to Nancy's position. From Nancy's perspective, in fact, all three tendencies are fully compatible:

1. there is no cosmos in the sense of a well-ordered totality (although this does not imply that we must abandon the ideal of worldliness);
2. genuine worldliness is lost due to historical factors (technology and capitalism);
3. worldliness can be regained by fully affirming the plurality of its singular origins.

This unity of the three tendencies is supported by Nancy's insistence on the phenomenological ideal of worldliness as sense-making. Other approaches to the concept of world within the third tendency, however, move beyond sense to points of real divergence and incompossibility between worlds. This necessitates the abandonment, not of the concept of world, but of the ideal of worldliness. Even though Nancy manages to break through the phenomenological inclination to construct worlds around the central point of a Husserlian ego or a Heideggerian Dasein, his conception of plurality still converges around a shared sense of worldliness. In contrast to this, I argue that in order to truly think the multiplicity of worlds, one must examine this multiplicity in its excessive divergence that does not necessarily provide the phenomenological horizon of a shared sense-making experience. My own perspective on the relation of the three tendencies thus looks like this:

1. there is no cosmos in the sense of a well-ordered totality (although this does not imply that we must abandon the concept of world);
2. what is lost is not world but the ideal of worldliness;
3. there is an actual multiplicity of divergent worlds.

The third tendency ultimately entails leaving behind not only the concept of world as a totality, dismissed by the first tendency, but also the phenomenological concept of world as the lost horizon of meaningful experience, affirmed by the second tendency. Understanding the multiplication of worlds requires a different concept of world. In the next chapter, I trace its genealogy back to Leibniz.

Notes

1. Alexandre Koyré, *From the Closed World to the Infinite Universe* (Baltimore: Johns Hopkins University Press, 1957), 2.
2. Jacques Lacan, *On Feminine Sexuality: The Limits of Love and Knowledge: The Seminar of Jacques Lacan, Book XX: Encore*, trans. Bruce Fink (New York: W. W. Norton, 1998), 30. Other places where Lacan mentions world as fantasy include *Television: A Challenge to Psychoanalytic Establishment*, trans. Denis Hollier, Rosalind Krauss, Annette Michelson and Jeffrey Mehlman (New York: W. W. Norton, 1990), 6, and *The Triumph of Religion, Preceded by Discourse to Catholics*, trans. Bruce Fink (Cambridge: Polity, 2013), 61–2.
3. Lacan, *On Feminine Sexuality*, 36.

4. Sigmund Freud, *New Introductory Lectures on Psycho-Analysis and Other Works*, trans. James Strachey, in *The Standard Edition of the Complete Psychological Works of Sigmund Freud, Vol. 22 (1932–1936)*, ed. James Strachey and Anna Freud (London: Hogarth Press, 1964), 158.
5. Ibid. 160.
6. Lacan says: 'what I ironically called a world view [. . .] has a more moderate and more precise name: ontology'. *On Feminine Sexuality*, 31.
7. Ibid. 43.
8. Ibid. 41–3.
9. Ibid. 43. Regarding Joyce, see ibid. 36–7.
10. Samo Tomšič, 'From the Orderly World to the Polluted Unworld', in *Objective Fictions: Philosophy, Psychoanalysis, Marxism*, ed. Adrian Johnston, Boštjan Nedoh and Alenka Zupančič (Edinburgh: Edinburgh University Press, 2022), 65–6.
11. Ibid. 65.
12. Jacques Lacan, 'The Third', trans. Philip Oravers, *The Lacanian Review: Hurly-Burly* 7 (2019): 90.
13. Ibid. 90.
14. Ibid. 89.
15. Slavoj Žižek and Glyn Daly, *Conversations with Žižek* (Cambridge: Polity Press, 2004), 97.
16. Slavoj Žižek, *Less Than Nothing: Hegel and the Shadow of Dialectical Materialism* (London: Verso, 2012), 149.
17. Adrian Johnston, '"Naturalism or Anti-Naturalism? No, Thanks – Both Are Worse!": Science, Materialism, and Slavoj Žižek', *Revue internationale de philosophie* 261, no. 3 (2012): 321. Johnston himself develops this kind of ontology further with his idea of a 'weak nature'.
18. Alain Badiou, 'Logology Against Ontology', in *The Adventure of French Philosophy*, ed. and trans. Bruno Bosteels (London: Verso, 2012), 317.
19. Markus Gabriel, *Why the World Does Not Exist*, trans. Gregory S. Moss (Cambridge: Polity Press, 2015), 1. Bryant develops a similar argument for the inexistence of the world to Gabriel's, but connects it to a different version of realist ontology. See *The Democracy of Objects* (Ann Arbor: Open Humanities Press, 2011), 270–9. Végső also calls for an affirmative understanding of worldlessness beyond loss. See *Worldlessness After Heidegger: Phenomenology, Psychoanalysis, Deconstruction* (Edinburgh: Edinburgh University Press, 2020), and 'On Acosmic Realism', in 'The Concept of World in Contemporary Philosophy', ed. Rok Benčin, special issue, *Filozofski vestnik* 42, no. 2 (2021): 71–92, https://doi.org/10.3986/fv.42.2.04.
20. Markus Gabriel, *Fields of Sense* (Edinburgh: Edinburgh University Press, 2015), 187.
21. Gabriel, *Why the World Does Not Exist*, 85.

22. Gabriel, *Fields of Sense*, 188.
23. Ibid. 166.
24. Gabriel, *Why the World Does Not Exist*, 69.
25. Gabriel, *Fields of Sense*, 157–8.
26. Gabriel, *Why the World Does Not Exist*, 79.
27. Ibid. 65.
28. Gabriel, *Fields of Sense*, 123.
29. Gabriel, *Why the World Does Not Exist*, 65.
30. Gabriel, *Fields of Sense*, 123; Bryant, *The Democracy of Objects*, 271–2; Végső, *Worldlessness After Heidegger*, 270.
31. Edmund Husserl, *Ideas Pertaining to a Pure Phenomenology and to a Phenomenological Philosophy, Second Book: Studies in the Phenomenology of Constitution*, trans. Richard Rojcewicz and Andre Schuwer (Dordrecht: Kluwer Academic Publishers, 1989), 192, 194, 199.
32. Ibid. 195.
33. Ibid. 196.
34. Ibid. 201.
35. Edmund Husserl, *The Crisis of European Sciences and Transcendental Phenomenology*, trans. David Carr (Evanston: Northwestern University Press, 1970), 299.
36. Ibid. 5–6.
37. Ibid. 142.
38. Ibid. 130.
39. Martin Heidegger, *Being and Time*, trans. Joan Stambaugh (Albany: State University of New York Press, 2010), 39.
40. Ibid. 64 (see also ibid. 54–5).
41. Ibid. 65.
42. Ibid. 66–7.
43. Ibid. 72, 86.
44. Ibid. 169.
45. Végső, *Worldlessness After Heidegger*, 46.
46. Heidegger, *Being and Time*, 181.
47. Ibid. 184.
48. Végső, *Worldlessness After Heidegger*, 25.
49. Martin Heidegger, *The Fundamental Concepts of Metaphysics: World, Finitude, Solitude*, trans. William McNeill and Nicholas Walker (Bloomington: Indiana University Press, 1995), 177.
50. Ibid. 270–1.
51. Ibid. 238–40.
52. Ibid. 198.
53. Ibid. 274.
54. Ibid. 285; Heidegger, *Being and Time*, 39.
55. Heidegger, *The Fundamental Concepts*, 350.

56. See, for example, Martin Heidegger, 'The Origin of the Work of Art', in *Basic Writings*, ed. David Farrell Krell (San Francisco: Harper, 1993), 200, and 'Letter on Humanism', ibid., 252.
57. Heidegger, *The Fundamental Concepts*, 172, 21.
58. Martin Heidegger, *Introduction to Metaphysics*, trans. Gregory Fried and Richard Polt (New Haven: Yale University Press, 2014), 29.
59. Ibid. 48.
60. Martin Heidegger, 'The Age of the World Picture', in *Off the Beaten Track*, ed. and trans. Julian Young and Kenneth Haynes (Cambridge: Cambridge University Press, 2002), 57–85.
61. Heidegger, *Introduction to Metaphysics*, 40.
62. See Hannah Arendt, *The Human Condition* (Chicago: University of Chicago Press, 1958).
63. Jean-Luc Nancy, *Being Singular Plural*, trans. Robert D. Richardson and Anne E. O'Byrne (Stanford: Stanford University Press, 2000), 93.
64. Ibid. 2–3.
65. Jean-Luc Nancy, *The Creation of the World, or Globalization*, trans. François Raffoul and David Pettigrew (Albany: State University of New York Press, 2007), 34.
66. Jean-Luc Nancy, *The Sense of the World*, trans. Jeffrey S. Librett (Minneapolis: University of Minnesota Press, 1997), 4.
67. Jean-Luc Nancy, *The Possibility of a World: Conversations with Pierre-Philippe Jandin*, trans. Travis Holloway and Flor Méchain (New York: Fordham University Press, 2017), 26.
68. For two very informative readings of Derrida's critique of Husserl and Heidegger in relation to the concept of world, see Sean Gaston, *The Concept of World from Kant to Derrida* (London: Rowman & Littlefield, 2013), 99–133, and Végső, *Worldlessness After Heidegger*, 193–244.
69. Jacques Derrida, *The Beast and the Sovereign, Volume II*, trans. Geoffrey Bennington (Chicago: University of Chicago Press, 2011).
70. Ibid. 8.
71. Ibid. 264.
72. Gaston, *The Concept of World*, 131.
73. Derrida, *The Beast and the Sovereign*, 9.
74. Ibid. 9.
75. Ibid. 8–9.
76. Ibid. 265–6.
77. Ibid. 266.
78. Ibid. 266.
79. Jacques Derrida, 'Rams: Uninterrupted Dialogue – Between Two Infinities, the Poem', in *Sovereignties in Question: The Poetics of Paul Celan*, ed. Thomas Dutoit and Outi Pasanen (New York: Fordham University Press, 2005), 140.

80. Paul Celan, 'Vast, Glowing Vault', in *Poems of Paul Celan*, trans. Michael Hamburger (New York: Persea Books, 1988), 267. In the original, the poem 'Grösse, Glühende Wölbung' appears in Celan's collection *Atemwende* (Frankfurt: Suhrkamp, 1967), 93, and ends with the line '*Die Welt ist fort, ich muß dich tragen*'. Another crucial text in which Derrida analyses this poem is the already mentioned 'Rams: Uninterrupted Dialogue', 35–163.
81. Derrida, *The Beast and the Sovereign*, 9.
82. Ibid. 9.
83. Ibid. 268.
84. Végső, *Worldlessness After Heidegger*, 234. Végső is critical of this 'fetishisation of the world', which pretends that there is nevertheless a world despite the knowledge that there is none. Ibid. 241.
85. Derrida, *The Beast and the Sovereign*, 268.
86. Végső, *Worldlessness After Heidegger*, 3, 5.
87. Alain Badiou, 'The Caesura of Nihilism', in *The Adventure of French Philosophy*, 64.
88. Ibid. 61.
89. Alain Badiou, *The Meaning of Sarkozy*, trans. David Fernbach (London: Verso, 2008), 53–70. An interesting postcolonial version of this imperative was proposed by Achille Mbembe in *Critique of Black Reason*, trans. Laurent Dubois (Durham, NC: Duke University Press, 2017); see especially the Introduction and the Epilogue.
90. Gilles Deleuze, *Cinema 2: The Time-Image*, trans. Hugh Tomlinson and Robert Galeta (Minneapolis: University of Minnesota Press, 1989), 169.
91. Nancy, *Being Singular Plural*, 93.
92. Nancy, *The Sense of the World*, 78.
93. Ibid. 155.
94. Nancy, *Being Singular Plural*, 5.
95. Nancy, *The Sense of the World*, 155.
96. Ibid. 4.
97. Ibid. 7–8.
98. Ibid. 8.
99. Nancy, *Being Singular Plural*, 4.
100. Nancy, *The Sense of the World*, 8.
101. Ibid. 9.
102. Ibid. 3.
103. Nancy, *The Possibility of a World*, 27.
104. Badiou, 'The Caesura of Nihilism', 62.
105. Alain Badiou, *Being and Event*, trans. Oliver Feltham (London: Continuum, 2005), 9–10.

106. Alain Badiou, *Logics of Worlds: Being and Event, 2*, trans. Alberto Toscano (London: Continuum, 2009), 101.
107. Badiou refers here to Plato's *Timaeus* in which the world is described both as 'the perfection of sense' and as 'a logic of visibility, a topology of the visible'. Badiou, 'The Caesura of Nihilism', 63–4.
108. Ibid. 63.
109. Badiou, *Logics of Worlds*, 325–30.
110. Ibid. 114.
111. Ibid. 114.
112. See Alain Badiou, *Conditions*, trans. Steven Corcoran (London: Continuum, 2008).
113. Badiou, *Logics of Worlds*, 10.
114. Gilles Deleuze, *Difference and Repetition*, trans. Paul Patton (London: Continuum, 2001), 51, and *The Fold: Leibniz and the Baroque*, trans. Tom Colney (London: Athlone Press, 1993), 81.
115. Deleuze, *The Fold*, 82.
116. Jacques Lacan, *Anxiety: The Seminar of Jacques Lacan, Book X*, trans. A. R. Price (Cambridge: Polity, 2014), 32.
117. Ibid. 33.
118. Ibid. 34.
119. Ibid. 34, 38, 108.
120. Ibid. 37.
121. Ibid. 40.
122. Ibid. 88. This identification does not, however, happen outside of any frame. While imaginary identification, for Lacan, takes place in front of the mirror, the identification with the object *a* takes place through the window. It would be interesting to address the mirror and the window as two different structures of the frame and its relation to subjectivity, especially in relation to the Leibnizian topic of the windowless monad. However, I leave this discussion for elsewhere.
123. Jacques Rancière, *Modern Times: Essays on Temporality in Art and Politics* (Zagreb: Multimedijalni institut, 2017), 13. A new edition of this book has recently appeared as *Modern Times: Temporality in Art and Politics* (London: Verso, 2022).
124. Jacques Rancière, *Disagreement: Politics and Philosophy*, trans. Julie Rose (Minneapolis: University of Minnesota Press, 1999), 27.
125. Végső, *Worldlessness After Heidegger*, 270, 278–9.

2   The Leibnizian Turn

LEIBNIZ IS OFTEN OVERLOOKED when the history of the idea that there is a multiplicity of worlds is discussed.[1] There is a good reason for this, for although he advocated the idea of an infinite universe, he firmly maintained that only one world can exist. In cosmological terms, Leibniz finds the debate over whether one or more worlds exist irrelevant. Regardless of how many stars and planets there are, they should all be considered parts of the same world or universe. In this sense, it seems that Leibniz is using a standard concept of world as the totality of everything that exists, even if that totality is infinite, multi-centred and multi-layered.

If not in cosmological terms, the discussion on the multiplicity of worlds is all the more relevant to Leibniz in a modal sense. To find multiple worlds, there is no need to look at the sky. Rather, one must become aware of the contingency of our own world being as it is. If other worlds can be imagined, they are different possible versions of *this* world, all the stars and planets included. There is thus a multiplicity of possible worlds, that is, all the different ways the one existing universe could have been constructed. For any possibility, there is an alternative, and where there are alternative possibilities, there is contingency of actualisation.

Leibniz makes the distinction between the cosmological and the modal multiplicity of worlds clear in *Theodicy*:

> I call 'World' the whole succession and the whole agglomeration of all existent things, lest it be said that several worlds could have

existed in different times and different places. For they must needs be reckoned all together as one world or, if you will, as one Universe. And even though one should fill all times and all places, it still remains true that one might have filled them in innumerable ways, and that there is an infinitude of possible worlds among which God must needs have chosen the best, since he does nothing without acting in accordance with supreme reason.[2]

Arguably, the interest shown in the second part of the last sentence has historically overshadowed the first part. Leibniz's theory of worlds is most often discussed in the context of the nature of God's choice of the best of all worlds and its philosophical and theological implications. What will be of interest to us in this chapter, however, are the innumerable ways in which all the times and places could have been filled. It is here that a new way of conceptualising the notion of world takes shape, one that does not focus on the totality of what is, but on how this totality is constructed. Any possible world – including the actually created one – is a specific combination of an infinite number of substances. Substances are ontologically real; yet, to constitute a world, they have to be coordinated and arranged in a particular way. Leibniz's theory of possible worlds reveals a specific conception of what a world (any world) is in the first place, regardless of how God chooses among them.[3]

It has to be noted that even if matters of theodicy are put into brackets, the modal multiplicity of worlds remains limited by the cosmological limitation of the sole existing world. As Leibniz claimed in the 'Monadology', 'there is an infinity of possible universes in God's ideas', but 'only one of them can exist'.[4] The idea that every possible world might actually exist somewhere is foreign to Leibniz. Such parallel realities would again have to be counted as parts of the same universe, which would make this universe full of what Leibniz calls 'incompossibilities'. The universe would, for example, include an Adam that sinned, but also an Adam that did not, a Caesar that crossed the Rubicon, but also a Caesar that did not. This, of course, would go against the supreme reason that God is acting in accordance with. Leibniz's multiple worlds are thus forever reduced to the modal status of possibilities and their existence is limited to the ideal sphere of God's mind.

Possible worlds are not the only multiplicity of worlds found in Leibniz. To a cosmological multiplicity, which Leibniz strictly denies, and a modal multiplicity, which he affirms, a perspectivist multiplicity of worlds should be added. This multiplicity is, in fact, double, since it exists on two levels of reality, namely, the ontological level of individual substances or monads and the phenomenological level of matter and bodies. Each individual substance, as Leibniz repeatedly claims, is 'like a world apart',[5] a world within a world, not only because it mirrors the whole universe within its windowless closure, but also because its specificity is defined by the unique perspective it has on the world as a whole. Even though such perspectives are ultimately views on the one and the same world within which these substances exist, Leibniz cannot resist the image of a proliferating multiplicity of worlds resulting from these perspectives. The same image appears again on the level of matter and bodies, this time connected to the different layers at which they can be observed. Any part of the world, if observed closely enough, reveals another world within itself. Again, there is no need to point our gaze at distant planets, since a multiplicity of worlds is present right where we are.

Although for Leibniz there could ultimately be only one world, his work marks a significant turn in the way the very concept of world can be understood. The multiplicity of possible worlds and world-perspectives, combined with the contingency of any actualised world, reveals a concept of world that is defined not by totality but by a particular arrangement of or perspective on ontological multiplicity. From this point on, the possibility of thinking the multiplicity of worlds in a transcendental sense is open. In the first part of this chapter, we will look more closely at Leibniz's concept of world. In the second part, we will observe how Gilles Deleuze and Alain Badiou – the two principle heirs of the Leibnizian turn in thinking the concept of world in contemporary philosophy – release into actuality the multiplicity of worlds that Leibniz discovered but confined to possibility.

From the Multiplicity of Substances to the Multiplicity of Worlds

At first glance, as we have seen, Leibniz adopts a standard conception of world as the totality of 'all existent things' in a spatial ('agglomeration') and temporal ('succession') sense. Yet, the path from all things to a world is not simply one of addition. Leibniz holds that 'the accumulation of an infinite number of substances, is, properly speaking, not a whole',[6] since for any conceived whole there are always substances that can be added to it. The idea of a whole of all wholes is contradictory, which means that the world cannot be defined as such a whole.[7] It is not the totality itself that defines what a world is for Leibniz. What makes a world out of an infinite pile of substances is the manner of coexistence between them. Substances can only be said to constitute a world when they are made to coexist in an arranged and coordinated way. This specific arrangement of an infinite series of substances is what constitutes a possible world and distinguishes it from others.

The fact that substances have to be arranged into a certain order of coexistence to form a world reveals a slight, if always-already surmounted gap between a series of substances and a world. It is the very plurality of substances as an ontological given that opens the concept of world as a problem for Leibniz. From a monist position, such as Spinoza's, according to which only one substance exists, the problem of world cannot arise since the equation between the world as a whole and the one necessarily existing substance is immediate. From a dualist position, such as Descartes's, there already arises the question of how the two substances (*res extensa* and *res cogitans*) are connected. The problem of substance dualism, however, is limited to the mind-body interaction and does not extend to the concept of world. Only from a position of substance pluralism – which Leibniz held against Spinoza and Descartes – can the question of how a world might be composed be raised. On the ontological level, any world is composed of an 'infinite multitude of simple substances',[8] which begs the question of how such a multitude can be united into a world. God contemplates not only an infinity of possible substances, but also the 'infinitely infinite combinations' of substances that distribute them into separate worlds.[9] Although the problem of world revolves around the unification of substances, ontological multiplicity entails a multiplicity of combinations of substances and therefore a multiplicity of possible worlds.

Even though the multiplicity of worlds is consigned by Leibniz to the realm of possibility, the one and only created world is itself only one among the possible worlds, that is, the infinitely many possible arrangements of the ontological multiplicity of substances. God reviews all these worlds in order to compare them and choose the best possible one: 'this is the cause of the existence of the best, which wisdom makes known to God, which his goodness makes him choose, and which his power makes him produce'.[10] Even though the criteria for

God's choice are clear, there is no metaphysical necessity that made the best possible world come into existence. God's choice is a matter of will. The actual existence of this possible world rather than another is not necessary but contingent, regardless of the good reasons God had to create it. According to Leibniz's definition from the 'Monadology', contingent truths differ from necessary ones in that their opposite is possible.[11] The creation of another, less good world would be possible, even though it would contradict God's wisdom and goodness. In his correspondence with Clarke, Leibniz insists that it is wrong to claim that what God does not choose is impossible: we can be certain in God's choice of the world, but it is a matter of contingency.[12]

From what we have said so far, a misunderstanding might arise that substances constitute an already given ontological multiplicity that must at a later stage be somehow arranged into a world in the best possible way. Rather, Leibniz understands God's creation of substances as a process that already takes their coexistence within a world into account:

> For God, so to speak, turns on all sides and in all ways the general system of phenomena which he finds it good to produce in order to manifest his glory, and he views all the faces of the world in all ways possible, since there is no relation that escapes his omniscience. The result of each view of the universe, as seen from a certain position, is a substance which expresses the universe in conformity with this view, should God see fit to render his thought actual and to produce this substance.[13]

We see in this quotation from the 'Discourse on Metaphysics' that God does not create substances prior to considering their position within the world as a whole. Thus, the constitution of a world is neither temporarily nor logically secondary with respect to substances; rather, substances are from the beginning created as belonging to a particular world. In the 'Monadology' we learn that what God finds in his mind before creation is a multiplicity of worlds and not substances.[14] In a sense, then, worlds precede substances, since substances are only considered for creation as belonging to infinite series that form possible worlds among which God makes his choice. There is thus, for Leibniz, at once a gulf and an indissoluble bond between substances and their worlds. On the one hand, substances must be arranged in a certain way to form a world. On the other hand, their arrangement into a world predetermines the very creation of substances.

In order to explain the difference between a possible substance as such and considerations related to the potential coexistence of substances within a world, Leibniz introduces the term 'compossibility'. Making notes on Spinoza's direct equation between possibility and existence, which makes God's choice among possibilities redundant, Leibniz argues that for something to exist, it must not only be 'possible within itself' but also 'compossible with other things'.[15] In a letter to Louis Bourguet, Leibniz further explains this distinction. He argues that the universe is not 'a collection of all possibles [...] since all possibles are not compossible'; rather, 'the universe is a collection of a certain order of compossibles only'.[16] Possibility is defined as the absence of contradiction, the presence of which would immediately rule out any possibility of the existence of a substance. Compossibility, on the other hand, refers to the intra-worldly compatibility of substances. For the existence of a substance to be possible in a particular world, it must be compossible with other substances in that world. While possibility is absolute, compossibility is relative to a particular world: 'And since there are different combinations of possibilities [...] there are many possible universes, each collection of compossibles making up one of them.'[17]

Yet, even a set of compossible substances alone is not enough to constitute a world. The necessity to order the substances into a world arises from the fact that they have no causal relation to each other. This is one of the mainstays of Leibniz's theory of substance, which changes in several other ways throughout his work. If substances could interact, their world could simply be equated with the totality of what results from these interactions. However, 'one particular substance never acts upon another particular substance nor is acted upon by it'.[18] For Leibniz, the very notion of substance still implies its complete self-sufficiency and inner determinacy.[19] Substances are the sources of their own actions and perceptions according to their inner law, which is inscribed in them by God. However, they do not act upon each other. In the 'Monadology' Leibniz provides the famous image of the monads having 'no windows through which something can enter or leave'.[20] Thus, in addition to creating substances, God also has to provide for the 'interconnection or accommodation of all created things to each other'.[21] Since monads have no interaction between each other, they have to be arranged and harmonised to form a coherent world.

Leibniz solves the problem of coexistence of independent substances with the concept of pre-established harmony. Like musicians playing in different places following the same notes, or different clocks telling the same time, although their mechanisms are not causally connected, the actions of substances are harmonised in perfect reciprocity. Without any physical influence between them, substances are coordinated with each other due to following God's predetermined design of the world in which they coexist. God has created each substance 'in such a way that everything must arise for it from its own depths, through a perfect *spontaneity* relative to itself, and yet with a perfect *conformity* relative to external things'.[22] The immanent law of any substance is harmonised with the general law of the world, which means that in each substance, the design of the whole world can be discerned. As Leibniz explains in a letter to Antoine Arnauld, 'every individual substance or complete being is, as it were, a world apart, independent of everything else excepting God'; yet, at the same time, 'all created substances are a continual production of the same sovereign being according to the same plans, and are an expression of the same universe or of the same phenomena'.[23] The same harmony runs through all substances, which means that in their separate existence, they nevertheless express all other substances and thereby represent the whole world (even though only the closest parts can be represented clearly).[24]

Although God designs and programmes substances to fit seamlessly with others, Leibniz is careful not to passivise them as mere cogs in the clockwork of the world to which they belong. As explained in the 'Monadology', the activity of monads results from their inner drive or appetition.[25] This gives rise to complex, ever-changing perceptions within each monad. It is this complexity that makes each monad unique compared to others. Even if a monad has no windows, the perceptions that arise within it through auto-affection are coordinated with the perceptions of all other monads. Through the harmonious connection of each monad with all others, the monad expresses the whole world from the specific perspective of its own uniqueness. The point, therefore, is not only that monads are parts of a world (arranged according to the principle of pre-established harmony), but also that the whole world is present in each monad.

From the combination of the separation of each monad, which acts like a world apart, and the fact that each monad also expresses the whole world, the perspectivist multiplication of worlds results:

> Just as the same city viewed from different directions appears entirely different and, as it were, multiplied perspectively, in just the same way it happens that, because of the infinite multitude of simple substances, there are, as it were, just as many different universes, which are, nevertheless, only perspectives on a single one, corresponding to the different points of view of each monad.[26]

As Leibniz makes clear, the monadic points of view are of the same universe or world; however, the persistent image of monads and their points of view as being worlds in their own right suggests a strong version of perspectivism and therefore indicates a tendency towards an actual multiplicity of worlds. We saw above in a long quotation from the 'Discourse on Metaphysics' that points of view logically precede substances; any favourable view of the world God contemplates for creation results in a substance that expresses that view. By this logic, paradoxically, monads are both views on the city and the 'buildings' of the observed city itself. The world that unites the created monads consists of just such views, each of which is defined as a perspectivist multiplication of that world. Leibniz's strong perspectivism suggests that a world is a union of a multiplicity of worlds from which it is composed.

Another kind of perspectivism emerges when we move from the ontological level of substances to the phenomenological level of bodies. The harmony that unites the substances into a world also synchronises the actions and perceptions of substances with the bodies that constitute the material world of phenomena. The way matter and bodies emerge in a world constituted solely of monads, which are themselves immaterial, remains unclear. Leibniz provides several lines of reasoning on this question but no definite answer.[27] It is clear, however, that any immaterial monad is bound to a body, which should be understood both as an aggregate of other substances and as a part of the material world. Unlike monads, which are immaterial undividable unities, matter is infinitely divisible and actually divided into an infinite multiplicity of bodies. Leibniz's search for substance as the ultimate unity is starkly contrasted by his fierce opposition to physical atomism. Each body can be divided into parts, which can themselves be considered as bodies consisting of parts and so on *ad infinitum*.

While at the ontological level monads provide singular (if only partially clear) perspectives on the world as a whole, at the phenomenological level perspective is defined by the framing of materiality. This means that material entities (bodies) can be recognised depending on how closely or at what level materiality is observed. The more we zoom in, so to speak, the more bodies we find: 'Each portion of matter can be conceived as a garden full of plants, and as a pond full of fish. But each branch of a plant, each limb of an animal, each drop of its humors, is still another such garden or pond.'[28] There is thus 'a world of creatures [. . .] in the least piece of matter'.[29] In order to find new worlds, it is not necessary to look at the sky, but to look more closely at what is right here, not only right next to us, but also as part of us. It turns out that the invention of the microscope was more important to Leibniz in this regard than the invention of the telescope. As Michel Serres notes in his book on Leibniz, the telescope only allowed us to see more clearly the world we already knew, while the microscope allowed us to discover a new world of creatures which we were not aware of.[30] In other words, the telescope refers to the world in a cosmological sense, while the microscope helps us discover a perspectivist multiplicity of worlds. The subjectivist perspective of a monad is thus joined by an objectivist perspective of a microscope, which reveals an infinite number of worlds within worlds.

Monads are indivisible and thus 'true atoms of nature' only in a strictly ontological sense; at the level of material reality, no indivisible unity of an ultimate building block can be found. An interesting implication of this is that the more we zoom in on matter and discover smaller and smaller 'ponds of fish', there will always have to be monads there to constitute these bodies. Thus, the world consists of an infinite multiplicity of monads not only in the sense of a limitless expansion but also in the sense of an infinite stratification of every part of the world. An infinity of monads is thus present in each grain of sand and again in each part of the grain of sand and so on.[31]

In the face of infinite divisibility, the task of ontology for Leibniz is to ensure unity in multiplicity. Due to the infinite multiplicity of substances, as we have seen, the world cannot constitute a whole. However, there is an ontological unity that makes this multiplicity consistent. We can speculate that without such a unity, all that existed would be matter as pure division – a division that would not even be a division into parts, since there would be no unity that would allow us to conceive of what is thus divided as parts at all. 'Monadology' thus presents an infinity of discernible unique monads that structure ontological multiplicity. The unification and division of matter into bodies is made possible by the fundamental unity provided by each body's dominant monad. Having no parts of their own, monads make possible the very existence of parts. We can also speculate that without the unity inscribed in ontological multiplicity, there would be no world as the ultimate, if non-whole, accumulation of parts. The concept of world ultimately refers to a kind of unification of what is, which would not be possible if all there was was pure division.

This complicated interplay of the one and the many, of unity and multiplicity, characterises Leibniz's thought on both substance and world. On the one hand, only one world can exist and it is the best possible one. Yet, the fact that the world has to be chosen from an infinite multiplicity of possible worlds immediately leaves the stamp of contingency even on the sole actual world. If the created world is only one of the many possible worlds, it is defined not primarily by its wholeness or existence, but by what distinguished it from other worlds before creation, namely its specific composition and arrangement of substances. The latent multiplication of worlds appears again in the guise of perspectivist multiplicity within the one actual world. Each substance is a world apart, a micro-world defined as a perspective on the macro-world of which it is a part. Each part of material reality can also be seen as its own world full of creatures, if one looks closely enough. While every possible world is defined by God's view of the multiplicity of which it is composed, every world is itself multiplied by partial perspectives. Leibniz's worlds are thus always contingent and partial, defined by a particular perspective, as though it would be formed by the frame through which it is viewed.

Beyond Leibniz with Leibniz

We now turn to contemporary readings of Leibniz, in particular to the two philosophers that can – as I try to show below – most assuredly be considered as heirs of the Leibnizian concept of world. In 1988, Deleuze published his book on Leibniz, *The Fold: Leibniz and the Baroque*, while Badiou issued his seminal *Being and Event*, in which Leibniz is also discussed. The following year, Badiou responded to Deleuze's book with a review, which – according to Badiou's own account – Deleuze acknowledged favourably and which eventually initiated a correspondence between the two philosophers who were previously quite hostile to one another.[32] Leibniz thus becomes a point of departure for a contemporary discussion on the nature of ontological multiplicity and its relation to worlds, which I will discuss more closely in Chapter 3.

What matters here is how Deleuze and Badiou read Leibniz and position themselves with respect to his concept of world. Both turn to Leibniz as the crucial and singular reference for thinking the concept of world today. They also mark their point of divergence from Leibniz in the same way: while Leibniz claimed that only the best of all worlds could ever be created, it is now essential to admit that an incompossible multiplicity of worlds exists. Nevertheless, it is still the concept of world in Leibniz's definition and his vision of an infinity of possible worlds that allow us to theorise this multiplicity, which in the meantime became actualised.

The importance of Leibniz for Deleuze is not limited to the book he wrote about the philosopher at a late stage of his work. Leibniz – and in particular his concept of world in connection with ontological multiplicity – appears in the two early fundamental books of Deleuze's philosophy, *Difference and Repetition* and *The Logic of Sense*. Developing the foundations of his own philosophy, Deleuze turns to Leibniz and the way 'he distributes [. . .] the differential elements of a multiplicity throughout the ground, and [. . .] discovers a play in the creation of the world'.[33] For Deleuze, following Leibniz, the construction of worlds 'presupposes the distribution of pure singularities according to the rules of convergence and divergence'.[34] A convergently distributed series of singularities composes a particular world according to the principle of compossibility. Divergence, on the other hand, marks the difference between possible worlds (for example, a world with Adam-the-sinner and a world with Adam-the-non-sinner).

Deleuze, however, performs a double subversion of Leibniz. First, on account of the distributed multiplicity of singularities, and second, on account of the worlds they compose. According to Deleuze's reading, to start with the former, it is not primarily the individuals as monads that constitute worlds, but singular elements, events, affections and properties that precede the constitution of individuals:

> We see that the continuum of singularities is entirely distinct from the individuals which envelop it in variable and complementary degrees of clarity: singularities are pre-individual. If it is true that the expressed world exists only in individuals, and that it exists

there only as a predicate, it subsists in an entirely different manner, as an event or a verb, in the singularities which preside over the constitution of individuals. It is no longer Adam-the-sinner but rather the world in which Adam has sinned.[35]

Singularities such as the event of sinning (or not-sinning) in relation to an only partially defined Adam precede the existence of Adam-the-sinner in the created world. Such pre-individual singularities constitute the nomadic 'pluralism of free, wild or untamed differences'.[36] This ontological multiplicity forms 'the real transcendental field' on the basis of which singularities are distributed in order to form particular worlds in which defined individuals exist.[37]

For Deleuze, worlds are the result of a process in which infinite convergent series of actualised singularities are formed on the basis of a virtual transcendental field of untamed differences. Accordingly, the Leibnizian concept of world is transcendental, but in a way that strongly differs from how transcendentalism is usually understood in the Kantian sense: 'A Leibnizian transcendental philosophy, which bears on the event rather than the phenomenon, replaces Kantian conditioning by means of a double operation of transcendental actualization and realization.'[38] The transcendental does not refer to the conditions of our approach to an otherwise unknowable ontological reality; rather, it refers to the process of actualisation and realisation of a virtuality: 'The world is a virtuality that is actualised in monads or souls, but also a possibility that must be realized in matter or in bodies.'[39] In Leibniz, however, the pure nomadic multiplicity is immediately filtered so that the many become one. A screen is placed in front of ontological multiplicity, which 'only allows compossibles – and only the best combination of compossibles – to be sifted through'.[40] This screen enables the formation of worlds as convergent and consistent series of singularities and ultimately allows only one – the best – world to be created. Nevertheless, even the best world is only one among a multiplicity of 'unique and relative' ones.[41] A new conceptualisation of world is thus invented, by way of which the Baroque 'transformation of the cosmos into a "mundus"' takes place.[42]

This transformation is a consequence of the collapse of the theological ideal and the classical reason that takes place in the Baroque.[43] At this point, Deleuze addresses Leibniz the theodician. Leibniz acts as God's 'lawyer' in an attempt to save the world constructed by theological reason, but only manages to suggest a 'schizophrenic reconstruction'.[44] This is where Leibniz's multiplicities ultimately come from. They are representative of Baroque's attempt to defend the theological ideal by multiplying principles that explain away any case made against it.[45] Leibniz's concept of world, as Deleuze sees it in this context, 'represents the ultimate attempt to reconstitute classical reason by dividing divergences into as many worlds as possible, and by making from incompossibilities as many possible borders between worlds'.[46] Leibniz might be the philosopher that discovered the play of the world, but also the philosopher that tried to restrain the divergences that ensue from it.

Here is where Deleuze performs his other subversion of Leibniz and argues for a 'neo-Leibnizianism' that would correspond to the era of the 'neo-Baroque' we find ourselves in today.[47] We have seen that the world, for Leibniz, was a result of a process of a transcendental selection. Now, the play of the world has changed due to the ultimate collapse of theological reason. Selection gives way to an affirmation of divergences.[48] The transcendental field can no longer be contained by boundaries between possible worlds. Incompossibilities can now occur within the same world: 'In a same chaotic world divergent series are endlessly tracing bifurcating paths.'[49] We are thus confronted with a vision of an actualised multiplicity of worlds, or a coexistence of incompossibilities within the same world, which – for Deleuze – amounts to the same thing. Deleuze offers this image whenever he discusses the Leibnizian concept of world, from his early to his late work.[50] Leibniz's discoveries are undoubtedly insufficient for what Deleuze wants to show, yet play a significant role in the development of his own arguments. It is Leibniz's novel concept of world that allows Deleuze to formulate his own conceptualisation of a chaotic world of incompossibilities, which we will examine more closely in Chapter 3.

Badiou's reading of Leibniz in *Being and Event* has a similar starting point to Deleuze's reading published in the same year. Leibniz's thought offers 'radical anticipations', but only on the basis of 'a conservative will' that simultaneously enables such anticipations and prevents them from fully developing their implications.[51] Badiou, however, only offers a glimpse into the anticipations and is much more interested in the way Leibniz restrains the excesses of the infinite ontological multiplicity he discovers. According to Badiou, Leibniz 'assumes the infinite divisibility of natural being without concession; he then compensates for and restricts the excess that he thus liberates within the state of the world [...] by the hypothesis of a control of singularities'.[52] Leibniz's multiplicity is ultimately a multiplicity of unities as nameable parts in which no void or excess can exist. In contrast to this, as we will observe in more detail in the next chapter, Badiou's own ontological project, based on mathematical set theory, develops a concept of pure multiplicity of multiplicities, founded on the void and characterised by an excess of parts. However, the most important consequence of Leibniz's ontological conservativism for Badiou lies not in ontology itself, but in the prohibition of the occurrence of an event that could contradict a given presentation of ontological multiplicity. For Leibniz, 'there is no event, since everything which happens is locally calculable and globally placed in a series whose reason is God'.[53]

Badiou's review of *The Fold*, published in 1989, provides an insight into how his reading of Leibniz compares to Deleuze's. Badiou welcomes Deleuze's effort to look beyond Leibniz's emphasis on the best of all worlds and describe our contemporary world as one in which incompossibilities coexist.[54] After this introductory salute, however, Badiou draws a line of demarcation between his own philosophy and the one Deleuze develops on the basis of his appropriation of Leibniz. The differences between their philosophical undertakings can be traced back to two opposite paradigms of multiplicity, the mathematical (or set-theoretical) and the organicist (or vitalist). According to Badiou, the world constructed by Deleuze-Leibniz (as Badiou calls the merged author of these thoughts) is a divergent totality. Due to the vitalist dynamism of this totality – 'the anarchic World-Animal' – there is constant 'immanent activity against the backdrop of totality; a creation or novelty, certainly, but thinkable from within the interiority of the continuous'.[55] For Deleuze, the movements of actualisation and realisation make of everything an event. In Badiou's understanding, contrary to Deleuze's intentions, this makes events indistinguishable from facts. According to Badiou's own account of multiplicity, on the contrary, there is no immanent activity and certainly no totality. True divergence only occurs if an event performs a radical rupture with the law of the world it takes place in. It is questionable, however, if such a law of the world, which definitely exists in Leibniz, can also be attributed – as Badiou seems to imply here – to Deleuze's understanding of the bifurcation of worlds. Does Deleuze's chaotic world even obey a law that could be disturbed by an event? Be that as it may, it is on the basis of such ruptures with a given world that truths emerge, according to Badiou. If the proper role of philosophy is to follow such truths, as he concludes, it 'must renounce the world'.[56]

While in that period Badiou mostly used Leibniz to demonstrate how his ontological project diverges from philosophical tradition and from his contemporaries (Deleuze), he returns to Leibniz in a more affirmative light in *Logics of Worlds*, the sequel to *Being and Event*. Although this work continues Badiou's persuasion that truths occur on the basis of an eventual rupture with a given world, the concept of world now acquires a crucial significance in its own right as the way ontological multiples come to appearance. Leibniz too thus gains in importance, since Badiou shares with him 'the same orientation with respect to the theory of the world'.[57] In fact, Leibniz is the only philosopher whose concept of world Badiou discusses affirmatively in relation to his own. In Badiou's account, this common orientation of thinking the concept of world relies on an ontological foundation composed of a multiplicity of monads (Leibniz) or pure multiplicities (Badiou) understood through mathematics (differential calculus in the case of Leibniz, set theory in the case of Badiou). Worlds, then, signify the way this ontological multiplicity comes into existence. Multiples come to form a world through a particular rule that sets their 'intensities of existence as well as the relations of identity and difference' between them. Leibniz called this rule pre-established harmony, while Badiou calls it the transcendental.[58]

Badiou then turns to differences, acknowledging that Deleuze has already stated all that needs to be said in this regard:

> Gilles Deleuze already acutely noted that it is on this point that we moderns diverge from Leibniz's classical-baroque stance. For us, it is effectively indisputable that there are multiple worlds, a divergent series of worlds, and that none may claim to be the best.[59]

Badiou fully agrees with this assessment and regrets that Leibniz subordinated the many to the power of the one. Nevertheless, he acknowledges that 'Leibniz is beyond doubt the thinker who has most enduringly meditated on the hypothesis of an infinite plurality of essential worlds'.[60]

Deleuze and Badiou thus both develop their respective conceptualisations of world in direct continuity with Leibniz. Both understand Leibnizian worlds as constituted by a transcendental principle that arranges ontological multiplicity in a particular way. Both also suggest that contemporary thought, going beyond Leibniz, should rethink the multiplicity of worlds as actual. Yet, as we will see in the next chapter and – from a different perspective – again in Chapter 5, Deleuze and Badiou understand this actuality in very different ways. The contrast between their respective conceptions of ontological multiplicity leads to completely different understandings of its transcendental arrangement into worlds.

Notes

1. See, for example, the limited role Leibniz plays in Steven J. Dick, *Plurality of Worlds: The Origins of the Extraterrestrial Life Debate from Democritus to Kant* (Cambridge: Cambridge University Press, 1982), or Mary-Jane Rubenstein, *Worlds Without End: The Many Lives of the Multiverse* (New York: Columbia University Press, 2014). In studies on the history of cosmology, the two books above included, Leibniz is most often mentioned in relation to his correspondence with Clarke, in which he attacks Newton's position on the absolute nature of space and time and the active role of God in the created universe.
2. G. W. Leibniz, *Theodicy: Essays on the Goodness of God, the Freedom of Man and the Origin of Evil*, trans. E. M. Huggard, Project Gutenberg, 2005, § 8, https://www.gutenberg.org/files/17147/17147-h/17147-h.htm.
3. The Leibnizian concept of world in a purely modal sense has found an afterlife in modal logic as developed in contemporary analytic philosophy. In these discussions, however, Leibniz takes only the role of a distant predecessor. For Leibniz himself, possible worlds were not a cosmological reality (since only one universe was created), but neither did they have a purely logical status – on the contrary, they played a crucial role in his metaphysical apparatus.
4. G. W. Leibniz, 'The Principles of Philosophy, or, the Monadology', in *Philosophical Essays*, trans. Roger Ariew and Daniel Garber (Indianapolis: Hackett, 1989), 220 (§ 53).
5. G. W. Leibniz, 'A New System of the Nature and Communication of Substances, and of the Union of the Soul and Body', in *Philosophical Essays*, 143.
6. Leibniz, *Theodicy*, § 195.
7. For a detailed discussion on Leibniz's notion of the infinite and its implication for his concept of world see Laurence Carlin, 'Infinite Accumulations and Pantheistic Implications: Leibniz and the *Anima Mundi*', *Leibniz Society Review* 7 (1997): 1–24; Richard Arthur, 'Infinite Number and the World Soul; in Defence of Carlin and Leibniz', *Leibniz Society Review* 9 (1999): 105–16.

8. Leibniz, 'Monadology', 220 (§ 57).
9. Leibniz, *Theodicy*, § 225.
10. Leibniz, 'Monadology', 220 (§ 55).
11. Ibid. 217 (§ 33). See also G. W. Leibniz, 'Discourse on Metaphysics', in *Philosophical Essays*, 44–6 (§ 13).
12. G. W. Leibniz, 'Mr. Leibniz's Fifth Paper', in *The Leibniz-Clarke Correspondence*, ed. H. G. Alexander (Manchester: Manchester University Press, 1956), 57.
13. Leibniz, 'Discourse on Metaphysics', 46–7 (§ 14).
14. Nicholas Rescher even claims that in Leibniz, 'God does not make the conception of the world, he finds it fully formed, so to speak, in his mind – along with the conception of innumerably many other alternative worlds. In relation to the actual world, God is the creator: he selects it for actualization. But in relation to the manifold of possible worlds, God plays no creative role.' Nicholas Rescher, 'Leibniz on Possible Worlds', *Studia Leibnitiana* 28, no. 2 (1996): 131–2, http://www.jstor.org/stable/40694300.
15. G. W. Leibniz, *Philosophical Papers and Letters*, trans. Leroy E. Loemker (Dordrecht: Kluwer, 1989), 169.
16. Ibid. 662.
17. Ibid. 662.
18. Leibniz, 'Discourse on Metaphysics', 47 (§ 14).
19. Leibniz, 'Monadology', 215 (§ 18).
20. Ibid. 214 (§ 7).
21. Ibid. 220 (§ 56).
22. Leibniz, 'A New System', 143.
23. G. W. Leibniz, 'Leibniz to Arnauld. Hanover, 4/14 July 1686', in *The Leibniz-Arnauld Correspondence*, ed. and trans. H. T. Mason (Manchester: Manchester University Press, 1967), 64.
24. Leibniz, 'Monadology', 220–1 (§ 59–60).
25. Ibid. 215 (§ 15).
26. Ibid. 220 (§ 57).
27. Daniel Garber provides a comprehensive overview of these lines of reasoning in chapter 9 of his *Leibniz: Body, Substance, Monad* (Oxford: Oxford University Press, 2009), 351–88. 'There are texts that suggest that bodies are aggregates of monads, and others that suggest that bodies are just the common coherent dreams of an infinity of monads. There are texts that suggest that all there are are monads in the world, and that everything else is just phenomena, while other texts suggest that there are, in addition, composite or corporeal substances.' Ibid. 382.
28. Leibniz, 'Monadology', 222 (§ 67).
29. Ibid. 222 (§ 66). In a letter to Foucher from 1693, which pre-dates the 'Monadology' by more than twenty years, Leibniz claimed that 'the

smallest particle [of matter] must be considered as a world filled with an infinity of different creatures'. G. W. Leibniz, quoted in Nicholas Rescher, G. W. Leibniz's Monadology: An Edition for Students (Pittsburgh: University of Pittsburgh Press, 1991), 228.
30. Michel Serres, *Le système de Leibniz et ses modèles mathématiques* (Paris: PUF, 1968), 376–7.
31. 'Because monads are presupposed in every actual part of matter, and matter is infinitely divided, there are actually infinitely many monads.' Richard T. W. Arthur, 'Leibniz's Actual Infinite in Relation to his Analysis of Matter', in *G. W. Leibniz, Interrelations between Mathematics and Philosophy*, ed. Norma B. Goethe, Philip Beeley and David Rabouin (Dordrecht: Springer, 2015), 154, https://doi.org/10.1007/978-94-017-9664-4_7.
32. Alain Badiou, *Deleuze: The Clamor of Being*, trans. Louise Burchill (Minneapolis: University of Minnesota Press, 2000), 4–5.
33. Gilles Deleuze, *Difference and Repetition*, trans. Paul Patton (London: Continuum, 2001), 51.
34. Gilles Deleuze, *The Logic of Sense*, trans. Mark Lester and Charles Stivale (London: Athlone Press, 1990), 111.
35. Ibid. 111.
36. Deleuze, *Difference and Repetition*, 50.
37. Deleuze, *The Logic of Sense*, 109.
38. Gilles Deleuze, *The Fold: Leibniz and the Baroque*, trans. Tom Colney (London: Athlone Press, 1993), 104.
39. Ibid. 120.
40. Ibid. 77.
41. Ibid. 60.
42. Ibid. 29.
43. Ibid. 67, 81.
44. Ibid. 68.
45. Ibid. 67.
46. Ibid. 81.
47. Ibid. 82, 136.
48. Ibid. 137.
49. Ibid. 81.
50. Deleuze, *Difference and Repetition*, 51; Deleuze, *The Logic of Sense*, 114, 172–4; Gilles Deleuze, *Cinema 2: The Time-Image*, trans. Hugh Tomlinson and Robert Galeta (Minneapolis: University of Minnesota Press, 1989), 131.
51. Alain Badiou, *Being and Event*, trans. Oliver Feltham (London: Continuum, 2005), 315.
52. Ibid. 320.
53. Ibid. 319.

54. Alain Badiou, 'Gilles Deleuze, *The Fold: Leibniz and the Baroque*', in *The Adventure of French Philosophy*, ed. and trans. Bruno Bosteels (London: Verso, 2012), 242.
55. Ibid. 254–5.
56. Ibid. 266.
57. Alain Badiou, *Logics of Worlds: Being and Event, 2*, trans. Alberto Toscano (London: Continuum, 2009), 327.
58. Ibid. 327.
59. Ibid. 329.
60. Ibid. 329.

3 Between Ontological and Transcendental Multiplicity

THIS CHAPTER PRESENTS A parallel reading of Gilles Deleuze and Alain Badiou as contemporary heirs of the Leibnizian concept of world. Leibniz's philosophy, as we saw in Chapter 2, opened a radically different way of conceptualising the notion of world, one based on an interplay between the ontological multiplicity and the multiplicity of worlds. Deleuze and Badiou fully accept these parameters, but also identify the limitations of Leibniz's thought that must now be superseded. While Leibniz discovered a new way of thinking the concept of world, he did not fully develop its implications due to his insistence on the one and only actual world and his commitment to the primacy of convergence as an exclusive world-making principle. In their readings of Leibniz – surprisingly convergent considering the strong divergence between their philosophical projects – Deleuze and Badiou both emphasise that the multiplicity of worlds can no longer be contained within the realm of possibility. We are now dealing with an actualised multiplicity of worlds, formed through transcendental structures or processes. For both Deleuze and Badiou, ontological multiplicity entails transcendental multiplicity. There is an excess of being that has the power to subvert the consistency needed to support the construction of a world. On the other hand, however, the proliferation of worlds produces its own excess as beings find themselves inhabiting several worlds at once. How to articulate this double excess, the excess of being over any world on the one hand and the excess of worlds over beings on the other? Developing a Leibnizian concept of world beyond the limitations imposed on it by Leibniz is an endeavour these two philosophers share, although their approaches, as we will see, differ greatly.

Deleuze or Badiou? Thinking Multiplicity Beyond Representation

What I have been schematically calling 'ontological multiplicity' marks a crucial theoretical interest shared by Deleuze and Badiou, but also the point where their paths emphatically split. As the history of the heated exchanges between them testifies, each sees in the other's work an impoverished version of such multiplicity.[1] For Badiou, Deleuze's vitalist paradigm of multiplicity is inferior to the complex forms of thinking multiplicity made available by mathematical set theory.[2] Deleuze (together with Félix Guattari), on the other hand, sees in Badiou's ontology a reduction of multiplicity to a mathematical set ('even mathematics has had enough of set-theoreticism'); against this reduction, at least two types of multiplicities should be taken into account, the actual and the virtual.[3] While Badiou accuses Deleuze of ultimately subsuming multiplicity to the one (which only set theory can avoid), Deleuze thinks that Badiou's notion of truth fails to think multiplicity in its immanence and makes his philosophy reach for a transcendent event. The accusations that Deleuze and Badiou address to each other are basically the same: the failure to properly conceptualise ontological multiplicity leads to an unintentional reaffirmation of transcendence. As Badiou himself summarises: 'The result is that Deleuze's virtual ground remains for me a transcendence, whereas for Deleuze, it is my logic of the multiple that, in not being originally referred to the act of the One, fails to hold thought firmly within immanence.'[4]

Ever since Badiou's book on Deleuze, there has been a growing body of literature that compares the two thinkers, sometimes taking sides with one against the other and pointing out their misreadings of each other's work.[5] It is clear, however, that these misreadings are conditioned by the pressures of the conceptual apparatuses each was developing. Deleuze can indeed be seen as a philosopher of the one if and only if we fully accept the way Badiou defines multiplicity. On the other hand, Badiou can indeed be seen as presenting a radically diminished understanding of multiplicity (reduced to sets) if we accept a

Deleuzian understanding of immanence. Asking the question whether one was 'right' about the other outside of these specific frameworks makes no sense, as there is ultimately no neutral middle ground where such judgements could be made. The question of the ontological multiplicity in opposition to the representational construction of reality can only be seen as a 'virtual' problem they both share, although the problem is in actuality posed and solved differently by each philosopher. Deleuze and Badiou thus represent two very different ways of thinking being as multiplicity – different to the extent that the common denominator 'being as multiplicity' should itself be questioned. In fact, while the designation of being as multiplicity may serve as a valuable comparative starting point, it is not completely accurate for either of them.

To say that being is multiplicity in Deleuze is not entirely accurate in the sense that the primary characteristic of being is 'univocity': being 'is said in one and the same "sense" of everything about which it is said'.[6] Being is the same for all that exists and for all that happens; it is common to the real, the possible and the impossible.[7] This is Badiou's prime evidence that Deleuze reinvents a metaphysics of the one.[8] In Deleuze's *The Logic of Sense*, however, the discussion of univocity immediately follows the discussion on the affirmation of divergences and thus the coexistence of Leibnizian incompossibilities. The univocal sense of being can only be expressed through divergent multiplicity. The univocity of 'Being does not mean that there is one and the same Being; on the contrary, beings are multiple and different, they are always produced by a disjunctive synthesis, and they themselves are disjointed and divergent, *membra disjuncta*'.[9]

The coexistence of all divergences, however, is only possible in a virtual sphere in which even contrary events are compatible and express each other. Incompossibility in the sense of incompatibility only emerges when the virtual is actualised: 'Incompatibility is born only with individuals, persons, and worlds in which events are actualized, but not between events themselves or between their *a-cosmic*, *impersonal*, and *preindividual* singularities.'[10] The line of ontological difference is thus drawn between the virtual compatibility of all events and pre-individual singularities on the one hand and the actualisation of individuals and events in particular worlds on the other.

The relation between the virtual and the actual is the key issue in the context of which Deleuze reflects on the concept of world. In

Difference and Repetition, he presents this relation as the opposition between the world of representation and the world of impersonal and pre-individual singularities.[11] For Deleuze (as for Badiou, as we will see) the fight against representation is not a fight against reproducing the world but against a specific way of constructing it. Singularities are turned personal and individual through the principles of representation (identity, analogy, opposition and resemblance).[12] For Deleuze, the break with representation is what defines the task of a truly contemporary philosophy: 'modern thought is born of the failure of representation, of the loss of identities, and of the discovery of all the forces that act under the representation of the identical'.[13] We have to find a way to escape representational actuality to unleash, once again, a nomadic redistribution of singularities beyond identities, recalling the univocity of being.

Contrary to Deleuze's, Badiou's ontological project is specifically designed to think multiplicity beyond any notion of the one. Badiou finds the means for carrying out such a project in set theory, according to which no multiple of all multiples can exist. Nevertheless, Badiou does not directly equate being with multiplicity. It is not being itself that is multiple – being only *presents* itself as multiple. Badiou is committed to a radically 'subtractive' vision of ontology, in which being is 'foreclosed not only from representation but from all presentation'.[14] This means that being-qua-being is neither one nor multiple; it can only be known in ontology as a void and mathematically addressed as an empty set. The presentation of being, however, can be thought of as multiplicity – and there is no better way to think multiplicity than mathematical set theory. This is why philosophy, Badiou claims, should acknowledge mathematics as ontology.

The subtractive character of being is another crucial trait through which Badiou distinguishes his own ontological thought from Deleuze's. As we have already seen in Chapter 1, he presents his project as an alternative to the Heideggerian 'poetic ontology', which looks for expressions of being beyond representation. However, Badiou will later reveal that he eventually came to realise that his aim was actually to present an ontology of multiplicity (based on set theory) that would rival the 'vitalist' one developed by Deleuze.[15] Similarly to Deleuze, Badiou draws the line of ontological difference between representational constructions (what he calls 'situations') and pure multiplicity. Nevertheless, the subtractive nature of Badiou's ontology does not allow for a possibility of finding an immediate presentation of being beyond the veil of representation. Juliette Simont rightly observes that here is where the difference between Deleuze's and Badiou's ontologies lies: while for Deleuze there is always a thread that connects the virtual to its actualisations, which allows for the movement in the opposite direction, for Badiou no such thread exists, which means that no revelation of being is possible.[16] For Badiou, in any case, this is not what philosophy is after. The subtractive approach to ontology ultimately 'un-binds the Heideggerian connection between being and truth',[17] a bond that still exists in Deleuze in the form of counteractualisation in which representational constructions are dissolved back into the virtual. According to Badiou, truth cannot be found in an expression, a revelation or a becoming of being.

For Badiou, truth is a (political, scientific, artistic or amorous) subjective procedure in fidelity to an event, which is defined precisely as 'that-which-is-not-being-qua-being'.[18] Events are not expressions of being, as they are for Deleuze; on the contrary, they are pure contingent ruptures with no ontological consistency. Events undermine the consistency of the (re)presentationally structured situations in which they occur. Having no being of their own, however, events disappear as soon as they take place. This is why it takes a subject to declare that an event has indeed taken place. The subject's fidelity to the event in a truth procedure will consist of the efforts to transform the situation. This assures that the event will be 'recognized in the situation by its consequences'.[19]

This also implies a different relation between pure multiplicity and representation to the one seen in Deleuze. In its inaugural intervention in the situation, according to Badiou, the subject names the event, thereby affirming its existence. Badiou calls this first consequence of the event – its name – 'a representative without representation'.[20] It is a *representative*, since the event can have no immediate being of its own within the situation; it is *without representation* because it defies and challenges the regime of representation that structures the situation. By its very existence, the event reveals the inconsistency of the situation – the void around which it is structured: 'It is only *for the event*, thus for the nomination of a paradoxical multiple, that the term chosen by the intervenor represents the void.'[21] The pure non-representational multiplicity can never be directly presented; it can only be retrospectively alluded to from the perspective of an event as the void of the situation: 'The event will be this ultra-one of a hazard, on the basis of which the void of a situation is retroactively discernible.'[22] By its very occurrence, the event indicates being as inconsistent multiplicity, but is in no way its effect or expression. Being as inconsistent multiplicity beyond representation cannot be directly revealed; instead, it can only be retroactively represented by the consequences of an event, which reveals the inconsistencies of representation. Therefore, representation cannot be challenged by what escapes it (a pure presentation), but only by an *additional representation*, a 'risky supplementation'[23] that rivals the dominant regime of representation.

Beyond the well-known controversy between Deleuze and Badiou over how to understand ontological multiplicity, there is a less explored issue of how this debate relates to the transcendental multiplicity of worlds. I explore this issue that both authors share in more detail below, first through Deleuze and then through Badiou. The two philosophers under consideration again part ways at this point.[24] The questions over the one and the multiple, transcendence and immanence, again come into sight, but cannot fully account for the differences between their approaches when it comes to the concept of world. This chapter is devoted to tracing the additional dividing lines that will help us distinguish between the philosophers' understandings of the actual multiplicity of worlds. The main question concerns the status of the transcendental formation of worlds in relation to being. In Deleuze, ontological multiplicity is itself the transcendental field in which worlds are generated as actualisations of series of singularities, which can also be drawn back into the acosmic univocity. The cosmogonic process in Deleuze can be described as a process of *transcendental folding*: worlds are folded from the continuous ontological multiplicity and dissolved back into it. In Badiou, on the other hand, the transcendental is not an immanent unfolding of being-qua-being. Worlds are contingent appearances of being arranged according to objective transcendental structures that select which multiples will appear in a given world and with what level of intensity. I propose to call this process *transcendental framing*: the transcendental acts as a frame imposed upon ontological multiplicity, thereby determining its partial local appearance within a world.[25]

Ontological Multiplicity and the Surplus of Worlds in Deleuze

Delineating the concept of world in Deleuze is not without its difficulties since it is a concept that appears throughout his writings in

BETWEEN ONTOLOGICAL AND TRANSCENDENTAL MULTIPLICITY | 75

different guises but never seems to achieve the status of a central component of his philosophy. Deleuze sometimes gives the impression of arguing for a two-worlds perspective as a kind of inverted Platonism, where the world of representation is opposed to the world of untamed differences and pre-individual singularities. Most often, however, Deleuze gives the concept of world a Leibnizian definition of a system of converging series of singularities, which he sometimes juxtaposes with or opposes to the Husserlian or the Kantian understanding of the concept.[26] The Leibnizian concept of world is then surpassed through the affirmation of divergences, which Deleuze sometimes describes as a multiplication of worlds, sometimes as the coexistence of incompossibles within the same world or universe, and still other times as the death of the world (alongside the death of God and the soul – the three Kantian transcendental ideas). Alternatively to these neo-Leibnizian attempts, Deleuze also detects a loss of belief in the world and mourns it as the outcome of historical atrocities and everyday banality. Is it possible to reconcile these intertwined meanings of the word 'world' under a common conceptual denominator? Or, do these different meanings rather converge from the perspective of another concept, ultimately superior to that of the world?

Something similar to a two-worlds perspective can be found at the beginning of *Difference and Repetition*, where Deleuze introduces his ontological project through a distinction between the world of representation and the forces that lie underneath it and constitute the world of simulacra.[27] As we have already stated, for Deleuze (as for Badiou) representation describes a way of constructing a world, not imagining it. Deleuze presents his version of the ontological difference as a descent from the world constituted by the principles of representation (identity, analogy, opposition and resemblance) to a world of impersonal and pre-individual singularities. It is therefore necessary to enter 'a world of differences [. . .], a complicated, properly chaotic world without identity'.[28]

It would be wrong, however, to understand this world beyond representation merely as a chaotic underworld. It only seems to be such from the perspective of the representational order, which sees it as an undifferentiated abyss, as Hegel objected to Schelling, of a dark night in which all cows are black. If we take it for what it is, Deleuze claims contra Hegel, we see the night become bright, which allows us to distinguish a world of differences and singularities.[29] The multiplicity thus revealed is not entirely chaotic, since it is ordered according to 'an organisation belonging to the many as such'.[30] Ontology thus entails an exploration of this immanent organisation of the seemingly chaotic world beyond the world of representation. As such, it can no longer be a part of 'the Platonic project of opposing the cosmos to chaos', since it is 'indeed the very opposite: the immanent identity of chaos and cosmos'.[31] Deleuze finds the perfect word for this immanent identity in Joyce's *Finnegans Wake*: the chaosmos. It is in the chaosmos that ontology finds its proper realm, where it places being within what could be called a chaosmogonic process: 'Ontology is the dice throw, the chaosmos from which the cosmos emerges.'[32]

The anti-Platonic character of Deleuze's ontology suggests that the two-world model – even though it is a part of Deleuze's rhetoric – is ultimately unsuitable for understanding the nature of the chaosmos. From an ontological perspective, there can be no two worlds, since being – for all its multiplicity – has to be thought of as univocal. The world of representation and the world of unbound singularities are not two separate worlds but the actual and the virtual dimension of the chaosmos in constant flux. The supposed two worlds have to be understood as a continuum. Even in a representational situation of seemingly complete actualisation, something of the virtual resists actualisation: 'Something of the ground rises to the surface, without assuming any form but, rather, insinuating itself between the forms; a formless base, an autonomous and faceless existence.'[33] A process of becoming can always occur in which singularities get redistributed and chaosmic dice recast.

This is also the reason why a distinction between being and appearance such as the one found in Badiou cannot exist in Deleuze. The transcendental that delimits a world is not imposed upon ontological multiplicity but stems immanently from it. The world of differences and singularities should itself be understood as 'an impersonal and pre-individual transcendental field, which does not resemble the corresponding empirical fields, and which nevertheless is not confused with an undifferentiated depth'.[34] Within this transcendental field, Deleuze explains in *The Logic of Sense*, singularities are constantly distributed and redistributed. The transcendental is therefore not a frame that would select discrete elements of ontological multiplicity for their appearance within a world but a board on which the cosmogonic dice are thrown. For Deleuze, ontological multiplicity is not composed of sets; it is rather a continuum that can be folded in several directions at once, depending on transcendental events. For Deleuze, therefore, the transcendental is not limited to conditioning (as it is in Kant and to a certain extent still in Badiou); instead, it is a field in which singularities get distributed and actualised.[35]

The discovery of the transcendental field of pre-individual and pre-cosmic singularities then leads to the question of the 'static ontological genesis' in which worlds and the individuals that belong to them are generated.[36] Singularities are actualised by extending themselves over a series of points, which brings them in the vicinity of other series. Neighbouring series form a world as 'an infinite system of singularities selected through convergence'.[37] Deleuze thus defines the concept of world in a stricter, Leibnizian sense. Convergence is the basis of Leibnizian compossibility, which excludes contradiction and establishes a continuity of the series. Divergences, on the other hand, mark the genesis of other worlds.

The adoption of a Leibnizian concept of world confirms the rejection of the two-world model in favour of a multiplicity of worlds. In Leibniz, of course, this multiplicity remains merely possible – but even so, it changes the way the concept of world can be understood:

> By thus positing an infinity of possible worlds, Leibniz in no way reintroduces a duality that would turn our relative world into the reflection of a more profound, absolute world: to the contrary, he turns our relative world into the only existing world, a world that rejects all other possible worlds because it is relatively 'the best.' God chooses between an infinity of possible worlds, incompossible with each other, and chooses the best, or the one that has the most possible reality. While the Good was the criterion of the two worlds, the Best is the criterion of the unique and relative world.[38]

Worlds should now be thought of as 'unique and relative', that is, unique in comparison with (or relative to) other possible worlds. The Baroque transformation from cosmos to *mundus* is thus complete.

While a world exists through the individuals that express it, individuals are themselves dependent on the world they express. Deleuze emphasises Leibniz's assertion that God primarily creates the world and not individual monads. God does not create Adam as a sinner but a world in which Adam sins. This 'ideal preexistence of the world' precedes the individualised parts of the world and the events that take place there.[39] In *The Fold*, Deleuze sides with Leibniz against Heidegger's characterisation of Dasein as being-in-the-world. For Leibniz, according to Deleuze, the monad is not 'in' but 'for' the world, which 'makes subjects all relate to this world as if to the virtuality that they actualize'.[40]

The process of actualisation, however, is characterised by entropy with regard to the divergent possibilities of the virtual. The potentiality of pre-individual singularities is exhausted when they are attributed to individuals. Individuals only have a very limited power to initiate local renewals of potentiality in the world they belong to. Deleuze claims that 'the question whether the world itself has a surface capable of forming again a potential of singularities is generally resolved in the negative'.[41] A world's capacity to change is therefore questionable.

If worlds as actualisations are marked by entropy with regard to their virtual intensity, what sustains the thread that connects actualisations back to the virtual and thus guarantees the univocity of being within the chaosmos? In order to answer this question, we must first understand how Deleuze takes the Leibnizian concept of world beyond Leibniz himself. With his unique and relative worlds, Leibniz discovered 'a play in the creation of the world' but this discovery was marked by a severe limitation 'because he linked the series to a principle of convergence, without seeing that divergence itself was an object of affirmation, or that the incompossibles belonged to the same world'.[42] Jorge Luis Borges and Friedrich Nietzsche led Deleuze beyond Leibniz. While Borges's literature showed how bifurcating storylines are unfolding simultaneously, making incompossible worlds a part of the same story, Nietzsche's philosophy showed how different perspectives on a city reveal the existence of other cities within the city.[43] The true play of the world consists of an affirmation of divergences and the coexistence of incompossibilities. It could thus be said that there is no need for Deleuze, at this level, to raise the question of how to re-potentialise and change a world, since what matters is the chaosmogonic play that simultaneously actualises different worlds and thus makes incompossibilities coexist. Affirmation of divergence takes the place of change.

It is from this perspective that Deleuze announces the death of the world. The multiplicity that comes with divergence no longer allows for the formation of a closed, convergent totality. In this sense, the

BETWEEN ONTOLOGICAL AND TRANSCENDENTAL MULTIPLICITY | 79

'divergence of the affirmed series forms a "chaosmos" and no longer a world'.[44] Chaosmos thus replaces world as the ultimate conceptualisation of the chaosmogonic formation that takes place on the basis of ontological multiplicity. The true play of the world no longer leaves any place for the Kantian idea of the world as a totality but still recognises the Leibnizian conceptualisation of worlds as systems of singularities – even though their formation is no longer limited to the principle of convergence.

In *The Fold*, Deleuze describes the modern condition as one in which we are witnessing the 'unfurling of divergent series in the same world' and 'the irruption of incompossibilities on the same stage'.[45] In this sense, it could be said that the very constitution of individual worlds has changed so that it no longer excludes divergences. Furthermore, Borges's dream 'to have God pass into existence all incompossible worlds at once' has become true.[46] The multiple worlds Leibniz consigned to the realm of possibility are now actualising simultaneously. Monads are now 'astraddle over several worlds' at the same time and thus 'kept half open as if by a pair of pliers'.[47] Deleuze also comes to these conclusions in *Cinema 2*, where he claims that nothing prevents us any longer 'from affirming that incompossibles belong to the same world, that incompossible worlds belong to the same universe'.[48]

But how to understand divergences and incompossibilities in relation to the same world or universe that they can now belong to? Are divergences and incompossibilities a part of the same world – the only one we truly have – which is no longer constituted based on the principle of convergence? Or is there a multiplicity of divergent worlds, which are only a part of the same universe in the sense that they coexist? As we can see in the quotes above, Deleuze gives indications of both options. The lack of a straight answer to this question, however, could simply be down to both being true. The two positions can be reconciled from the perspective of the chaosmos as the common background on which convergent and divergent series now constitute worlds. The same world or universe, constructed on the basis of divergence, is the chaosmos itself: 'the world is now made up of divergent series (the chaosmos)'.[49]

The multiplication of worlds reaffirms the unity of the chaosmos, but also changes the nature of the individual worlds themselves. The divergence that makes worlds multiply also effaces borders between individual worlds. For Leibniz, divergences constituted 'genuine borders between incompossible worlds', borders that are no longer possible if divergence is affirmed and the multiple possible worlds become actual.[50] Multiple worlds as results of the chaosmogonic game can no longer be clearly distinguished.

The coexistence of incompossibilities requires a common ontological background upon which divergent actualisations intertwine. If divergences would be absolute, we would again end up in a Leibnizian situation of separated worlds. If worlds would be fully isolated from each other, we would lose both the univocity of being and divergence itself, considering that the latter can only be truly affirmed if divergences coexist. The coexistence of incompossibilities presupposes that there is something common to several worlds; something that belongs to various worlds in different ways. A specific kind of objectivity thus connects different worlds:

> We must therefore understand that incompossible worlds, despite their incompossibility, have something in common – something objectively in common [...] Within these worlds, there is, for example, an objectively indeterminate Adam, that is, an Adam positively defined solely through a few singularities which can be combined and can complement each other in a very different fashion in different worlds.[51]

Deleuze describes this kind of object with the Kantian formula 'object = x'.[52] Such objects constitute inter-worldly phenomena that signal the effacement of borders between worlds but also reaffirm the necessity of still thinking the chaosmic reality in terms of Leibnizian worlds. They allow for the very link between chaos and cosmos: the pure distribution and redistribution of singularities on the one hand, and the prolongation of singularities into series and the organisation of series into systems on the other. Such virtual objects are actualised in a different way in various worlds and temporal sequences – without there being an 'original' Adam.[53] They connect the bifurcated events (to sin or not to sin, for example) and provide the thread that links actualisations back to the virtual. The fully individuated Adams are thus connected to the pre-individual singularities whose actualisations constitute them within a given world.

Apart from the obsoleteness of world (the death of the world as a totality) and its multiplication (into coexisting divergent worlds), Deleuze also presents the third destiny of the world we examined in

Chapter 1, namely its loss. In *Cinema 2*, Deleuze goes from presenting his Leibnizian perspective on the coexistence of incompossibilities to declaring that the 'link between man and the world is broken'.[54] In the introduction to the English translation of the book, Deleuze attributes this break to World War II, during and after which people often found themselves in situations in which they did not know how to react – a condition registered in cinematography by the break between classical and modern cinema.[55] The classical cinema was based on a sensory-motor schema which presupposed an active link between people and the world. This link was broken when people started finding themselves in pure optical and sound situations in which they were overwhelmed by sensation to which they could not react. Since then, there has been a lack of belief in what is in front of us, belief as what links a self to the world it finds itself in: 'The modern fact is that we no longer believe in this world. We do not even believe in the events which happen to us, love, death, as if they only half concerned us.'[56] The state we find ourselves in in such situations, however, cannot be described as completely indifferent. The stupor to which we are subjected is a result of being 'struck by something intolerable in the world and confronted by something unthinkable in thought'.[57] What makes the world intolerable and unthinkable can still affect us and leaves open the possibility of restoring belief: 'Which, then, is the subtle way out? To believe, not in a different world, but in a link between man and the world, in love or life, to believe in this as in the impossible, the unthinkable, which none the less cannot but be thought.'[58] Restoring and filming this belief is the task Deleuze bestows on contemporary cinema. Belief, he claims, is what can bridge the gap between people and the world in a time when action that could bring forth a different world seems implausible. It is not a belief in another world, either in heaven or on earth, that is required. What we lack and need is a 'belief in this world, as it is'.[59] Similarly to Hannah Arendt, Deleuze characterises modernity not with the loss of a transcendent world, but with the loss of belief in this world.[60]

How are we to understand Deleuze's elaboration of the loss of humanity's link to the world and the possibility of its restoration with respect to the multiplicity of Leibnizian worlds, whose existence he also affirms? Considering the eruption of incompossibilities in the chaosmos, how are we to understand the claim that, suddenly, there seems to be a world out there to believe in? The lost world in which we should believe cannot be the stable representational totality whose death Deleuze has previously declared with joy. And if there is a multiplicity of actualised divergent worlds, which world exactly should we believe in? Is Deleuze here switching from a Leibnizian to a phenomenological concept of world as a horizon of authentic existential experience, which is most often associated with loss?

As I have already mentioned, the Leibnizian concept of world is also present in *Cinema 2*. Deleuze claims that after Nietzsche and Borges we know that Leibnizian incompossible worlds actually belong to the same universe.[61] While Leibniz attempted to save the ideal of truth by placing divergences within different possible worlds, Nietzsche abandoned such attempts 'in favour of the false and its artistic, creative power', and Borges understood that incompossible events belong to the same story.[62] This indicates that Deleuze sees no contradiction between the multiplication and loss of world. The belief in the world should therefore not be thought of separately from the coexistence of incompossibilities. If we are to believe in this world and not in a different or a transcendent one, it is because this world is already bifurcated. The link to be restored here is a link to a divergent world through the creative powers of the false. As Allan James Thomas rightly observes: 'To *believe in this world as it is*, then, means neither submission to the existing reality or the cynicism of *realpolitik*, nor a messianic faith in a world or a people to come. It is, rather, to affirm being as vital difference, as creation.'[63] To this, we could add that being as difference amounts precisely to the chaosmic divergence of worlds. Belief should be thought of as an affirmation of divergences.

One final use of the concept of world remains in Deleuze which can be approached through the question of the individual's role in the chaosmos. This question is already posed in *The Logic of Sense*, where after revealing his subversion of the Leibnizian concept of world Deleuze wonders how a fully actualised individual might reverse the process and reach for the virtual in an act of 'counteractualization':

> The problem is therefore one of knowing how the individual would be able to transcend his form and his syntactical link with a world, in order to attain to the universal communication of events, that is, to the affirmation of a disjunctive synthesis beyond logical contradictions, and even beyond alogical incompatibilities.[64]

The individual would thus have to put their own actualised existence at stake and join the game of the world in the transcendental field, risking that their own singularities would get redistributed. The name Deleuze assigns to this process is 'becoming'. Becoming, for Deleuze, is not a process of achieving a predefined design or form; on the contrary, it is a process of counteractualisation: 'To become is not to attain a form (identification, imitation, Mimesis) but to find a zone of proximity, indiscernibility, or indifferentiation.'[65]

In *A Thousand Plateaus*, Deleuze and Guattari reassess the concept of becoming by toying with different senses of *le monde*, the French word for world. Becoming-imperceptible (or indiscernible or impersonal) – the ultimate stage of becoming – is defined as becoming like everybody else (*comme tout le monde*).[66] While being like everybody could be understood as the height of representational construction of world that reduces difference to sameness (the Heideggerian '*man*'), Deleuze and Guattari understand becoming-everybody as the release of impersonal singularities from their actualisations and realisations. This brings individuals close to the chaosmogonic game: 'Becoming everybody/everything (*tout le monde*) is to world (*faire monde*), to make a world (*faire un monde*).'[67] Becoming allows individuals to counteractualise and thus exchange their singularities with other individuals. Such redistributions of singularities, however, also produce re-actualisations, new prolongations of singularities into series and systems. Becoming is thus a destroyer but also a creator of worlds. It is the activation – through individuals – of the true (chaosmogonic) play of the world: 'If one reduces oneself to one or several abstract lines that will prolong itself in and conjugate with others, producing immediately, directly *a* world in which it is *the* world that becomes, then one becomes-everybody/everything.'[68]

Death, loss and multiplication – all different destinies of world in Deleuze – ultimately converge within the concept of the chaosmos. Each unique and relative world (*a* world) – in the Leibnizian sense of an arrangement (assemblage) of ontological multiplicity – is an expression of the same chaosmos (*the* world) as the virtual transcendental field. With the multiplication of worlds, the one and the same chaosmos, which coincides with the univocity of being, is affirmed in its divergent multiplicity.

The Double Excess of Badiou's Ontology

Despite Badiou's insistence on the subtractive nature of his ontological project, which is supposed to be strictly opposed to Heidegger's 'poetic' and Deleuze's 'vitalist' ontology, some commentators have claimed that, in fact, Badiou has more in common with these rival ontologies than he would like to admit.[69] The basis for this claim is that for Badiou, just as for Heidegger or Deleuze, there is an irreducible excess of being over any kind of structured representation – and that an expression of this excess is what ultimately brings us to the truth of being. In *Being and Event*, indeed, a series of (partly overlapping) distinctions follows this basic structure: the pure multiple and the count-as-one, inconsistent and consistent multiplicity, presentation and representation, the situation and the state of the situation. Badiou attaches the possibility of truth to a revelation of pure inconsistent multiplicity, to something that is presented, but not represented, a part of a situation not acknowledged by the state of that situation. Therefore, a justification for a 'poetical' reading of these distinctions in Badiou's texts does not seem difficult to find. In the *Manifesto for Philosophy*, for example, Badiou seems clear:

> Inasmuch as the unfathomable depths of what is present is inconsistency, a truth will be that which, from inside the presented, as *part* of this presented, makes the inconsistency – which buttresses in the last instance the consistency of presentation – come into the light of day.[70]

On this basis, one could easily conclude that truth is on the side of the excess of inconsistent multiplicity that escapes any representational structuring. In the following pages, however, I will present a different reading of Badiou, emphasising another kind of excess that is equally important to his ontology, namely the excess of oneness and representation over multiplicity and presentation. Badiou's subtractive ontology is essentially characterised by this double excess.

According to Badiou, ontology historically starts out from the assumption (first formulated by Parmenides and later reaffirmed by Leibniz) that beyond the multiplicity of everything that presents itself to us, there must be some one in which the multiplicity of what is is grounded.[71] Badiou announces that he will take the opposite road, claiming that beyond the oneness that presents itself to us, there must be some multiplicity. *Being and Event* does not actually start with the identification of being with multiplicity. What presents itself at this basic level is a multiplicity already structured by oneness, a multiplicity of unified beings or 'several-ones'.[72] The Leibnizian unification of everything is the primary ontological factuality. Despite acknowledging the fact that oneness is all around us, so to speak, Badiou declares that 'the one *is not*'.[73] The apparent oneness must be the result of an operation which makes the many into one. Badiou calls this operation the count-as-one: 'there is no one, only the count-as-one'.[74] Even though it appears as a primary fact, oneness will thus be considered as a result of an operation, the operation of the count that unifies multiplicity. The assumption is that the operation of unification is implemented upon a domain of some evasive multiplicity, which is only 'retroactively legible'.[75]

The primary ontological distinction Badiou makes is between a multiplicity of unities that has already been structured by the count-as-one ('consistent multiplicity') and a pure ('inconsistent') multiplicity beyond oneness, which can only be retroactively assumed.[76] The question for Badiou at this point is if inconsistent multiplicity can somehow be consistently presented in theory. If not, it can only be mystically experienced or poetically expressed. Badiou's answer, of course, is affirmative: it is via mathematical set theory that pure multiplicity is accessible to thought. Ontology as 'the theory of inconsistent multiplicities as such' is only possible as mathematics.[77] The challenge of ontology is then how to present this inconsistency in a consistent way without reducing multiplicity to oneness: 'What is required is that the operational structure of ontology discern the multiple without having to make a one out of it, and therefore without possessing a definition of the multiple.'[78] We saw in Chapter 2 that for Leibniz, the task of ontology was to establish substances as ultimate unities. For Badiou, it is the opposite: the presentation of being should be thought of as pure multiplicity, without any kind of metaphysical atoms that would provide primary unity. As Peter Hallward explains, 'Badiou's pure multiplicity must have no limit to its extension, neither intrinsic nor extrinsic, neither from above nor from below'.[79]

Even on the level of the pure presentation of being, which set theory allows us to understand, being itself (beyond its presentation as multiple) can only be marked by the empty set.[80] Yet, even though being is thus identified with the void, Badiou has to be credited, as Tzuchien

Tho has argued, for 'his commitment to rejecting the occultation of the void', since it is the novelty of the event and not the void itself that allows for the emergence of truth.[81] The void, Badiou concludes, is 'merely the subtractive face of the count'.[82]

Badiou turns to the Zermelo-Fraenkel (ZF) system of set theory, in which the search for a definition of a set is abandoned in favour of a relational description. Instead of featuring the property 'to be a set', the ZF system is based on the relation of 'belonging to' a set, marked by the sign $\in$.[83] A set is thus not defined as a primary entity, but as something that belongs to (is an element of) another set. This is why every multiple is but a multiple of multiples. In ontological terms, 'something' is defined solely as an element that belongs to another 'something'. Multiplicity itself is thus a relation that precedes its terms: 'being an "element" is not a status of being, an intrinsic quality, but a simple relation to-be-element-of, through which a multiplicity can be presented by another multiplicity'.[84] Belonging is the condition of being, not the other way around. There can be no definition of a primary entity of being, since being is only a presentation of a multiplicity by another multiplicity.

We can now understand the two theses that Badiou prescribes as 'prerequisites for any possible ontology':

> 1. The multiple from which ontology makes up its situation is composed solely of multiplicities. There is no one. In other words, every multiple is a multiple of multiples.
> 2. The count-as-one is no more than the system of conditions through which the multiple can be recognized as multiple.[85]

The argument I am proposing here is that this understanding of multiplicity entails that there is in fact no primary antagonism between the pure multiple and the count-as-one and therefore no room for a 'poetical' understanding of Badiou's ontology as an excess of multiplicity over oneness. If a multiple has no being before being counted as one by another multiple, then the two sides of the ontological difference – the inconsistent and the consistent multiplicity – are the two sides of the Möbius strip of the count-as-one:

> The one is assigned to the sign $\in$ alone, that is, to the operator of denotation for the relation between the 'something' in general

and the multiple. The sign ∈, unbeing of any one, determines, in a uniform manner, the presentation of 'something' as indexed to the multiple.[86]

The operation of belonging is the process of unification that produces multiplicity as such. What constitutes pure multiplicity is thus also what drives the count-as-one. Yet, it follows from this that the process of unification is also what makes any figure of the one non-existent on the ontological level. This is why the sign ∈, as Badiou claims, is at the same time what 'the one is assigned to' and the 'unbeing of any one'. From this perspective, multiplicity is nothing but a self-deconstructing oneness. Translated in Leibnizian terms, this means that ontological multiplicity does not consist of windowless monads that could be structured into a world. The operation of belonging is better understood as an ontological monadless window that both frames and deframes the presentation of being. As a frame that precedes that which is being framed, the window itself is at the same time an excess of oneness and an excess of multiplicity.

According to this reading, a clear distinction between inconsistent and consistent multiplicity is only established with the stabilisation of the count. In a situation of a presented consistent multiplicity, the oneness no longer self-deconstructs but presents consistent sets and elements, the successful results of the count-as-one. Once consistency is established, there is no excess of pure multiplicity that would allow us to climb back toward inconsistency (no 'thread' that would connect both sides of the ontological difference, which still exists in Deleuze). Badiou makes it clear that within a situation of consistent multiplicity, 'there is no rebel or subtractive presentation of the pure multiple upon which the empire of the one is exercised', which also entails that 'within a situation, the search for something that would feed an intuition of being qua being is a search in vain'.[87] Pure inconsistent multiplicity can never erupt within a situation; its non-presence remains one of a 'phantom remainder', an 'unperceivable gap', an 'unlocalisable void'.[88] Nevertheless, through this gap 'between the one as result and the one as operation', inconsistency haunts presented situations and therefore remains a threat to any consistent situation.[89]

At this point, Badiou introduces the last distinction, namely the distinction between presentation and representation. Since any structured presentation is 'exposed to the danger of the void', there is a need to double the count.[90] Presentation thus has to be represented, which means that for any situation, there is a state of that situation. This additional operation is mathematically grounded in the relation of inclusion: a multiple can therefore belong to a situation (as an element, presented in the situation) and be included in it (as a 'subset', recognised or represented by the state of the situation).[91] Based on this distinction, Badiou introduces a 'typology of being', which lists normal, singular and excrescent multiples.[92] While normal multiples are both presented and represented, singular multiples are presented, but not represented, and excrescent multiples are represented, but not presented.

This typology becomes important in what Badiou calls historical (as opposed to natural) situations, in which a double chasm between presentation and representation appears. While in natural situations, all multiples are normal, historical situations also introduce singularities and excrescences. Badiou gives a Marxist illustration of these terms.[93] The ruling class is a 'normal' term of a historical situation since it both belongs to and is included in the situation (it is presented as well as represented politically, on the level of the state). The working class, on the other hand, is a 'singular' term since it belongs to the situation without being included in it; it is presented, but not represented politically. The state (as an instrument of the ruling class it stands for the regime of representation that excludes the working class) is an 'excrescent' term – an excess of representation. This political example indicates that the truth is on the side of the singular term, that is, those who are present in the situation but excluded from any representation. Yet, what Badiou also emphasises here is the power of the excess of representation, evident in the persistence of the state even in communist countries. To return to ontology, the excess of representation has its grounding in set theory. As Badiou demonstrates, subsets outnumber the elements themselves, marking an irreducible 'point of excess' of representation over presentation.[94] Badiou's ontology can therefore not be understood solely in terms of the excess of multiplicity that escapes the count (or is repressed by it), but also in terms of the excess of the count itself. Apart from the (singular) excess of presentation over representation, there is also an (excrescent) excess of representation over presentation.

The question that must now finally be answered is, how does Badiou formulate his idea of truth in relation to being? As mentioned above, truth as a subjective process is not directly related to being, but rather defined as the fidelity to an event. The event is not an expression of being; on the contrary, it has no ontological existence. It occurs as a pure rupture with the regimes of presentation and representation within a given situation. As such, it cannot be accounted for by the count-as-one that dictates what can belong to or be included in a particular situation.

Nevertheless, events are indirectly related to singular multiples as 'evental sites' in which situations border on the void.[95] It is here that the consistency of situations is vulnerable. The existence of such sites on its own cannot cause an event, but does define its possible locations. So how does an event relate to the inconsistency of the situation? While the void of a situation – its imperceptible inconsistency – cannot be seen as the cause of the event, it is the event that makes 'the void of a situation [...] retroactively discernible'.[96] By its very occurrence, the event – a pure contingency with no grounding in being – indicates inconsistent multiplicity. It is only from the perspective of the event that the inconsistency of the situation can be retroactively discerned without being made present.

Eventually, inconsistent multiplicity – without it ever being present in the situation – can be represented by its consequences, which are the result of the activities of an emerging collective subject, faithful to the event.[97] What is thus 'positively connected to the event' forms a new, 'generic multiplicity' that 'forces the situation to accommodate it', thereby transforming the situation by changing its representational regime.[98] The truth of the situation as a generic multiplicity is thus 'at once something new' and 'the closest, ontologically speaking, to the initial state of things'.[99] It is closest to being-qua-being, since it challenges the given regime of exclusive representation by referring to the universality of belonging as such. Going back to the political example given by Badiou, this evokes Marx's notion of the proletariat, which is not merely a specific class, but the egalitarian dissolution of class society. As Jelica Šumič has proposed, the subject of truth (an emancipatory political collective) is generic in the sense of 'a paradoxical collectivity that is at one and the same time not-all, nontotalizable, and for all'.[100]

The dominant regime of representation can therefore not be challenged by the mere existence of what it excludes, but only by what supplements it – an additional 'representative without representation' that works to reframe the situation. A truth is thus not defined as an eruption of inconsistency as such but as a 'minimal consistency' which has 'to be produced' as 'the infinite multiple-horizon of a post-eventful procedure'.[101] Tzuchien Tho has argued that 'in contrast to other contemporary thinkers', Badiou develops 'a figure of novelty that would not be the "other" of structure (void or gap), but rather a generic existence which is inscribed through its self-grounding (generic) character'.[102] Or, as Magdalena Germek has put it: 'Based on inconsistency as the being of the situation, the truth procedure creates a new consistency, an extension of the situation, and thus establishes a new formalization of the existing.'[103]

Even though Badiou emphasises the inconsistency of what escapes the count-as-one as the condition of any truth, this should not be understood in terms of a dualism of consistency and inconsistency that would bring Badiou's ontology back to the 'poetic' revelation of being. On the contrary, as my reading tries to show, there is, in Badiou's ontology, a certain monism of the count as the pure excess of multiplicity framing itself. The excess of multiplicity that destabilises the count is an effect of the count itself. The monadless window that ultimately constitutes multiplicity as such allows Badiou to present an understanding of truth not as a complete *de*framing of multiplicity that escapes any representational bonds, but rather as its radical *re*framing. It is through the introduction of a new frame, a new formalisation, that truth can emerge within a situation.

Badiou has often been criticised, from both Marxist and Lacanian perspectives, for lacking a theory of a primary antagonism, lack or negativity, which would make his theory of truth more dialectically sound. For example, Slavoj Žižek has asked whether the progression, in Badiou, from inconsistent to consistent multiplicity and then from being to world does not presuppose 'a kind of "negativity" that has to be somehow operative in the midst of Being itself'.[104] According to the reading I developed here, the answer is that the count-as-one is dialectical in itself, since it is what makes a one out of a multiple and what at the same time destabilises any unity of the one. This self-destabilising excess of framing is what drives the (inherently inconsistent) progression from being to its (re)presentation and ultimately to its unification within a world.

The Surplus of Worlds in Badiou

Badiou develops his theory of worlds in *Logics of Worlds*, published eighteen years after *Being and Event* as its sequel. From the systematic perspective of Badiou's philosophy, this second instalment moves from 'the level of pure being' to 'the level of being-there, or of appearing, or of worlds'.[105] The focus thus shifts from ontology to phenomenology – although phenomenology is not meant here in the sense of the philosophical orientation following Husserl and Heidegger, but is given a technical definition as the logic of appearance. Again, Badiou reaches for a formal, mathematical articulation of his propositions, with set theory now being supplemented by category theory.[106] To the series of levels already presented in *Being and Event* – being as neither one nor multiple, the presentation of being as inconsistent multiplicity, the presentation of being within situations as consistent multiplicity, the representation of being as states of situations – another level is added, the level of the appearance of being within worlds. Above, we have already answered Žižek's question on the negativity that drives this progression, but how does what we have called the excess of framing apply to worlds?

Even though the level of appearance is presented as an additional level, there is some overlap with what has already been theorised in *Being and Event*, since – as Badiou admits – the concept of world has a similar function to that which the concept of situation had in the previous book.[107] The question that governs the theory of worlds is the following: 'how can the essential unbinding of multiple-being give itself as a local binding and, in the end, as the stability of worlds?'[108] From this perspective, being and worlds are juxtaposed in a similar fashion to how inconsistent and consistent multiplicity were addressed in *Being and Event*. The passage from being to appearance, however, would be misunderstood if interpreted as a passage from the multiple (being) to the one (world). For all the similarities Badiou sees between his own concept of world and Leibniz's, the difference is – as we saw in Chapter 2 – that appearance should not be consigned to the power of the one. Being appears within a multiplicity of worlds that are irreducible to any one universe. To *Being and Event*'s 'the one is not', *Logics of Worlds* adds '*there is no* Whole' or '*there is no* universe'.[109]

The non-existence of the universe as a whole entails that being can only appear locally, within a multiplicity of worlds. The relation between the ontological multiplicity and the multiplicity of worlds should be understood as a relation between particular multiples and particular worlds:

> We will say that a multiple, related to a localization of its identity and of its relations with other multiples, is a being [*étant*] (to distinguish it from its pure multiple-being, which is the being of its being

[*son pur être-multiple, qui est l'être de son être*]). As for a local site of the identification of beings, we will call it [. . .] a world.[110]

What I have been calling 'framing' is conceptualised in *Logics of Worlds* as the transcendental. In opposition to the Kantian transcendental, which is subjective and unique, Badiou envisions his own concept of the transcendental as objective and multiple. It is objective, since it determines how beings are identified in a particular world, and multiple, since each world is constructed according to its own transcendental.[111] The way beings appear is not inscribed in their multiple-being, but dictated by the objectivity of a world in which they appear: 'the fact that such and such multiple-beings appear in such and such a world is contingent with regard to the transcendental laws of appearing'.[112] Ontological multiplicity can thus only appear (and therefore exist) through the transcendental frame of a given world, which determines which beings will appear within a particular world and how.

The transcendental – which Badiou compares, as we have seen, to Leibniz's pre-established harmony – is defined by a series of logical operations that establish the cohesion and immanent organisation of beings within a world. It identifies beings in relation to themselves and other beings so that a world is formed as 'a relational network' on the basis of which the differentiation of beings and the intensity of their appearance can be determined.[113] Two additional concepts are then introduced by Badiou, which help further explain the composition of worlds. First, beings appear within worlds as objects: 'by "object" we must understand that which counts as one within appearing, or that which authorises us to speak of *this* being-there as inflexibly being "itself"', relative to the transcendental of a given world.[114] Second, objects within worlds form mutual relations, which explains the logical completeness of a world.[115] The transcendental, object and relation are thus the three concepts Badiou uses to define the logics of worlds.

Badiou's objective phenomenology, however, does not stop at explaining the consistency of worlds. Its final aim – just as in his ontology – is rather to account for the contingent events in which the inconsistency of transcendentals is manifested via truth procedures. While *Being and Event* examined the being of truths, *Logics of Worlds* explores their appearance. Just like in the first book, truths emerge at the site of discrepancies between the two basic levels under consideration. The ontological discrepancy between inconsistent and consistent multiplicities is now replaced by the discrepancy between being and appearance. As we will see, a double excess again comes to the fore: on the one hand, there is an excess of being over what appears within a world, and on the other, there is an excess of worlds over beings. The question that then remains to be answered is, how does Badiou articulate his conception of truth to this double excess in *Logics of Worlds*?

To prepare for a theory of truth in relation to worlds, Badiou introduces the concept of 'the inexistent', which marks the point of the irreducible excess of being over appearance. This concept takes the place of singular multiples from *Being and Event*. In any appearance of a multiple within a world, there is 'a reserve of being which, subtracted from appearance, traces within this appearance the fact that it is always contingent for such a being to appear there'.[116] The transcendental frame necessarily limits the appearance of beings, whose multiple-being can never fully appear within any one world. To illustrate this, Badiou again uses a political example of a population deprived of political rights (the indigenous population in the world of Quebec between 1918 and 1950).[117] Even though this population is ontologically present, the transcendental that organises (political) appearance within this world assigns them a minimal (nil) degree of existence. Such inexistents mark the hidden presence of inconsistency within any transcendental order.

The excess of being over appearance allows Badiou to formulate truth as the result of a subversion of the transcendental order, which ultimately constitutes an event. For such an occurrence to take place, being must appear within a world in violation of this world's transcendental. The Paris Commune – another political example offered by Badiou – can thus be seen as 'the appearance of worker-being' in the world of 'political and governmental capacity' in which it was previously inexistent.[118] A multiple-being 'rises "in person" to the surface of objectivity', which means that it dictates its own transcendental value.[119] This can be understood both as an apparition of an excess of being (it proves that being can never be contained by any transcendental frame) and as an additional framing (the event consists of a transcendental revalorisation of an ontological multiple). Subjectivity again enters the stage at this point, since truth is identical to the process of establishing the consequences of such a paradoxical apparition within a particular world. The ultimate aim of a subjective 'body' – as Badiou defines the worldly appearance of the subject of truth – is to reframe the world within which it exists, to enforce 'a different distribution of what exists and what does not'.[120] Badiou addresses the process of redistributing appearances in his theory of points.[121] A truth procedure proceeds through 'points' at which the subjective body has to make a decision on how to act, which will have consequences for the way the transcendental of the world in question will be transformed. A new, non-teleological consistency is materially built based on the fidelity to an event. This is how the inexistent, which came to appearance under its own terms, bypassing the transcendental order, changes the world through subjective intervention: 'Under the pressure that being exerts on its own appearing, the world may be accorded the chance [...] of an other world.'[122]

Despite this remark on making another world in place of the old one, the emergence of truth in *Logics of Worlds* remains fundamentally intra-worldly. Badiou emphasises the way in which a truth *transforms* a given world based on the 'pressure' of being, but leaves aside the question of how events and truth procedures can be articulated in terms of the multiplicity of worlds and thereby the excess of worlds over being. It thus remains partly unclear how the transformation of a world is to be understood in the context of the general multiplicity of worlds that is the starting point of Badiou's theory of appearance. By only presenting the event as a change within a given world, Badiou risks losing sight of the basic insight of *Logics of Worlds*, namely the infinite multiplicity of the said logics.

The problem stems from the fact that multiple-being is essentially inter-worldly, which is a consequence of the fact that multiples are not cleanly divided into separate worlds. Worlds overlap in the sense that multiples can belong to several worlds at once: 'Not only is there a plurality of worlds, but the same multiple – the 'same' ontologically – in general co-belongs to different worlds.'[123] If beings can appear in several worlds at once, there is a surplus of worlds over being (similarly to how representation is in excess over presentation in *Being and Event*, since there are more subsets than elements within a set). This is especially true for human beings, who can appear 'in a very great number of worlds', more than other kinds of beings.[124] The new transcendental developed by the subjective procedure of truth is thus necessarily only one of the multiple transcendentals in which the same beings appear. The 'stability of worlds' which was supposed to bind ontological multiplicity thus seems radically undermined by this surplus of worlds even before the appearance of events.

The problem I am posing here is not related to the acknowledgement of a diversity of worlds. Badiou has always insisted that the appearance of a truth as singular universality puts the differences between those who enter the composition of the faithful subject into brackets.[125] The problem relates to transferring this insight into Badiou's theory of the worldly appearance of truth: how the universal truth is established in relation to the multiplicity of worlds among which it emerges. The question that remains unanswered is how truths interrupt what Badiou himself describes as the 'egalitarian indifference of an infinity of worlds'.[126] Badiou resolves this issue by referring to the standard definition of universality as validity in all possible worlds, even though – given the polemical nature of Badiou's notion of truth, which should always be considered as a radical break with the laws of a given world – the trans-worldly existence of truths should not be understood as a sphere of neutral universality. On the one hand, Badiou claims, truths have a clear origin within a given world (as resistance to its transcendental laws) and are marked by their origin within this world, which means that they are polemical rather than abstractly universal. On the other hand, truths 'let themselves be identified at a distance (from another world) as universal, or trans-worldly'.[127] Therefore, truths are both singular (marked by the event and the world in which they originate) and universal (they can be identified in any world).

This solution still seems insufficient, since it only addresses truths 'at a distance', after they have already been established and not in the moment of their emergence and development. When the subject of a truth procedure fights in the name of the inexistent that has appeared in a particular world, does it not, in fact, wage its battle at a crossroads of worlds? Does it not, with its attempt to transform the transcendental of a world, introduce a further bifurcation of worlds? As a body, does the subject of truth not itself exist in multiple worlds at once? From this perspective, those who see the event as a non-event, or constitute themselves as reactive subjects in response to the event, should be understood as trying to enforce their own world as the true world of this event, a world in which a certain degree of existence is assigned to the appearance of the inexistent in a way that renders it irrelevant or inconsequential. The forces that want to suppress this insurgent subject want to present the novelty that it stands for by framing it according to the old transcendental. To continue with the Marxist example Badiou himself uses, the workers that aim to unite in an emerging new common world they are building (as *The Communist Manifesto* famously states) appear within the capitalist world as a band of lazy thugs. If the appearance of the inexistent is to have strong consequences, so that the event truly becomes an event, then the world relative to which the inexistent is inexistent needs to be enforced as the relevant one. The struggle of the truth procedure is therefore the struggle to define what world exactly is at stake in the first place. It is a struggle between different framings of the ontological multiples in question. Should *Logics of Worlds*, therefore, be supplemented by a theory of the conflict of worlds? Even in other types of truth – artistic ones, for example – the trans-worldly truth-status of art presupposes that an artwork – as a product of a specific world – can appear (that is, be known and appreciated) within other worlds. This presupposes a kind of aesthetic interference in which an object can appear within one world, even though it is formed according to another transcendental.

Logics of Worlds is presented by Badiou as both a theory of the existence of multiple worlds and a theory of the worldly existence of truths. Yet, the appearance of truths is for the most part defined as intra-worldly (by the gap between being and its appearance within a particular world) and trans-worldly (their universal reach), while its inter-worldly dimension (their existence as articulated with a multiplicity of worlds) is somewhat neglected.[128] For the truth procedure to have any effect, it has to, first, introduce a bifurcation of worlds (the clash between the old and the new transcendental), and, second, make its presence (the new transcendental being developed) felt within the phenomenal field organised by other transcendentals that involve the same ontological multiples. Emphasising the gap between being and appearance, *Logics of Worlds* does not, in fact, provide the conceptual resources needed to think truth from the perspective of the gaps between worlds or the conflictual relations between them.[129] To really grasp what trans-worldliness entails, we first have to understand inter-worldly phenomena, that is, objects that mark the presence of one world within another.

Intra-worldly, Inter-worldly or Trans-worldly?

Some conclusions regarding the difference but also complementarity between Deleuze's and Badiou's approaches to ontological and transcendental multiplicity can now be made. Just as for Deleuze the one does not exist outside of its production of multiplicity (its events), for Badiou multiplicity does not exist outside of the production of its oneness, which is occasionally interrupted by events. Worlds arise from this ontological multiplicity on the basis of its transcendental folding (Deleuze) or transcendental framing (Badiou). While the former is immanent to being and testifies to a continuity between being and worlds, the latter is always contingent with regard to being and displays a gap between being and its appearance within worlds.

For Deleuze, the proliferation of worlds is directly related to ontological multiplicity as the virtual transcendental field in which divergent series of singularities get actualised. He offers an image of the chaosmos, in which incompossible worlds coexist. Their coexistence, however, blurs the boundaries between worlds. Deleuze is ultimately interested in the inter-worldly phenomena of singularities divergently distributed and actualised over several worlds. The task at hand is to transgress our actualisations and unleash the becomings in which ontological multiplicity is refolded and its singularities redistributed.

In Badiou, in contrast, multiple transcendentals frame ontological multiplicity in a multitude of distinct but overlapping worlds. Worlds overlap since the same ontological multiples can coexist in several worlds. However, there is no ultimate totality that would unite either the multiplicity of being or the multiplicity of worlds. Although Badiou (just as Deleuze) affirms the simultaneous coexistence of beings in several worlds at once, the inter-worldly reality is not what ultimately interests him. The truth philosophy is after is not a becoming of being beyond its actualisations (which he rejects as vitalism), but a subjective procedure in which the transcendental parameters of a world are radically transformed. While for Deleuze, individuals should seek to affirm an inter-worldly state of divergence, for Badiou subjective truth is intra- and trans-worldly. It is intra-worldly in the sense that a truth is based on an event that occurs within a specified world; it is trans-worldly because a truth, once it is developed, has universal value for many (or perhaps all) worlds.

I will come back to reconsider Deleuze's and Badiou's different views on the multiplicity of worlds from an aesthetic perspective (their fictional structure) in Chapter 5. For now, my conclusions are the following. Although their works display a philosophical urgency of conceptualising a multiplicity of actual worlds, both Deleuze and Badiou seem to place the ultimate purpose of this endeavour beyond the realm of multiple worlds itself. For Deleuze, the highest philosophical stakes are attributed to the realm of the virtual as the chaosmos of becoming in which worlds are formed but also dissolved. For Badiou, multiple worlds are the background on which intra- and trans-worldly truth procedures emerge and develop, while their articulation with the inter-worldly dimension of transcendental multiplicity is left unexplored.

In order to put more emphasis on the multiplicity of worlds itself, my approach in the second half of this book will be based on a combination of both perspectives. If we are to truly think world *as world*, we have to subscribe to a Badiousian subtractive ontology. If not, the transcendental realm of divergent worlds dissolves into a chaosmic becoming of being itself and loses its distinction. However, if we are to truly think the *multiplicity* of worlds, Deleuze's inter-worldly perspective should be retained above Badiou's intra- and trans-worldly one. If multiple worlds can truly be said to coexist, it is on the basis that there are inter-worldly phenomena that appear in several worlds at once. What will interest me in the remaining chapters is how such phenomena interrupt what Badiou calls the indifferent coexistence of worlds. At what point does the coexistence in several worlds produce political conflicts and aesthetic interferences that make us feel the presence of one world within another? It is in such instances that the multiplicity of worlds is actually experienced. Such conflicts and interferences are the sights of transcendental reframing in which new worlds can emerge.

Notes

1. Badiou recounts this history in *Deleuze: The Clamor of Being*, trans. Louise Burchill (Minneapolis: University of Minnesota Press, 2000), 1–5.
2. See ibid. 47–8.
3. Gilles Deleuze and Félix Guattari, *What Is Philosophy?*, trans. Hugh Tomlinson and Graham Burchell (New York: Columbia University Press, 1996), 151–3. It should be noted, however, that Deleuze does not oppose the ontological use of mathematics, but uses mathematical models of a different kind.
4. Badiou, *Deleuze*, 45.

BETWEEN ONTOLOGICAL AND TRANSCENDENTAL MULTIPLICITY | 99

5. See, for example, Jon Roffe, *Badiou's Deleuze* (London: Routledge, 2014); Clayton Crockett, *Deleuze Beyond Badiou: Ontology, Multiplicity, and Event* (New York: Columbia University Press, 2013); Becky Vartabedian, *Multiplicity and Ontology in Deleuze and Badiou* (London: Palgrave Macmillan, 2018).
6. Gilles Deleuze, *The Logic of Sense*, trans. Mark Lester and Charles Stivale (London: Athlone Press, 1990), 179.
7. Ibid. 180.
8. Badiou, *Deleuze*, 11.
9. Deleuze, *The Logic of Sense*, 179.
10. Ibid. 177.
11. Gilles Deleuze, *Difference and Repetition*, trans. Paul Patton (London: Continuum, 2001), xx–xxi.
12. Ibid. 29.
13. Ibid. xix.
14. Alain Badiou, *Being and Event*, trans. Oliver Feltham (London: Continuum, 2005), 10.
15. Badiou, *Deleuze*, 3.
16. Juliette Simont, 'Critique de la représentation et ontologie chez Deleuze et Badiou (Autour du "virtuel")', in *Alain Badiou: Penser le multiple*, ed. Charles Ramond (Paris: L'Harmattan, 2002), 463–4.
17. Badiou, *Being and Event*, 15.
18. Ibid. 184.
19. Ibid. 207.
20. Ibid. 206.
21. Ibid. 206.
22. Ibid. 56.
23. Alain Badiou, *Manifesto for Philosophy*, trans. Norman Madarasz (Albany: State University of New York Press, 1999), 106–7.
24. Deleuze and Badiou's discussion on the concept of world can only be staged retrospectively, since Deleuze died before Badiou wrote his *Logics of Worlds*, in which he discusses Deleuze's concept of event, but not his concept of world.
25. 'Transcendental folding' and 'transcendental framing' are not terms Deleuze or Badiou would explicitly use. I believe, however, that they accurately reflect their descriptions of world-building procedures. The fold is the main concept Deleuze uses in his book on Leibniz (Gilles Deleuze, *The Fold: Leibniz and the Baroque*, trans. Tom Colney (London: Athlone Press, 1993)), while in *Logics of Worlds* Badiou uses the term 'transcendental framework', a translation for *'cadre transcendental'* (Alain Badiou, *Logics of Worlds: Being and Event, 2*, trans. Alberto Toscano (London: Continuum, 2009), 38; Alain Badiou, *Logiques des mondes. L'être et l'événement 2* (Paris: Seuil, 2006), 47).

26. See Deleuze, *The Logic of Sense*, 109–17, 176.
27. Deleuze, *Difference and Repetition*, xx–xxi.
28. Ibid. 57.
29. Ibid. 277.
30. Ibid. 182.
31. Ibid. 128.
32. Ibid. 199.
33. Ibid. 275.
34. Deleuze, *The Logic of Sense*, 102.
35. Ibid. 105.
36. Ibid. 109.
37. Ibid. 109.
38. Deleuze, *The Fold*, 60.
39. Ibid. 106.
40. Ibid. 26.
41. Deleuze, *The Logic of Sense*, 110.
42. Deleuze, *Difference and Repetition*, 51.
43. Deleuze, *The Logic of Sense*, 114, 174.
44. Ibid. 176.
45. Deleuze, *The Fold*, 82.
46. Ibid. 62.
47. Ibid. 137.
48. Gilles Deleuze, *Cinema 2: The Time-Image*, trans. Hugh Tomlinson and Robert Galeta (Minneapolis: University of Minnesota Press, 1989), 131.
49. Deleuze, *The Fold*, 137. The sameness or oneness of the chaosmos could be seen, from Badiou's perspective, as proof that multiplicity in Deleuze ultimately collapses into a figure of the one. Yet, as Anna Longo emphasises, the set-theoretical conception of multiplicity and totality cannot be applied to Deleuze's Riemannian understanding of these notions. The 'possibilities of the nomadic distribution of singularities [. . .], as a continuum, cannot be exhausted as if it was a discrete totality'. In this manner 'any throw of the die, as a brand new and ideal event, consists in the selection of some of the more-than-infinite points of the continuum'. Longo's text does not discuss Deleuze in comparison to Badiou, but in comparison to Quentin Meillassoux's objections to Deleuze inspired by Badiou. Nevertheless, Longo articulates very well the Deleuzian multiplicity of worlds beyond the Badiousian reductive perspective. Anna Longo, 'Virtual Time and Possible Worlds: The Madness of the Real', *Scenari* 8 (2018): 122.
50. Deleuze, *The Fold*, 81.
51. Deleuze, *The Logic of Sense*, 114.
52. Ibid. 113.
53. Deleuze, *Difference and Repetition*, 105, 124.

54. Deleuze, *Cinema 2*, 171–2.
55. Ibid. xi.
56. Ibid. 171.
57. Ibid. 169.
58. Ibid. 170.
59. Ibid. 172.
60. The similarity between Deleuze's and Arendt's position has been emphasised by Frank Fischbach in *Sans objet. Capitalisme, subjectivité, alienation* (Paris: Vrin, 2009). I believe that this similarity is only apparent, since Arendt's conception of world is essentially phenomenological, while Deleuze – as I show in what follows – nevertheless stays within the framework of a Leibnizian concept of world.
61. Deleuze, *Cinema 2*, 131.
62. Ibid. 131.
63. Allan James Thomas, *Deleuze, Cinema and the Thought of the World* (Edinburgh: Edinburgh University Press, 2018), 249.
64. Deleuze, *The Logic of Sense*, 178.
65. Gilles Deleuze, *Essays Critical and Clinical*, trans. Daniel W. Smith and Michael A. Greco (Minneapolis: University of Minnesota Press, 1997), 1.
66. Gilles Deleuze and Félix Guattari, *A Thousand Plateaus: Capitalism and Schizophrenia*, trans. Brian Massumi (Minneapolis: University of Minnesota Press, 1987), 279.
67. Ibid. 280.
68. Ibid. 280.
69. See, for example, Alenka Zupančič in *What Is Sex?* (Cambridge, MA: MIT Press, 2017), 130.
70. Badiou, *Manifesto for Philosophy*, 106.
71. Badiou, *Being and Event*, 23.
72. Ibid. 25.
73. Ibid. 23.
74. Ibid. 24.
75. Ibid. 24.
76. Ibid. 25.
77. Ibid. 28.
78. Ibid. 29.
79. Peter Hallward, *Badiou: A Subject to Truth* (Minneapolis: University of Minnesota Press, 2003), 82.
80. Badiou, *Being and Event*, 58, 66–9.
81. Tzuchien Tho, 'The Void Just Ain't (What It Used to Be): Void, Infinity, and the Indeterminate', in 'The Structure of the Void', ed. Mladen Dolar et al., special issue, *Filozofski vestnik* 34, no. 2 (2013): 47, https://ojs.zrc-sazu.si/filozofski-vestnik/article/view/3252/2969.

82. Badiou, *Being and Event*, 55.
83. Ibid. 43.
84. Ibid. 44–5. A resonance with Lacan's definition of the subject can be detected here. According to Lacan, a signifier represents the subject for another signifier. In a similar way, being is, according to Badiou, what a multiplicity represents for another multiplicity. See Jacques Lacan, *The Four Fundamental Concepts of Psychoanalysis: The Seminar of Jacques Lacan, Book XI*, trans. Alan Sheridan (New York: W. W. Norton, 1981), 207.
85. Badiou, *Being and Event*, 29.
86. Ibid. 44.
87. Ibid. 54.
88. Ibid. 53–5.
89. Ibid. 54.
90. Ibid. 93.
91. Ibid. 94. It should be noted that in set-theoretical terms, inclusion is derived from belonging and not an additional operation. It does not, therefore, introduce a dualism of the count.
92. Ibid. 93–101.
93. Ibid. 104–11.
94. Ibid. 84–5.
95. Ibid. 173–7.
96. Ibid. 56.
97. Ibid. 206.
98. Ibid. 335, 342.
99. Badiou, *Manifesto for Philosophy*, 36.
100. Jelica Šumič, 'The For-All: Grappling with the Real of the Group', *Crisis and Critique* 6, no. 1 (2019): 338, https://www.crisiscritique.org/storage/app/media/2019-04-02/jsumic.pdf.
101. Badiou, *Manifesto for Philosophy*, 107.
102. Tho, 'The Void', 47.
103. Magdalena Germek, 'The Dialectic of Formalization', *Filozofski vestnik* 42, no. 1 (2021): 40, https://doi.org/10.3986/fv.42.1.02.
104. Slavoj Žižek, *In Defense of Lost Causes* (London: Verso, 2008), 397.
105. Badiou, *Logics of Worlds*, 8.
106. Ibid. 38. See also Alain Badiou, *Mathematics of the Transcendental*, trans. A. J. Bartlett and Alex Ling (London: Bloomsbury, 2014).
107. Badiou, *Logics of Worlds*, 36.
108. Ibid. 101.
109. Ibid. 102.
110. Ibid. 112–13.
111. Ibid. 101, 120.

112. Ibid. 238.
113. Ibid. 102, 118, 123.
114. Ibid. 193.
115. Ibid. 313–17.
116. Ibid. 322.
117. Ibid. 323–4.
118. Ibid. 365.
119. Ibid. 360.
120. Ibid. 453, 380.
121. Ibid. 397–447.
122. Ibid. 380.
123. Ibid. 114.
124. Ibid. 114.
125. On this, see Alain Badiou, *Saint Paul: The Foundation of Universalism*, trans. Ray Brassier (Stanford: Stanford University Press, 2003).
126. Badiou, *Logics of Worlds*, 328.
127. Ibid. 10.
128. This lack of attention to inter-worldly phenomena might also explain why Badiou – as we saw in Chapter 1 – resorts to describing the nature of contemporary social reality as worldless. Precisely because the emergence of truth is defined only as intra-worldly does the absence of a clear transcendental to be subverted present itself to Badiou as a sign of worldlessness instead of as riddled with a multiplicity of transcendentals. The incomplete theorisation of the universality of truth in relation to the multiplicity of worlds similarly makes the declaration of the one-world horizon of emancipatory politics seem too vague. The discrepancy between these views was first spotted by Alberto Toscano: 'whilst in Badiou's theoretical writings on the appearance of worlds he cogently argues that events engender the *dysfunction* of worlds and their transcendental regimes, in his "ontology of the present" Badiou advocates the necessity, in our "intervallic" or world-less times, of *constructing* a world'. Alberto Toscano, 'From the State to the World: Badiou and Anti-Capitalism', *Communication & Cognition* 37, nos. 3–4 (2004): 199–224.
129. The recent third part of the *Being and Event* trilogy does not seem to resolve this issue, as it moves from truths as they appear within a given world to the absolute character of truths, independent of particular worlds in which their origins lay. Alain Badiou, *The Immanence of Truths: Being and Event III*, trans. Susan Spitzer and Kenneth Reinhard (London: Bloomsbury, 2022), 24–5.

4 From Cosmopolitanism to the Conflict of Worlds

SINCE DIOGENES THE CYNIC proclaimed himself to be a citizen of the world, the concept of world has shaped the way Western philosophy thinks politics. Diogenes' statement is now often quoted as the dawn of cosmopolitanism, the idea that only an affiliation to the world can provide a true ethical and political standpoint. A tradition first fully formulated by the Stoics, cosmopolitanism posits the world as a political ideal. For the Stoics, this ideal was both humanist and metaphysical. Humanist, since it rested on an affective identification with all of humanity and the acknowledgement of reason as common to all human beings. Metaphysical, since this very humanism was linked to an organic and holistic understanding of the universe in which all of its parts are limbs of a single body, pervaded by the same *logos* and arranged by the same teleological grand design.[1] Stoic cosmopolitanism thus presupposed the very cosmos whose dissolution marks the beginning of modern philosophy. Modern reinventions of the world as a political ideal thus face an elementary conundrum: can there be a cosmopolitanism without the cosmos?

That the cosmic foundations of cosmopolitanism cannot simply be shaken off once we enter modernity is evidenced by the fact that they were taken seriously by Immanuel Kant, who gave cosmopolitanism its most influential modern formulation. Kant's philosophy displays the tension between accepting the consequences of modern acosmism and the ethical and political need to preserve an ideal of the world.

As he makes clear in the *Critique of Pure Reason*, the notion of world no longer refers to anything real. It is nothing more than a transcendental illusion, a fiction inscribed by default into pure reason. This kind of fiction, however, as Kant also argues, is not only impossible to completely overcome, but is also what makes pure reason useful in theoretical and practical terms. Such fictions become regulative ideas, that is, unverifiable assumptions that guide our thinking and action. These are the grounds upon which cosmopolitanism was reinvented by Kant: as a hypothetical perspective on history that presupposes (not as an ontological claim but merely as a useful fiction) a gradual achievement of a natural design. It is the fiction of providence that enables us to see history as a narrative leading up to the achievement of a 'universal cosmopolitan condition', a condition of peace and understanding among the nations.[2] We will see in what follows that while contemporary champions of cosmopolitanism believe that its humanist core can easily be salvaged from the grips of its outdated metaphysics, critics think that its metaphysical heritage still has dire political consequences for the cosmopolitan ideal in the shape of an inherently oppressive assumption of historical progress.

Yet, cosmopolitanism is not the only role the concept of world has played in political philosophy. World as a political ideal has also been elaborated in opposition to the global perspective, as can be seen in the work of Hannah Arendt. In *The Human Condition*, she develops a concept of world as the artificial environment humanity makes for itself. This man-made world of things provides a horizon of common experience and sets the stage for political action. For Arendt, the question of world is not the question of establishing a global political community, but rather the question of how the public sphere as such rests on the phenomenological experience of a surrounding world. In contrast to the cosmopolitans, Arendt's concept of world confronts the consequences of the modern destruction of the cosmos head on. Referring to Alexandre Koyré,[3] Arendt showed how modern science had not only metaphysical but also political implications. In combination with the development of global capitalism, it critically disturbed the sense of being-in-the-world and thereby undermined the foundations of political action proper. Modernity is thus synonymous with 'world alienation'.[4] For cosmopolitan authors, the challenges of globalisation make Kant's regulative ideal more urgent than ever. For Arendt, on the other hand, global realities turned Kant's ideal into a fact, but to devastating effect. The world cannot be globalised without destroying its very worldliness.

While Arendt is primarily concerned with the loss of mankind's world-making capacity, she also acknowledges a proliferation of worlds. Not only does the sense of being-in-the-world condition political action, the latter also has the power to create new worlds. Such multiplicity of worlds is more explicitly elaborated by Jean-Luc Nancy, who proposes another political application of the phenomenological concept of world. Sharing with Arendt the diagnosis that the social reality of global capitalism is worldless, he attempts to salvage worldliness in its singular plurality. According to Nancy, it is the very multiplicity of worlds that constitutes worldliness in opposition to globalised totalisation. Arendt and Nancy thus retain a political ideal of the world, yet not as a totality, but as a singularity.

In contrast to the positions described above, I will argue in this chapter that modern acosmism prevents us from retaining any ideal of worldliness. There can be no cosmopolitanism without the cosmos, not because the world would be lost in its very globalisation, but because modern acosmism results in an indifferent multiplicity of worlds. Even when considered in terms of a singular plurality of worlds, the ideal of worldliness misses the most important political implication of the modern proliferation of worlds, namely the conflicts between them. Since the multiple worlds share the same ontological reality, they cannot always coexist indifferently or complementarily. The multiplicity of worlds becomes a political realm as soon as something in the shared ontological multiplicity cannot coexist within two different worlds. These are the points where irreconcilable singularisations of the common world enter into conflict. To explore the multiplicity of worlds as a political realm we will turn to Jacques Rancière, who defines politics as a conflict of worlds. Far from positing the world as a political ideal, Rancière understands worlds as structures determining the coordinates of perception and intelligibility that define a common reality and the way various subjects can take part in it. For Rancière, the point is not only – as it was for Arendt – that political action establishes the world in which it takes place. Rather, political subjectivation stages a conflict between two worlds, that is, two irreconcilable framings of the common. While not denying the existence of a globalised social totality, the hypothesis of this chapter is that the role of the concept of world in emancipatory politics is not to remind us of the shared (social or natural) reality or experience, but to help us grasp divergent worlds in their dissensual singularisation.

Kant's Cosmopolitan Fiction

In the 'Idea for a Universal History from a Cosmopolitan Perspective', Kant is torn between introducing cosmopolitanism either as a scientific hypothesis or as a fictional tale. The question addressed by this short 1784 article published in the journal *Berlinische Monatsschrift* is whether the history of humanity can be understood as following a natural design. While at the beginning of the text this assumption is compared to Kepler's and Newton's discoveries of natural laws, which suddenly clarified seemingly 'eccentric' natural phenomena, at the end he admits that 'such a project could yield only a *novel*'.[5] Kant's hesitation is symptomatic, since it reflects a contradiction at the heart of his undertaking: resurrecting the cosmopolitan ideal after the destruction of the cosmos. The metaphysical and teleological assumptions of Stoic cosmopolitanism are not compatible with a post-Copernican critical approach to philosophy, although the speculative fantasy that a metaphysical assumption would reveal itself as a natural law remains tempting. Nevertheless, Kant acknowledges that such assumptions can only be considered a useful fiction. While we cannot critically confirm the existence of a natural design directing the course of history, making such an assumption in a practical sense reveals a powerful progressive vision of humanity. This is the Kantian critical compromise: while the cosmological assumption that underpinned the Stoic conception of cosmopolitanism is no longer acceptable metaphysically, it should still be preserved practically as a guiding principle.

The problematic assumption Kant has in mind is not only that nature has a plan, but that this plan is destined to be achieved. Since any 'creature's natural predispositions are destined eventually to develop fully and in accordance with their purpose', humans as creatures equipped with reason are destined to fully develop their rational capacities, which is only possible collectively, in a reasonable form of society on a global scale.[6] Just as individuals must come together to form a civil constitution, states too must eventually 'enter into a federation of peoples'.[7] The natural predispositions of humanity can only be fully achieved within a cosmopolitan condition.

Kant defines cosmopolitanism as a perspective upon history, or, more precisely, as a projection of a retrospective, a look back on history from its endpoint, the realisation of its natural design. Cosmopolitanism is thus not merely an ideal – a preferred goal – but the assumption of an actual process leading up to it. If the cosmopolitan ideal would merely be set as a moral goal, there would be no guarantee that its realisation can ever be hoped for. What Kant is looking for is some sort of evidence or at least a convincing argument that cosmopolitanism is not merely how reason imagines an ideal end to history, but that history is actually developing towards a reasonable end in which humanity's capacities will be fully developed. The beginning and the end of the tale can be set by reason alone, but the problem is progression from the former to the latter: does humanity actually pursue the purpose inscribed into its nature? From a critical perspective, reason cannot postulate this as a fact. Hence, the two alternative introductions. Progress can either be proven in experience, which would make it a scientific hypothesis. Or, it can be imagined, which makes it a fiction – history could thus be read as a novel.

In the article on cosmopolitanism from 1784, the second option prevails. The comparison to a novel is significant, not because the assumption that the history of humankind follows a natural design can only be considered a fiction, but because what is at stake is precisely to imagine history as a narrative. While history may at first glance seem like an absurd succession of events, the cosmopolitan perspective reveals it as a well-structured narrative in which humanity eventually manages to overcome all obstacles and finally achieve the purpose that was set for it at the start. The idea is thus that history has the structure of fiction, wherein fiction is understood according to a certain rationality of fiction, that is, as a narrative in which events make sense from the perspective of the end they inevitably lead to. The cosmopolitan 'novel' narrates history as a fiction of progress.

Yet, Kant also returns to the scientific path, alluded to at the beginning of the text: 'All that matters is whether experience can discover any evidence of such a purposeful process in nature. I submit: it can discover *a little*.'[8] Some 'faint signs' of progress can be identified within the emerging movement of the Enlightenment, but this falls short of convincing proof. If we are to retain the cosmopolitan perspective, it is therefore necessary to put our faith in providence. Results of the empirical research are underwhelming and the text ultimately sways towards fiction with the leading metaphor of history as a novel.

The question of whether the fiction of history could nevertheless be confirmed by experience as true will continue to haunt Kant throughout his political writings. Just a month later, another of Kant's articles appeared in the same journal, the famous 'An Answer to the Question What Is Enlightenment?'.[9] Here, Kant provides a more detailed explanation of what can be expected from the faint signs of progress coming from the Enlightenment. The slogan *Sapere aude!*, with which Kant opens his article, implies that reason can appear as a historical force not via a clandestine plan of nature but by its direct independent use. Kant's Enlightenment can be defined precisely as the subjectivation of reason; as having the courage to actually use, in an independent way, humanity's essential natural capacity. Michel Foucault will later claim that modern philosophy starts with the first pages of this text, in which Kant does not seem concerned with progress towards a future goal but with 'an ontology of the present'.[10] Yet, in the following pages, Kant condemns revolutions and immediately casts doubt on the capacity of individuals to subjectify reason by themselves, and puts the task in the hands of an Enlightened elite that will spread the spirit of Enlightenment in the sphere of public discourse. The question of progress is thus reintroduced: the true subject of Enlightenment is ultimately Friedrich, King of Prussia, because his tolerance of public discussion makes progress possible in the long run.[11] Discuss, but obey, is the principle of the Enlightened state, which Kant offers as the guarantee that the faint signs of progress will not fade away. Direct subjectivation of reason in the present moment thus retreats to make way for the providence embodied in the monarch, who guarantees that history is a reasonable process after all.

Kant returns to discussing cosmopolitanism in 'Toward Perpetual Peace' (1795), where he finds new ways of reconciling the fact and fiction of progress. In spite of its precarious epistemological status, providence still plays the role of guaranteeing the cosmopolitan ideal. In order to alleviate its fictional status, Kant further naturalises providence. Since the surface of the earth is limited, its peoples are faced with the necessity to eventually come to some sort of understanding. Now that 'the violation of right at any one place on the earth is felt in all places', the cosmopolitan idea is no longer 'fantastic or exaggerated' but is becoming 'a necessary supplement [. . .] for public human right in general'.[12] The question is no longer how to see a hidden order beyond the apparent chaos of history. Now history itself, driven by the natural conditions of life on earth, is seen as producing the social conditions that make cosmopolitanism a reality. Potential objections that the globally interconnected social reality can also be seen from the perspective of deepening antagonisms rather than as anticipating cosmopolitan peace are disqualified in advance since it is precisely through antagonisms that the plan of nature operates: 'The mechanical course of nature visibly reveals a purposive plan to create harmony through discord among people, even against their own will.'[13] The path to peace leads through war, which enables Kant to argue for cosmopolitanism from a supposedly realist rather than a moral position.

Kant addresses the question of historical progress once more in the 'Contest of Faculties' (1798). The original question of whether the hypothesis of historical progress can be confirmed in experience now receives a stunning new answer. While his earlier article on the cosmopolitan perspective could only deliver faint signs of actual progress, Kant now discovers a 'historical sign' that proves, 'even for the most rigorous of theories', that the capacity nature bestows upon humanity is indeed historically active and therefore that the fiction of progress is real.[14] While in the texts on the Enlightenment and perpetual peace Kant tried to embody or naturalise providence by realistically referencing actual social processes and natural conditions of social life, he now claims that it is impossible to assume 'the perspective of *providence*' – from which such processes and conditions appear as leading to a historical *telos* – since it 'lies beyond the grasp of all human wisdom'.[15] Progress can therefore not be confirmed by empirical facts and processes but by something much more elusive and precarious – an affect triggered by an event. The French Revolution helped Kant to finally prove that progress is not merely a fantasy. Yet, it is not the event itself that proves it, since its immediate effects are disastrous and its achievements can still prove to be reversible. The proof is in the enthusiasm of the spectators that sympathise with the revolutionary efforts from abroad. The Revolution might be local, but the participation in sentiment that followed spread throughout the world with an intensity that will never be forgotten, regardless of the consequences of the particular event itself. Even though Kant does not discuss cosmopolitanism explicitly here, the revolutionary enthusiasm becomes a cosmopolitan affect. It proves that what happened in France 'can happen among all the peoples on earth'.[16]

This affective cosmopolitanism is what ultimately makes the fiction of progress real. Yet, the evidence Kant finally finds might not actually confirm what Kant was looking for. Perhaps the political affect brought about by the Revolution is indicative of another kind of fictional rationality. What the event proves is that humanity's natural predisposition, which requires a cosmopolitan condition to fully develop, can be historically effective. Despite what Kant claims, however, enthusiasm does not actually prove that the cosmopolitan condition will ever actually be achieved. It only proves the cause of progress, not its continuity. It proves that reason can appear as a historical force if it is directly politically (revolution) or at least affectively (enthusiasm) subjectivised. Kant thus comes back to what was implied in his initial definition of Enlightenment as direct subjectivation of reason. Another kind of fictional rationality is at work here: not the fiction based on narrative progression from a beginning to its inevitable end, but fiction as organised around an exceptional kind of event, an event that condenses all of human history in one fragile moment of uncertain destiny.

Kant's writings on history clearly display the political consequences of the modern destruction of the cosmos. Cosmopolitanism originally rests on the idea that nature or the world itself is the subject of progress. Positing the world as a political ideal entails an understanding of history as the unfolding of nature's plan. Discarding this metaphysical assumption is not as simple as it may appear since the question of the subject of progress remains topical, as Kant was duly aware. His solution was to hold on to cosmic teleology by introducing providence as a fictional character which guarantees that history remains structured as a narrative. This solution, however, implies problems that Kant struggles to resolve in a series of texts. It implies a split between two different rationalities of fiction: a plot-driven fiction in which all events make sense from the perspective of the end inscribed in the beginning and an event-driven fiction in which an exceptional event breaks the story into two parts but provides no guarantees regarding the end to which it might lead. In the first kind of fiction, the lack of a subject of progress is resolved by objectifying progress. The state or empirical social processes can be viewed as materialisations of providence, the real-world guarantee that history is a reasonable process. The second kind of fiction, on the other hand, is radically subjective, since it is driven by a political subjectivation of reason in the present. The price to be paid for this is that progress itself is hung in the balance. Exceptional events can only be signs of progress, signs that cannot be objectified as stable processes. Kant oscillates between the two rationalities of fiction and often produces contradictory compromises, at the same time justifying and condemning dissent and revolution. As Foucault noted, Kant's texts on history seem to betray their own more radical insights.[17]

The cosmic legacy of cosmopolitanism is still a matter of fierce debate. Contemporary champions of cosmopolitanism, such as Martha C. Nussbaum, argue that the humanist core of cosmopolitanism (belief in a shared humanity based on reason) can be disentangled from its metaphysical (cosmological and teleological) traits without any harm done to the idea itself.[18] This humanist core provides the ground for ethical and political principles of contemporary normative cosmopolitanisms, such as those of Nussbaum, Jürgen Habermas or David Held. In the work of these authors, normative reflections on principles are often supplemented by proposals for their institutional implementation. Cosmopolitanism is thus no longer consigned to teleological projections. Instead, it can rely on realist assessments of global social issues and crises and the already existing international institutions, which should be reformed in order to be able to address them. Taking this line of argument further, Ulrich Beck proposes a move from philosophical reflections on cosmopolitanism as a normative ideal to the analysis – within the framework of social science – of actual processes of cosmopolitisation in the face of global risks.[19] Yet, as we have seen above, this kind of objectivation of the cosmopolitan ideal is nothing new as it was already present in Kant's philosophical account. Since Kant, the cosmopolitan ideal has already been understood as an actual historical process leading up to its own eventual realisation. Despite seemingly renouncing philosophical assumptions and identifying a material basis for their proposals, this kind of cosmopolitanism can be seen as a continuation of Kant's attempts to present providence as an empirical fact.[20]

Contemporary critics of cosmopolitanism warn that its hidden metaphysical assumptions contribute to the contradictions and perversions that more often than not burden the application of its ideals. Costas Douzinas, for example, claims that cosmopolitan designs get derailed precisely due to their secularised and disavowed metaphysics. Instead of addressing real social antagonisms, cosmopolitanism promotes an ideal of unity employed at best as the moral remedy for the negative effects of globalisation and at worst for the purposes of legitimising imperial ambitions.[21] Similarly, many postcolonial critics point out that contemporary theoreticians of cosmopolitanism fail to take into account the colonial and imperial histories of the principles they defend.[22] As hegemonic universalisations of particular principles and interests, cosmopolitan projects tend to succumb to the vicissitudes of progress that see elites enforcing their world order on those less favoured by the unfolding course of history. Progress becomes a problematic idea when Kant's call for Enlightenment as the emancipation from intellectual immaturity is understood as a legitimation for the rich and powerful to infantilise 'immature' nations, groups or critical views in order to impose measures, presented as the unfolding of history itself.[23]

Contrary to what Nussbaum suggests, Kantian providence is not a metaphysical leftover we can simply discard. It cannot easily be discarded because it is rooted in the very fantasy of modern cosmopolitanism, the fantasy that history is structured as a narrative. The acknowledgement that there is no cosmic subject of progress does not eliminate the assumption that history can be read as a reasonable process. It remains crucial for normative cosmopolitanisms to identify the embodiments and materialisations of progress, the values and institutions that define the modern progressive legacy as the ground on which cosmopolitan thinkers can develop their proposals. This explains what David Harvey describes as

> an odd tendency in much of the new cosmopolitanism to assume that more or less adequate models of democracy have already been constructed within the framework of the leading nation-states and that the only problem remaining is to find ways to extend these models across all jurisdictions.[24]

This assumption, Harvey adds, obscures the problems with these democratic models themselves, but also legitimises disastrous interventions into 'immature' states. As many critics have argued, this kind of thinking not only leads to perversions of universalism but also tends to replace any kind of emancipatory political movement with humanitarian interventions.

As political ideals such as the Enlightenment or cosmopolitanism get turned into 'legacies' to be defended, they are often defended against more radical versions of social critique. When Habermas, for example, defends the legacy of the Enlightenment, he does so through the critique of Theodor W. Adorno, Max Horkheimer, Foucault and others, whose critique supposedly goes too far and threatens to undermine the very foundations of progressive modern ideals.[25] In a similar vein, some contemporary cosmopolitan theoreticians spend much of their energy attempting to prove that the association of the cosmopolitan ideal with colonial and imperial practices is largely coincidental and does not undermine the ideals themselves.[26]

Such defences of progressive legacies recall Karl Marx's objection to philosophers that the task at hand is not to 'anticipate the world with our dogmas but instead attempt to discover the new world through the critique of the old'.[27] This brings us back to the split in Kant between direct subjectivation of reason and the objectivation of progress as a historical narrative. Instead of truly dismissing cosmic providence, cosmopolitan thinkers materialise it in the form of institutions that might need reforms and a refreshment of their narratives – ideas for which philosophers are keen on offering – but that for all their shortcomings are still what constitutes the legacy that radical critique or radical new subjectivations should not undermine. This reduces the cosmopolitan ideal to what Alain Badiou calls democratic materialism, for which no truths can exist, only bodies and languages.[28] For the cosmopolitans, we can paraphrase, there are no political subjectivations, only institutions and narratives.

Nevertheless, postcolonial critiques of the normative cosmopolitan ideal have brought about new versions of cosmopolitanism based on specific conditions and subjectivations. Concepts such as 'rooted' (Kwame Anthony Appiah), 'vernacular' (Homi K. Bhabha) or 'subaltern' (Boaventura de Sousa Santos) cosmopolitanism, 'whole-world' (Édouard Glissant), 'afropolitanism' (Taiye Selasi, Achille Mbembe) and so on, aim to preserve the world as a political ideal while discarding its normative basis of abstract universality often associated with colonial practices.[29] According to these approaches to cosmopolitanism, which range from humanist and liberal to radically anti-capitalist, the universality of the world can only be activated when articulated with some kind of particularity, singularity, multiplicity and/or marginality. In more radical versions, true cosmopolitan subjects are thus no longer the Enlightened intellectuals but the people on the margin, who are often forced into a cosmopolitan condition. In the introduction to their volume *Cosmopolitanism*, Sheldon Pollock, Homi K. Bhabha, Carol A. Breckenridge and Dipesh Chakrabarty argue:

The cosmopolitanism of our times does not spring from the capitalized 'virtues' of Rationality, Universality, and Progress; nor is it embodied in the myth of the nation writ large in the figure of the citizen of the world. Cosmopolitans today are often the victims of modernity, failed by capitalism's upward mobility, and bereft of those comforts and customs of national belonging. Refugees, peoples of the diaspora, and migrants and exiles represent the spirit of the cosmopolitical community.[30]

While some critics have warned that such experiences do not necessarily lead to any kind of cosmopolitan solidarity,[31] others hope that the subjectivities emerging in political struggles surrounding these conditions can be seen as forming a radical cosmopolitics from below.[32] From the latter perspective, cosmopolitanism can be observed in counter-hegemonic social movements and places where the antagonisms of global capitalism are most obviously on display. Cosmopolitanism is thus preserved on account of its singularisation, meaning that its universal horizon can only be opened up from specific perspectives within social struggles. In Marxist terms, one could say that the world in which proletarians unite can only exist from the perspective of the class struggle itself.[33]

Singularising the Common World

Turning away from the institutions and narratives that constitute the cosmopolitan ideal, another tradition of thought comes into sight, one that relates the actual unification of the world to the very loss of world as the horizon of common existential experience that conditions political action. From this perspective, the modern process of globalisation is seen not as a condition of either possibility or necessity of political cosmopolitanism, but as a direct threat to any worldly experience. Gaining the world as a global socio-economic totality is equated with the loss of what turns human coexistence into a world. Therefore, if world is to remain a political ideal, it must be divorced from any notion of a global totality. Yet, as we will see, this does not necessarily imply the regression to the closed worlds of national communities. According to the point of view we are about to present, it is neither the totality nor the particularity of human coexistence that makes a world, but its singularity: the common world exists as a singular common world, based on specific common experience and joint action, and as a world of singularities, unique beings who share the world in question. Curiously, however, this perspective does not seem to devote much consideration to the multiplicity of worlds that logically follows from their singular character. Emphasising the opposition between global worldlessness and a singular worldliness, the question of the relation between singular worlds and potential conflict between them remains somewhat sidelined.

Well before the discussion of globalisation accelerated after the fall of the Berlin Wall, Hannah Arendt proposed a reflection on global worldlessness. In the famous discussion of human rights in *The Origins of Totalitarianism*, she addresses the unwelcome effects of the realisation of Kant's regulative idea. As united humanity becomes an 'unescapable fact', the merits of cosmopolitanism are put to the test.[34] Just as the 'One World' becomes reality, the existence of the rightless, whose numbers have been increasing in the face of the two world wars, testifies to a radical form of exclusion.[35] When stateless people, reduced to their abstract humanity, are denied their rights, they are not merely excluded from a particular state, but from humanity itself and consequently 'deprived of expression within and action upon a common world'.[36] When world as framework of political coexistence becomes a generalised totality, it coincides with worldlessness.[37] Yet, what might still be understood here as a condition of the radically deprived turns out to be a particularly disturbing form of a much more general state of affairs. In *The Human Condition*, Arendt puts the concept of world in the centre of her political thought, which identifies modernity with world alienation. The interconnectedness of humanity across the globe in terms of economy, travel and communication unites humanity on a global scale but deprives it of a world.[38]

Before returning to the reasons for this loss, we should understand better what makes world a political concept for Arendt. For it is not at first introduced as such. Arendt presents world as a product of human work, the artificial environment of things humanity surrounds itself with: 'The man-made world of things, the human artifice erected by *homo faber*, becomes a home for mortal men, whose stability will endure and outlast the ever-changing movement of their lives and actions.'[39] To the natural cycles of mortal life and its needs, as well as to the perishable character of words and deeds, world opposes a realm of durability, objectivity and stability. As the correlate of work, world is thus opposed to the two other forms of *vita activa* Arendt explores in *The Human Condition*: labour, whose correlate is life, and action, whose correlate is the plurality of human beings as political animals capable of deeds and speech. Even though the fabrication of the world of things as such is not political *per se* (only action can be political),[40] it soon becomes clear that it is not only the material ground of action but has a much more intimate relation to the political realm. Work and action condition each other:

> Without being talked about by men and without housing them, the world would not be a human artifice but a heap of unrelated things to which each isolated individual was at liberty to add one more object; without the human artifice to house them, human affairs would be as floating, as futile and vain, as the wanderings of nomad tribes.[41]

The meaning of the common world for human affairs only becomes fully apparent with its loss. But how can it be lost, considering that humanity obviously still (and increasingly so) lives in an artificial world of things? Modern world alienation results from the fact that the principles of both labour and action invade the world-making principles of *homo faber*. On the one hand, things are no longer produced to be durable but become themselves objects of consumption, just like the goods necessary for the daily reproduction of life.[42] This erodes the durability of the world and pulls the public sphere of political action down into the field of social issues and reproduction. No longer a free activity of equal men, politics becomes subordinated to the necessities dictated by mass society of labouring animals and those who exploit them. On the other hand, modern science and advanced technology infect work with characteristics of action: unpredictability and irreversibility. Some of the things that *homo faber* now produces no longer offer worldly stability but threaten the very existence of a world. What started with the Scientific Revolution in the seventeenth century, Arendt claims, gets its conclusion with the atom bomb.[43] Without the stabilising force of worldliness, provided by work, the natural cycles of life and the unpredictability of action reveal their worldless character.

In Arendt, world thus appears as a political concept not in the sense of a political project or a regulative idea, but in the phenomenological sense as authentic existential experience. Without entering into Arendt's complicated position towards Heidegger, it is clear – as

Roland Végső argues – that 'she shares Heidegger's phenomenological investment in the idea (and the experience) of the world'.[44] As we have seen in previous chapters, it is part and parcel of the phenomenological concept of world that it is haunted by worldlessness, not only historically, through the onset of a worldless modernity, but also structurally, from within. Étienne Tassin notes that for Arendt, political action proper 'can rise against being-in-the-world'.[45] Even though world is both the condition (the stability of the man-made world of things) and the object (the public realm of coexistence) of politics, every free political act detaches itself from its conditions and therefore the world, redefining the field of possibilities with unpredictable consequences. Due to its power of separation from the world in which it takes place, action should be understood as existentially (Tassin) or structurally (Végső) worldless – it is a worldless power that precedes any historical epoch of world alienation.[46]

It should not be forgotten, however, that Arendtian action does not only disturb the world with its inherent worldlessness, but also with its power to bifurcate and multiply worlds. Action, for Arendt, is not only the bearer of worldlessness, but also what turns the heap of things humans produce into a world in the first place. Political action, in the sense of 'acting together', 'not only has the most intimate relationship to the public part of the world common to us all, but is the one activity which constitutes it'.[47] While it is true that the constitutive capacity for action is also what has the power to dismantle the stability of a world, this is not because of its structural worldlessness, but because every act constitutes the world anew. Rather than being committed within the world, an act has the character of opening up a new world, a new field of possibilities. The multiplicity of acts and therefore worlds coincides with the human plurality which is the condition of political life.[48] With every proper act, a bifurcation of worlds takes place.

For Arendt, the dynamic plurality of humanity is intimately related to natality, the constant appearance of new human beings. Arendt claims that 'action has the closest connection to the human condition of natality', which she proclaims to be 'the central category of political [. . .] thought'.[49] Arendt thus replaces the central position that mortality held for Heidegger with its opposite as the primary category of political phenomenology. Every new being (with its capacity to act) represents a new beginning of public life. Natality, which inserts 'a new world into the existing world', is the ontological condition of action.[50]

While it is true that an excess of new beginnings threatens the stability of the common world of political action, it is not worldlessness that is at the gates but a proliferation of a multitude of worlds. Action, therefore, is not the principle of structural worldlessness, but a principle of radical singularisation of worlds.

Arendt's focus on the loss of world in modernity, however, prevents her from following this thread and developing the implications of the excess of worlds. In a seemingly paradoxical manner, Arendt claims that the loss of world coincides with the process of its global unification. The unification of the globe in terms of travel and communication succeeded in 'alienating man from his immediate earthly surroundings', uprooting the experience of having one's defined place within a particular and limited world.[51] Expropriation in the context of accelerating capital accumulation is another central factor in modern world alienation for Arendt, which brings her close to Marx (although she claims Marx wrongly emphasised self-alienation over world-alienation).[52] Yet, even economic globalisation is 'of minor significance' compared to the 'alienation underlying the whole development of natural science in the modern age'.[53] Arendt thus comes close to Heidegger and his reflections on the darkening of the world. Science does not connect us to the world, Arendt believes, but alienates us from it, since it introduces an ontological split. With modern science, 'being and appearance part ways',[54] which undermines the very foundations of the phenomenological experience of worldliness. In a true phenomenological fashion, Arendt claims that the reality that science explores has nothing to do with the world as the horizon of meaningful experience, in which being (in its plurality) and appearance are one.

It could be said that Arendt thus reintroduces the cosmopolitan fiction of history, but in reverse. The narrative of modernity is no longer the narrative of progress towards the realisation of a globally shared world. This realisation itself coincides with the process of world alienation, which seems irredeemable. Regaining the possibility of a shared world – as singular and for singularities – in the midst of global worldlessness nevertheless remains the stake of politics, but how this task can be achieved is a difficult question. From an Arendtian perspective, this would entail not only countering the worldless effects of global capitalism – the end of which, as the saying goes, is harder to imagine than the end of the world itself – but also dismantling modern subjectivity, along with its forms of rationality and their ontological implications.

Another version of elaborating the political meaning of the phenomenological concept of world was proposed by Jean-Luc Nancy. The multiplication of worlds already suggested by Arendt receives in Nancy a more direct conceptualisation. His work crystallises the question of how the plurality of human beings constitutes a shared world, considering that this plurality itself implies a multiplication of worlds. Nancy sees no contradiction between the unity and the plurality of worlds:

> The unity of a world is nothing other than its diversity, and its diversity is, in turn, a diversity of worlds. A world is a multiplicity of worlds, the world is a multiplicity of worlds, and its unity is the sharing out [*partage*] and the mutual exposure in this world of all its worlds.[55]

Unity and multiplicity come together through the connection between sharing and mutual exposure, which – as we saw in Chapter 1 – are essential to Nancy's conception of being and world, which emphasises the dimension of the *mitsein*. Beings come into existence within an essentially shared plural world, each singular being offering a different access to the world, its own singularisation of the common world.

As we have already discussed, the phenomenological conceptualisations of world tend to present its object as on the verge of being lost. Nancy offers no exception here as he claims that 'the world has lost its capacity to "form a world" [*faire monde*]'.[56] Again, it is the very unification of the globe through globalisation that deprives us of a meaningful worldly experience. The paradoxical proximity of gaining and losing the world is even more apparent in French, where the word for globalisation (*mondialisation*) is based on 'world' (*monde*) rather than 'globe'. Nancy attempts to rehabilitate the worldliness inscribed in *mondialisation* from the process commonly referred to as globalisation. Addressing the intricate relation between world-making and world-deprivation, Nancy moves from Heidegger to Marx. Referring to Marx's comments on the making of the world market and the prospects of a communist takeover of world history and thus the fruits of global production, Nancy acknowledges that capitalist unification actually produces a globally shared world, but in an alienated form. Capitalism captures plural singularities within the uniformity of general equivalence and commodification: 'One could say that capital is the alienation of being singular plural as such.'[57]

In the face of such alienation, it is necessary to redeem the capacity of creation and 'create a world tirelessly'.⁵⁸ It is only in the mutual exposure of singularities within worlds they create and share that 'the real connection between existences', which capital establishes but obscures, can be reappropriated.⁵⁹ The political meaning of world no longer revolves around its unification but around the irreducible plurality of singularities, mutually exposed in their coexistence: 'what is necessary is a world that would only be the world of singularities, without their plurality constructed as a unitotality'.⁶⁰ And since every singularity also singularises the common world that it shares and therefore creates its own world, the world of singularities becomes a multiplicity of singular worlds. World thus remains a political ideal, but precisely in its singularity and multiplication. Political struggle becomes the 'struggle for a world', the struggle to configure 'a quantity of possible worlds in the world'.⁶¹

Bringing the phenomenological concept of world as a horizon of meaningful existential experience to the sphere of politics, Arendt and Nancy thus emphasise the plurality of singular beings as what constitutes common or shared worlds. Nancy seems to further integrate the two paths already opened by Arendt – the loss of world on the one hand and the proliferation of worlds on the other. Avoiding the trap of getting stuck in an inverted cosmopolitan narrative of loss (as in Arendt), Nancy uses the multiplication of worlds as the means of a potential reversal of the creeping worldlessness of modernity.

What I have proposed instead is to cast aside the ideal of worldliness – not to affirm worldlessness, but first of all to contemplate the multiplicity of worlds as a prosaic actuality. The crucial problem the opposition between worldliness and worldlessness leaves aside is the problem of relations and potential conflicts between multiple singular worlds. When the plurality of worlds is considered as an ideal in itself, it misses potential conflicts cutting through the very field of plurality. Antonia Birnbaum thus claims that Nancy's ontologisation of plurality equates conflict with 'a catastrophic destruction of the frame of compossibility', which excludes conflict from understanding plurality.⁶² While the task of politics is limited to keeping the field of the singular plural open, conflict closes the becoming of plurality. For Birnbaum, this indicates a powerless and inconsequential conception of politics. She claims instead that it is precisely through conflicts that a shared world is actualised. A similar critique, but of Arendt, was proposed by Tassin, according to whom Arendt has not paid sufficient attention to the social conflicts and political struggles that are constitutive of political action. Even though political action indeed presupposes the Arendtian 'being-with' and 'acting-together', it also implies 'being-in-conflict-with' and 'acting-against'.[63] The concept of world as plural singularity or singular plurality ultimately reduces the question of multiple worlds to the question of ethical and political coexistence within a common world. This deposits any notion of conflict or antagonism on the outside, into the intrusion of worldlessness, to which the ideal of worldliness is opposed.

Adding the conflictual dimension to the phenomenological concept of world is the task taken on by Tassin himself. While he retains the phenomenological concept of world, he understands it not as an existential given but as a realm emerging from social conflict. Staying within the Arendtian conceptual framework, he explores precisely the singularity and plurality of worlds, which Arendt indicates but does not explore further. For Tassin, a common world in the political sense is a world made of 'the intangible materiality' of human actions and relations that 'is born out of struggles and conflicts'.[64] It is within a common struggle in the midst of concrete social conflicts that a common world emerges. The concrete nature of political struggles gives such worlds a necessarily singular character, as opposed both to the particular nature of exclusive communities and to the abstract universal community of cosmopolitanism, which constitutes the '"transcendental illusion" of political reason'.[65] According to Tassin, cosmopolitan political projects aiming for the world as a whole in fact serve to distract from actual conflicts and emancipatory struggles.[66] His own version of 'cosmopolitics', on the other hand, goes beyond the cultural or communitarian conception of common worlds, defined by belonging, to the properly political common worlds, in which singularities, irrespective of their identities, are united in a common struggle.[67]

Tassin succeeds at dialecticising the opposition of political worldliness and worldlessness by understanding social conflicts – the very condensations of modern worldlessness – as the site of the emergence of common worlds. This way, he manages to reaffirm world as an Arendtian political ideal in terms of emancipatory political struggles. Looking closely at the way Tassin develops his argument, it becomes clear that what ultimately allows him to make this move is his adoption of a Rancièrian perspective.[68] His understanding of conflict follows

Rancière's notions of constitutive exclusion and the part with no part, while his conception of struggle owes a lot to Rancière's notion of political subjectivation. As we will see, however, Rancière's concept of world is not phenomenological, not even in an Arendtian sense. Tassin assumes the compatibility between the Arendtian and the Rancièrian framework of political thought without engaging with Rancière's own critique of Arendt. What thus remains unaddressed is the tension between two very different concepts of world, namely world as a phenomenological ideal of meaningful experience and world as a transcendental structure that determines what can appear within it, and how. In order to understand the multiplicity of worlds politically, but outside any affirmation of worldliness as a political ideal, we now turn to Rancière.

Two Worlds in One

Rancière's declaration that 'there is no world politics' makes it clear that he is not a thinker of the cosmopolitan ideal.[69] Broad political perspectives that encompass Europe, world citizens or humanity aim for 'a whole that is equal to the sum of its parts', a type of whole that Rancière considers to be essentially deprived of politics.[70] Political universality does not begin with a consensual perspective that puts together all the parts of a whole, but through 'the singular construction of disputes', which occur where there is a manifestation of 'a part of those who have no part'.[71] In politics, a whole can never be identical with the sum of its parts, since what constitutes the parts as having something in common is always characterised by a particular distribution of bodies and capacities that turns out to be contingent whenever bodies appear out of place or displaying capacities that should not belong to them. This also implies that the problem cannot be solved by opposing globalisation with a more meaningful experience of singular common worlds, as plural as they may be. The problem is that any sense of worldliness is predefined by the question of who can take part in such a world. If Rancière does not share the ideal of worldliness as developed by Arendt or Nancy, it is because he views political action not only as world-building, but also as a manifestation of a split within a given world. Those who have no part can only stake their claim by provoking a bifurcation of worlds. Instead of posing the world as a political ideal, Rancière understands politics through a paradoxical and conflictual coexistence of worlds: '*The essence of politics is the manifestation of dissensus as the presence of two worlds in one.*'[72]

According to Rancière, worlds are composed of forms of visibility and intelligibility that define the perception and understanding of phenomena, events and situations that shape a shared reality and the ways various subjects can take part in it.[73] Rancière does not hesitate to characterise such forms as fictions. These fictions, however, are not mere illusions; they are what produces our sense of reality:

> A fiction is not the invention of an imaginary world. Instead it is the construction of a framework within which subjects, things, and situations can be perceived as coexisting in a common world and events can be identified and linked in a way that makes sense. Fiction is at work whenever a sense of reality must be produced.[74]

Rancière's concept of world is closely related to what he calls the 'distribution of the sensible', which he describes as a Foucauldian historicisation of the Kantian *a priori* forms of sensible experience.[75] The distribution of the sensible allows us to understand how the apparently immediate facts of sense perception depend on historically variable transcendental structures that determine the way subjects perceive and occupy worlds. Dictating what can or cannot be seen, who can and cannot be heard, the distribution of the sensible can be described as 'the dividing-up of the world (*de monde*) and of people (*du monde*)'.[76]

We immediately see where this concept of world differs from the phenomenological one. Instead of establishing an authentic experience of being-in-the-world as an existential or political ideal, it describes how any experience of a world already depends on divisions and distributions dictated by its transcendental coordinates. From this perspective, the problem with political uses of the phenomenological concept of world is that they do not account for the political divisions, inscribed in the experience of worldliness. The forms of visibility and intelligibility that compose a world also 'determine the ways in which subjects occupy this common world, in terms of coexistence or exclusion, and their capacity to perceive it, understand it and act on it'.[77] Rancière's position, however, is not that the constitution of worlds is always political. The transcendental structures that arrange the distribution of parts and capacities fall under what Rancière prefers to describe as the order of the police (following Foucault's analysis of the seventeenth- and eighteenth-century use of the term as a mode of government).[78] Politics in its proper, emancipatory sense, on the other hand, begins when this order is challenged by those who are also present, but have no part. It is the manifestation of a dissensus that makes of the multiplicity of worlds a political realm.

Rancière's conception of politics opposes the 'inegalitarian distribution of social bodies' within a given world to 'the equal capacity of speaking beings in general', which means that anyone can display the capacity of taking part in the political framing of the common.[79] The equality of speaking beings, however, should not be equated with the Aristotelian link between the speaking animal and the political animal adopted by Arendt. While Arendt is interested in the way speaking beings construct the political world of public life in which they can freely express their singularity as equals, for Rancière politics is located precisely in the question of who counts as a speaking being.[80] As Arendt herself admits, not everyone is in a position to lead a public life.[81] Speaking beings, capable of constituting a political world, may only include adult men, freed from the necessities of the private sphere. Slaves, as is well known, were not considered by Aristotle as fully in possession of the capacity of speech.[82] As Rancière shows, the emerging workers' and women's movements of the nineteenth and twentieth centuries first had to deal with the fact that not only were they not considered as capable of public discussion, but also their issues and demands were not considered as a public matter, as a part of what constitutes the public sphere and thereby the common world in the political sense.[83]

This kind of egalitarianism does not posit the world as a political ideal. If, for cosmopolitanism, the recognition of humanity, common to everyone, implies a unification of the world, the universality implied by the equality of speaking beings is strictly connected to the singularity of dissensus. When the equality of subjective capacities is activated, it necessarily bifurcates the world in a dissensual way. The multiplication of worlds that Arendt discovered as essential to political action without fully considering the consequences of this discovery thus gains a new meaning and recognition in terms of Rancièrian dissensual understanding of politics: 'Modern politics holds to the multiplication of those operations of subjectification that invent worlds of community that are worlds of dissension.'[84]

But the question is not only how to move away from cosmopolitan consensualism by acknowledging the elementary political value of dissensus. The question is also why political conflict should still be formulated as a conflict of worlds. Rancière claims that the political dissensus is not merely a confrontation between interests or opinions. If it were so, there would be no need to articulate political conflict as a conflict of worlds, since the sides of the conflict could be considered as belonging to the same world. This would be a conflict between already constituted parties that negotiate their position and stake within the common whole. In contrast to this, dissensus is 'the demonstration of a gap in the sensible itself', which means that the issues it addresses concern the very constitution of partners, objects and stage of discussion.[85] Dissensus makes the gap between two transcendental renderings of the same situation become apparent:

> Political demonstration makes visible that which had no reason to be seen; it places one world in another – for instance, the world where the factory is a public space in that where it is considered private, the world where workers speak, and speak about the community, in that where their voices are mere cries expressing pain.[86]

When those who have no part display a capacity to participate in the common world, they manifest another world that lays the claim over the same sensible reality. The conflict, therefore, is not between two parties in the same world, but also not between two completely separate worlds that have nothing in common. What is manifested is rather a presence of two worlds in one.

The primacy of dissensus as the presence of two worlds in one is the reason why Rancière rejects Habermas's insistence on the distinction between the intra-worldly argumentation, necessary for communicative action, and the poetic, world-building function of language.[87] Reducing politics to the common world of communicative rationality, which is given as a moral ideal, necessarily ignores dissensus. It neglects the fact that 'the demonstration proper to politics is always both argument and opening up the world where argument can be received and have an impact – argument about the very existence of such a world'.[88] Rancière therefore proposes to think politics from the point of view of a split between two worlds, two rival transcendental framings of the common. Without suggesting a new transcendental, a redistribution of the sensible, the dissensual demonstration would only be perceived within the dominant transcendental as an expression of pain, deprived of public significance. It is only effective if it opens up a new world in which it can be perceived as addressing something in common. Another world emerges, a world that is not just another addition to an indifferent multiplicity of worlds, but a world formed in a dissensual (non-)relation with a specific already existing world. The world where the factory is a public space cannot coexist indifferently with the world in which it is considered private. In the Conclusion, I will call such objects 'contested objects'. Points of contestation emerge when the existence of an object in one world becomes incompossible with its existence in another.

The paradox of dissensus as the presence of two worlds in one is that it is simultaneously a demonstration of a split between two worlds and a demonstration of another common world that unites them. The workers that stage a discussion regarding their rights have to 'behave as though such a stage existed, as though there were a common world of argument – which is eminently reasonable and eminently unreasonable, eminently wise and resolutely subversive, since such a world does not exist'.[89] When the workers emerge as a political subject, they manifest, on the one hand, that there is no common world. The world they find themselves in does not include them and their cause as a public matter. On the other hand, however, they act as if such a world existed, as if they can act in the public sphere within the community of equals from which they are actually excluded. What their manifestation reveals is not only a separate world but also a reframing of the common one.

If what is at stake in political subjectivation is not merely a recognition of one's status in the world but a creation of an alternative world, we should also accept that the new transcendental changes those who are thus subjectivised:

> A political subject is not a group that 'becomes aware' of itself, finds its voice, imposes its weight on society. It is an operator that connects and disconnects different areas, regions, identities, functions, and capacities existing in the configuration of a given experience.[90]

Since identities and capacities are defined by the distribution of the sensible, they are necessarily challenged by the new transcendental.

Political subjectivation thus requires disidentification and the display of unforeseen capacities.

This also implies that there cannot be, strictly speaking, a world of achieved equality, where the sensible multiplicity would appear as unlimited by any transcendental. Rancière is critical of those political philosophies that substantialise multiplicity itself as an emancipatory political force: political subjectivity consists in 'the singularity of cases of division' and not in an evocation of a political entity 'unmarked by separation'.[91] Equality appears in processes of subjectivation and acts of redistribution in which the contingency of any social order in relation to the multiplicity it distributes is revealed. It exists as the activated capacity of anyone to take part in setting the transcendental coordinates of a common world. But does this mean that the redistribution put into motion by the process of political subjectivation merely aims to replace one distribution of the sensible with another, one police order with another, perhaps slightly less inegalitarian? And if this were the case, according to what idea of progress could such an improvement even be measured if we stay true to the dissensual definition of politics proposed by Rancière? Or, alternatively, does emancipatory political subjectivation engage in a different kind of world-building? This would mean that what is at stake in the conflict of worlds is not just a clash between two transcendentals but also between two kinds of transcendental.

With this question, we come back to the problem of history as a narrative of progress that we analysed in relation to the Kantian cosmopolitan ideal. Rancière is strongly opposed to 'the logic of Enlightenment in which the cultivated elites have to guide the ignorant and superstitious lower classes in the path of progress', a path 'of infinite reproduction of inequality in the name of the promise of equality'.[92] Kant's dilemma between a direct subjectivation of reason and the materialised fiction of progress returns with Rancière opting firmly for direct subjectivation against progressive representation. The idea of the mature guiding the immature is based on the assumption of inequality and thus betrays in its practice the equality it pronounces as its goal. The dependence of the idea of progress on a narrative structure is emphasised by Rancière with his inversion of Jean-François Lyotard's thesis on the end of grand narratives. According to Rancière, the grand narratives in fact never ended. In the aftermath of the 2008 financial crisis, Rancière states, we have seen the state authorities and financial elites take on the role of the mature acting in the name of progress, proposing a narrative of historical necessity in which the markets dictate urgent reforms.[93] On the other hand, we have seen the rise of new political subjectivations, such as the Occupy movement, which engage another kind of temporality, not the narrative temporality of progress, but rather the temporality of moments or events in which bodies and capacities are redistributed.[94]

Rancière traces the genealogy of the dilemma between subjectivation and progress, the event and the narrative beyond Kant to Aristotle and his preference for poetry over the historical chronicle. What is at stake in this famous passage from *Poetics* is in fact a dilemma between two types of fictional rationality that define two constructions of historical temporality as well as two kinds of participation in historical time. Poetry is truer, for Aristotle, since it causally links events according to necessity and verisimilitude, while the historical chronicle merely lists the empirical succession of events. The advantage of the former is precisely that it is capable of linking events into a narrative. Rancière shows how Aristotle's temporal hierarchy rests on a social hierarchy between two kinds of people:

> There are people whose present is situated within the time of the events that might arrive – the time of action and of its ends which is also the time of knowledge and of its leisure: in short the time of those who have time and who, for that reason, are called active men. And there are people who live in the present of the things which merely happen, one after another, the repetitive and narrow time of the everyday: in short the time of those who don't have the time: those men that are called passive, not because they do nothing, but because they passively receive time, without enjoying either the ends of action or the time of leisure which is an end in itself. In such a way the causal rationality of the temporal linkage between events ties up with a hierarchical distribution of temporalities which is a distribution of forms of life.[95]

Modern grand narratives, Rancière claims, applied the Aristotelian poetic rationality to history itself. History as a narrative of progress perpetuates inequality by drawing a division between two ways of participation in historical time: on the one hand, those who are well positioned to understand and use for their own ends the necessities and impossibilities dictated by the historical arc, and on the other, those to whom history merely happens as a succession of events, the rationality of which exceeds their capacity for knowledge and action.

The temporality of political subjectivation, on the other hand, is not the temporality of a narrative, but a temporality of exceptional events in which history is condensed. It occurs in moments of temporal fissure that have the power of 'engendering another line of temporality' along with a redistribution of spaces and bodies that occupy them.[96] As we will see in Chapter 5, this temporality of micro-events coincides, according to Rancière, with the new fictional logic introduced by realist and modernist novelists. It also coincides, we should add, with the unexpected findings of Kant's search for the evidence of progress. As I have claimed above, the enthusiasm regarding the French Revolution does not actually prove that history is structured as a narrative of progress but that reason can enter history as a moment of subjectivation, a moment that can connect to any other moment in any other place on the basis of the generic equality of speaking beings. This connectivity between moments or events is the alternative world-building principle to the narrative of progress. Political subjectivation redistributes time and space and thus establishes not only another transcendental, but another kind of transcendental.

This kind of world-building has two dimensions, an autonomous one and a heteronomous one. On the one hand, political subjectivation creates a world of its own, a collective already functioning according to the transcendental it introduces. Rancière's examples range from the Paris Commune to May '68 and the Occupy movement. As Rancière points out regarding May '68: 'The barricade is the self-affirmation of a community of equals rather than an efficient means of fighting against the enemy.'[97] In such micro-worlds, equality is immediately established as a principle of subjectivation, without any need for postponement and regulatory ideas. It thus exists not as a goal but as the assumption and condition of political action. This world-building principle could be called metonymical: it is based on the connection of equals within a moment and the expansion of a moment into a series of moments. In metonymy any part can take the role of the whole, and so the collective political subject builds its own world as universally addressed. Such worlds are not based on exclusion but on the equality of speaking beings, activated in temporal and spatial discontinuities carved into the dominant world-narratives. Such worlds can 'begin at any moment whatsoever' and expand 'by creating unexpected connections'.[98]

On the other hand, the political subject's world is not only its own world, a bubble within the social totality, but a rival transcendental projected beyond the subjective collective itself, a reframing of the common, an alternative singularisation of the world. This heteronomous world-building dimension is metaphorical in the sense it establishes a relation at a point where there is no relation. The political subject, as we have seen, does not only expose the supposedly common world as a fiction, it also creates its own fiction: the common world in which the political subject has a part, in which the factory, for example, is considered to be a public matter. The closed metonymical world is thus expanded in the sense of mimicking a relation with the outside: it projects the principles of its own separated world as the principles of a new common world, which is not merely anticipated but already enacted in the subject's own activities.

But to what extent can this new transcendental enforce itself in comparison to the world it is in conflict with, or, for that matter, to a number of other worlds with which it shares ontological or sensible multiples? Obviously, such micro-worlds exist within other worlds in a dissensual way and have very real forces staked against them. Criticisms of Rancière usually focus on this point: how do such local manifestations of subjective capacity and ephemeral openings in the dominant regime of the sensible produce any lasting and large-scale political effects?[99] Antonia Birnbaum offered perhaps the most nuanced elaboration of this problem as one of articulating the conflict of worlds with the conflict of forces.[100] An alternative transcendental may indeed emerge in the way Rancière describes it, Birnbaum claims, but it is itself inscribed in a field of forces and antagonisms. The conflict of forces should thus not be ignored, but also not be presented as the ultimate real world to which all fictions should be reduced. In the light of what I have been developing here, the question would be how such new transcendentals can be extended beyond the initially limited sphere of their emergence, inevitably taking into account the conflict of forces, but without wanting or being able to rely on the progressive narrative logic. The issue is not to reduce the multiplicity of worlds back to the world of social totality, but to understand and contribute to the expansion of dissensual worlds.

Notes

1. Martha C. Nussbaum, 'Kant and Cosmopolitanism', in *Perpetual Peace: Essays on Kant's Cosmopolitan Ideal*, ed. James Bohman and Matthias Lutz-Bachmann (Cambridge, MA: MIT Press, 1997), 34, 39.

2. Immanuel Kant, 'Idea for a Universal History from a Cosmopolitan Perspective', in *Toward Perpetual Peace and Other Writings on Politics, Peace, and History*, ed. Pauline Kleingeld, trans. David L. Colclasure (New Haven: Yale University Press, 2006), 14.
3. Hannah Arendt, *The Human Condition* (Chicago: University of Chicago Press, 1958), 258.
4. Ibid. 248–57.
5. Kant, 'Idea for a Universal History', 4, 15.
6. Ibid. 4.
7. Ibid. 10.
8. Ibid. 13.
9. Immanuel Kant, 'An Answer to the Question What Is Enlightenment?', in *Toward Perpetual Peace*, 17–23.
10. Michel Foucault, *The Government of Self and Others: Lectures at the Collège de France 1982–1983*, trans. Graham Burchell (New York: Palgrave Macmillan, 2010), 11–15, 21.
11. Kant, 'An Answer to the Question What Is Enlightenment?', 22–3.
12. Immanuel Kant, 'Toward Perpetual Peace: A Philosophical Sketch', in *Toward Perpetual Peace*, 84–5.
13. Ibid. 85.
14. Immanuel Kant, 'The Contest of the Faculties, Part 2', in *Toward Perpetual Peace*, 158.
15. Ibid. 154.
16. Ibid. 158.
17. Foucault, *The Government of Self and Others*, 39.
18. Nussbaum, 'Kant and Cosmopolitanism', 42.
19. Ulrich Beck, 'Cosmopolitanism as Imagined Communities of Global Risk', *American Behavioral Scientist* 55, no. 10 (2011): 1,346–61, https://doi.org/10.1177/0002764211409739.
20. As we have seen, Kant's position on possible proof of historical progress is highly ambivalent and complicated. This ambivalence, however, completely evaporates in some contemporary reaffirmations of the Enlightenment. An example can be found in Steven Pinker's best-seller *Enlightenment Now: The Case for Reason, Science, Humanism, and Progress* (New York: Viking, 2018). In an astonishing twist on the Kantian problem of confirming the idea of progress in experience, Pinker sets out to prove with extensive empirical data how humanity has indeed progressed remarkably in all aspects of life since the eighteenth century. When progress becomes a fact, the critics of the Enlightenment, such as Foucault or Adorno, can only be seen as the prophets of doom, spreading illusory pessimism – as Pinker is happy to conclude. As some critics have noticed, such arguments provide a seemingly centrist platform that serves to legitimate more controversial

ideas of the radical right. See James A. Smith, 'Steven Pinker and Jordan Peterson: The Missing Link between Neoliberalism and the Radical Right', *Open Democracy*, 1 November 2018, https://www.opendemocracy.net/en/steven-pinker-jordan-peterson-neoliberalism-radical-right. In this light, Pinker's heroic humanity evokes Kant's joke on account of his own discussion of progress, featuring a patient dying of improvement. Kant, 'The Contest of the Faculties', 163.

21. Costas Douzinas, 'The Metaphysics of Cosmopolitanism', in *After Cosmopolitanism*, ed. Rosi Braidotti, Patrick Hanafin and Bolette Blaagaard (Abingdon: Routledge, 2013), 57–76.
22. See, for example, Gurminder K. Bhambra, 'Whither Europe? Postcolonial versus Neocolonial Cosmopolitanism', *Interventions: International Journal of Postcolonial Studies* 18, no. 2 (2016): 187–202, https://doi.org/10.1080/1369801X.2015.1106964.
23. See David Harvey, *Cosmopolitanism and the Geographies of Freedom* (New York: Columbia University Press, 2009), particularly chapters 1 and 4.
24. Ibid. 86.
25. Jürgen Habermas, *The Philosophical Discourse of Modernity*, trans. Frederick G. Lawrence (Cambridge: Polity Press, 1987).
26. See, for example, David Held, 'Cosmopolitanism in a Multipolar World', in *After Cosmopolitanism*, 36.
27. Karl Marx, 'Letter from Marx to Arnold Ruge, September 1843', Marxists Internet Archives, accessed 13 September 2019, https://www.marxists.org/archive/marx/works/1843/letters/43_09-alt.htm.
28. Alain Badiou, *Logics of Worlds: Being and Event, 2*, trans. Alberto Toscano (London: Continuum, 2009), 1.
29. See Kwame Anthony Appiah, *The Ethics of Identity* (Princeton: Princeton University Press, 2005), chapter 6; Homi K. Bhabha, 'Unsatisfied: Notes on Vernacular Cosmopolitanism', in *Text and Nation: Cross-Disciplinary Essays on Cultural and National Identities*, ed. Laura Garcia-Morena and Peter C. Pfeifer (London: Camden House, 1996), 191–207; Boaventura de Sousa Santos, 'Beyond Neoliberal Governance: The World Social Forum as Subaltern Cosmopolitan Politics and Legality', in *Law and Globalization from Below: Towards a Cosmopolitan Legality*, ed. Boaventura de Sousa Santos and César A. Rodríguez-Garavito (Cambridge: Cambridge University Press, 2005), 29–63; Édouard Glissant, *Treatise on the Whole-World*, trans. Celia Britton (Liverpool: Liverpool University Press, 2020); Taiye Selasi, 'Bye-Bye Babar', *Callaloo* 36, no. 3 (2013): 529; Achille Mbembe, 'Afropolitanism', in *Cosmopolitanisms*, ed. Bruce Robbins and Paulo Lemos Horta (New York: New York University Press, 2017), 102–7. On the distinction between universal and plural cosmopolitanisms see also Harvey, *Cosmopolitanism*, 79.

30. Sheldon Pollock, Homi K. Bhabha, Carol A. Breckenridge and Dipesh Chakrabarty, 'Cosmopolitanisms', in *Cosmopolitanism*, ed. Carol A. Breckenridge, Sheldon Pollock, Homi K. Bhabha and Dipesh Chakrabarty (Durham, NC: Duke University Press, 2002), 6.
31. See Pheng Cheah, 'Cosmopolitanism', *Theory, Culture & Society* 23, nos. 2–3 (2006): 492–3, https://doi.org/10.1177/026327640602300290.
32. Sousa Santos, 'Beyond Neoliberal Governance', and James D. Ingram, *Radical Cosmopolitics: The Ethics and Politics of Democratic Universalism* (New York: Columbia University Press, 2013).
33. Would the socialist and communist internationalism be a more appropriate designation for this horizon of unification? Étienne Balibar writes that compared to the bourgeois ideal of cosmopolitanism, proletarian internationalism 'is no longer conceived as a regulatory ideal or as a tendency whose historical realisation one presumes, but a slogan of an actual struggle against the systems of power and domination, engrained in the present situation of a (majority) class'. Étienne Balibar, 'Cosmopolitisme et internationalisme: deux modèles, deux héritages', in *Philosophie politique et horizon cosmopolitique*, ed. Moufida Goucha (Paris: UNESCO, 2006), 55. In internationalism, subjectivation takes precedence over the narrative of progress. This makes it clear that the world in which the workers can unite is a world yet to be built.
34. Hannah Arendt, *The Origins of Totalitarianism* (San Diego: Harcourt Brace & Co., 1979), 298.
35. Ibid. 297.
36. Ibid. 302.
37. See Roland Végső, *Worldlessness After Heidegger: Phenomenology, Psychoanalysis, Deconstruction* (Edinburgh: Edinburgh University Press, 2020), 89.
38. Arendt, *The Human Condition*, 248–57.
39. Ibid. 173.
40. Ibid. 208.
41. Ibid. 204.
42. Ibid. 124.
43. Ibid. 6.
44. Végső, *Worldlessness After Heidegger*, 81.
45. Étienne Tassin, *Un monde commun. Pour une cosmo-politique des conflits* (Paris: Seuil, 2003), 147.
46. Ibid. 146; Végső, *Worldlessness After Heidegger*, 86.
47. Arendt, *The Human Condition*, 198.
48. Ibid. 7.
49. Ibid. 9.
50. Ibid. 242, 247.
51. Ibid. 251.

52. Ibid. 253–6.
53. Ibid. 265.
54. Ibid. 275.
55. Jean-Luc Nancy, *The Creation of the World, or Globalization*, trans. François Raffoul and David Pettigrew (Albany: State University of New York Press, 2007), 109.
56. Ibid. 34.
57. Jean-Luc Nancy, *Being Singular Plural*, trans. Robert D. Richardson and Anne E. O'Byrne (Stanford: Stanford University Press, 2000), 73.
58. Nancy, *The Creation of the World*, 112.
59. Ibid. 54, 36.
60. Ibid. 61.
61. Ibid. 54, 46.
62. Antonia Birnbaum, *Trajectoires obliques* (Paris: Sens & Tonka, 2013), 86.
63. Tassin, *Un monde commun*, 14, 143, 155.
64. Ibid. 295.
65. Ibid. 19.
66. Ibid. 211.
67. Ibid. 177, 297–8.
68. Ibid. 241, 277–8, 287–90.
69. Jacques Rancière, *Disagreement: Politics and Philosophy*, trans. Julie Rose (Minneapolis: University of Minnesota Press, 1999), 139.
70. Ibid. 125.
71. Ibid. 139, 123–5.
72. Jacques Rancière, 'Ten Theses on Politics', in *Dissensus: On Politics and Aesthetics*, ed. and trans. Steven Corcoran (London: Continuum, 2010), 37.
73. Jacques Rancière, *Modern Times: Essays on Temporality in Art and Politics* (Zagreb: Multimedijalni institut, 2017), 12.
74. Ibid. 13.
75. Jacques Rancière, *The Aesthetics of Politics*, trans. Gabriel Rockhill (London: Continuum, 2006), 12–13.
76. Rancière, 'Ten Theses on Politics', 36.
77. Rancière, *Modern Times*, 12.
78. Rancière, *Disagreement*, 28–32.
79. Ibid. 42.
80. Regarding crucial distinctions between Arendt and Rancière, see Jean-Philippe Deranty and Emmanuel Renault, 'Democratic Agon: Striving for Distinction or Struggle against Domination and Injustice?', in *Law and Agonistic Politics*, ed. Andrew Schaap (Farnham: Ashgate, 2009), 43–56, and Andrew Schaap, 'Enacting the Right to Have Rights: Jacques Rancière's Critique of Hannah Arendt', *European Journal of Political Theory* 10, no. 1 (2011): 22–45, https://doi.org/10.1177/1474885110386004.

81. Arendt, *The Human Condition*, 32–3.
82. For Rancière's comment, see *Disagreement*, 17.
83. Ibid. 51.
84. Ibid. 58.
85. Rancière, 'Ten Theses on Politics', 38.
86. Ibid. 38.
87. Rancière, *Disagreement*, 55–60.
88. Ibid. 56.
89. Ibid. 52.
90. Ibid. 40.
91. See Jacques Rancière, 'The People or the Multitudes', in *Dissensus*, 85–6.
92. Jacques Rancière, 'Communists Without Communism?', in *The Idea of Communism*, ed. Costas Douzinas and Slavoj Žižek (London: Verso, 2010), 167–8.
93. Rancière, *Modern Times*, 22–5.
94. Ibid. 39–42.
95. Ibid. 18.
96. Ibid. 33.
97. Jacques Rancière, 'Re-politicizing 68', *Crisis and Critique* 5, no. 2 (2018): 297, https://www.crisiscritique.org/storage/app/media/2018-11-29/ranciere.pdf.
98. Rancière, *Modern Times*, 34.
99. See, for example, Peter Hallward, 'Staging Equality: Rancière's Theatrocracy and the Limits of Anarchic Equality', in *Jacques Rancière: History, Politics, Aesthetics*, ed. Gabriel Rockhill and Philip Watts (Durham, NC: Duke University Press, 2009), 140–57.
100. Antonia Birnbaum, *Égalité radicale. Diviser Rancière* (Paris: Amsterdam, 2018), 178–235.

5 Worlds as Fictions, Artworks as Monadic Objects

AFTER HAVING ADDRESSED THE political aspects of the multiplicity of actual worlds, it is now time to take a closer look at its aesthetic dimension. I have insisted from the beginning of the book that there is a fictional element to the concept of world. This does not contradict the objective status of worlds but rather alerts us to the aesthetic dimension of their formation as transcendental frameworks. In this sense, aesthetics cannot be limited to a separate or independent register. We have seen in the previous chapter how fictional categories pervade the sphere of politics and how, vice versa, sensible perception is distributed according to transcendental coordinates that align with political divisions. In order to examine the aesthetic element of worlds, we will now move from politics to literature and art, not because they would in any way be exempt from social or political factors, but because they constitute a field where the transcendental coordinates of sensible experience and their transformations can be examined in a distilled form.

Literature and art allow us to confront the two meanings of aesthetics as defined by Gilles Deleuze: the theory of possible experience on the one hand and the theory of real experience as it is revealed in art on the other.[1] While the former limits sensible experience to *a priori* forms, the latter turns to literature and art to show how experience can go beyond such limits. Deleuze sees art as a field of experimentation with transcendental frameworks, which – as we will see in the next chapter – resonates with Marcel Proust's designation of art as a laboratory for the creation of worlds.[2] For Deleuze, real experience ultimately goes beyond all forms and beyond representation itself to reveal 'the being of the sensible', which amounts to 'a formless *ungrounded* chaos'.[3]

From my own perspective in this chapter, however, there is no need to understand real experience as anything more than the relativisation of the possible one, as evidence that the sensible can be reframed within different transcendental or representational coordinates. I thus understand art here as a device that allows us to observe experience as framed and as an experiment in reframing it. This goes against the grain of the onto-poetics that dominated aesthetics from Martin Heidegger to Deleuze. We saw in Chapter 1 how Alain Badiou defines his 'subtractive' ontological project as an alternative to Heidegger's 'poetic ontology' as well as Deleuze's 'vitalist' one. I have argued elsewhere that poetic and vitalist ontologies, which understand being as something to be revealed, find their aesthetical correlate in 'onto-poetics' – a philosophical understanding of art as the sphere of a revelation of being.[4] I claim that accepting Badiou's critique of poetic ontology also entails a necessary critique of onto-poetics. From this perspective, art does not reveal the being of the sensible, but a bifurcation of transcendental frameworks through which the sensible is given. If politics is the sphere in which the overlapping multiplicity of worlds can be examined in its conflictual state, art is where we can observe the aesthetic interferences between worlds. I call aesthetic interference the appearance of one world within another. This occurs through the perception of a certain kind of object that is perceived within one world, but seems moulded according to another transcendental. In line with a transformed traditional metaphor to which I will return in a slightly modified form below, artworks can be seen as windows that (re)frame our view of the world(s).

In this chapter, I will address these issues through a Leibnizian conceptual apparatus that I have already deployed earlier in this book. Given that most modern aesthetical debates pass through Kant, Leibniz might be seen as a curious fit for this purpose. Yet, there is a strong Leibnizian current in contemporary aesthetics that should not be understated. First, this entails acknowledging the important role the Leibnizian concept of possible worlds has had in contemporary aesthetics and literary theory, explaining narrative structure as world-construction. But if fictions can be described as worlds, does this not also entail that there is something fictional about the concept and experience of world as such? Returning to the discussion on the differences between Deleuze's and Badiou's conception of the multiplicity of worlds from an aesthetic perspective, I will indicate a passage from understanding fictions as possible worlds to understanding actual worlds in terms of their fictional structure.

Second, there is another Leibnizian concept that had a decisive role in one of the most important contributions to the twentieth-century philosophy of art. In *Aesthetic Theory*, Theodor W. Adorno describes artworks as windowless monads, marking their seclusion from the world, but also their ability to contain a truth about the world that can only be expressed at a distance. I will confront Adorno's views on the autonomy and heteronomy of the monadic artwork with Jacques Rancière's elaboration of these topics.

If we put these fragmentary uses of elements from Leibniz's philosophy together, we get a glimpse of a curious dismantled Leibnizianism of contemporary aesthetics, composed of a proliferation of fictional worlds that lack proper objectivity on the one hand and monadic objects that can only touch the world from a distance on the other. After examining both poles of this aesthetical Leibnizianism, the chapter aims to put the pieces back together. Combining both perspectives allows us to see artworks as monadic objects that seem alienated from the world, but only because they contain a transcendental of another world. Windowless monads thus become windows themselves, reshaping the transcendental coordinates of experience and thus producing aesthetic interferences between worlds.

From Fictions as Worlds to Worlds as Fictions

The idea that objects, events and characters depicted in literary texts (or in artworks in general, but especially narrative ones) can be considered as elements of a fictional world, constructed according to principles that can be reconstructed and analysed, often appears in criticism. In her book on the concept of possible worlds in literary theory, Ruth Ronen describes two major ways in which concepts of world have been used to explain fiction.[5] At first, world referred to the internal structure, organisation and coherence that integrates fictional objects so as to form a special domain, a distinct sphere specific to art. Conceived either phenomenologically (Roman Ingarden) or semiotically (Yuri

Lotman), worlds designated the way literary texts not only represent a set of objects, but model a fictional reality. More recently, a different concept of world emerged in literary theory (in the work of Lubomir Doležel, Thomas G. Pavel, Umberto Eco, Marie-Laure Ryan and others), this time in an attempt to define the fictionality of a literary text in relation to external reality. Instead of the internal organisation of works of fiction, such theories focus on what makes fictional worlds distinct from other types of worlds. This trend takes inspiration from the discussions on possible worlds in analytic philosophy in terms of both logic and ontology. This philosophical concept of possible worlds helped literary theory to turn away from the questions of mimesis towards reflections on the autonomous fictionality of literary texts. Yet, as Ronen points out, the philosophical concept was appropriated by literary theory at the price of its metaphorisation. If we strictly adhere to the concept of possible worlds as it was developed in philosophy, it turns out that it might not actually be the most appropriate means of addressing the specifics of fictional worlds.[6]

A careful examination of the Leibnizian concept of world in relation to fiction is therefore required. A number of differences appear between possible and fictional worlds. Ronen accounts for this distinction in terms of their relation to the actual world:

> Possible worlds are based on a logic of ramification determining the range of possibilities that emerge from an actual state of affairs; fictional worlds are based on a logic of parallelism that guarantees their autonomy in relation to the actual world.[7]

Possible worlds are derived from the actual world on the basis of alternative possibilities. While in the actual world, for example, Caesar crossed the Rubicon, we can imagine a possible world in which he did not. Everything that is not related to this event remains the same in both worlds. Fictional worlds, on the contrary, create their own autonomous reality, usually populated by otherwise non-existent characters and events. Fictional worlds do not necessarily refer to a possibility within the actual world and can even be impossible and contradictory. Even when the actual world is closely referred to and actual persons or events are described, the reality thus created remains fictional.

Not only do possible and fictional worlds differ on the basis of their relation to the actual world, they are also differently structured. A possible world has the same completeness as the actual world since it retains the same characteristics, except for the ones directly related to the distinct possibility that it realises (Caesar does not cross, for example). A fictional world, on the contrary, necessarily remains incomplete, since it is limited by what the literary text presents of it.[8] As Jean-Jacques Lecercle notes, fictional worlds are 'framed' and 'furnished': everything outside the frame remains unknown (and strictly speaking non-existent), while the frame is furnished by objects, events and characters that are singled out.[9] Lecercle adds that while it is in the nature of the idea of possible worlds that there are multiple possible worlds, only fictional worlds are truly singular. Possible worlds are still dependent on the actual world they are a variation of, while fictional worlds construct their own, singular fictional reality.

Given these differences between possible and fictional worlds, it is all the more interesting that Leibniz himself seems to have welcomed the comparison between the two. He discusses his conception of possibility in relation to works of fiction on several occasions, citing works such as d'Urfé's *Astrea* and Barclay's *Argenis*. In 'The Philosopher's Confession' (1672–73), Leibniz stages a dialogue between a theologian and a philosopher. The theologian proposes the thesis that whatever exists, exists necessarily, to which the philosopher objects with the idea of possible and contingent existence. The philosopher claims that actuality is determined contingently and 'contingent things are not necessary even if they follow from a necessary thing, the existence of God, i.e. the harmony of things'.[10] Two examples are given. The first example is in line with what we have described above as a possible world (even though Leibniz does not use the term in this text): there is nothing impossible about the idea that Judas would be saved – even though it is impossible according to the contingent harmony of things in this world. This means that other possibilities are imaginable and it is 'a mark of an elegant poet', the philosopher remarks, 'to devise something false yet possible'.[11] The second example Leibniz proposes is a fictional one: 'Barclay's *Argenis* is possible, i.e. it is clearly and distinctly imaginable although it is certain that she has never been alive, and I do not believe that she will ever be alive.'[12]

In a letter to Louis Bourguet from 1714 (which we have already touched upon briefly, in Chapter 2), a similar confrontation of views takes place. Leibniz again elaborates on his distinction between the notions of possibility and compossibility: for something to be possible (in an absolute sense), it does not necessarily have to be compossible with (that is, possible in) our own world. Leibniz does not agree with his correspondent's assertion that 'in order to know of the romance if "Astrea" is possible, it is necessary to know its connections with the rest of the universe'.[13] This would only be the case if one had to determine the 'compossibility' of Astrea with the actual universe. Since the story of Astrea never happened and most probably never will, one can claim with good reason that it is impossible in this world (that is, not compossible with it), although not impossible in the absolute sense:

> But whether the 'Astrea' is possible in an absolute sense is another question, to which I answer 'Yes', because it does not imply any contradiction. Yet in order for this novel to exist in fact, it would be necessary for the rest of the universe also to be entirely different from what it is – and it is possible that it should be otherwise.[14]

The concept of possible worlds is therefore not limited, for Leibniz, to the worlds derived or ramified from the actual one. This testifies to Leibniz's concept of world being properly singular and contingent. Even though contradictory (and therefore impossible) fictional worlds can be presumed excluded from consideration, worlds populated by the characters and stories in a work of fiction, given that they are clearly and distinctly imaginable and imply no contradiction in themselves, are just as possible as anything derived from imagining alternative possibilities derived from the actual world. A possible world for Leibniz is something 'clearly and distinctly imaginable' and centred on singularities such as Argenis and Astrea as fictional characters. The closeness of possible and fictional worlds implies that there is something inherently fictional about possible worlds.

We could thus stipulate that generation by ramification (possible worlds) might not be that different to generation by imagination (fictional worlds). Not only because, as Leibniz shows, other possible worlds are something to be imagined, but also because the function needed to derive a possible world from the actual one (inverting the truth value of a proposition) already singles out the events and characters that 'frame' this particular possible world. Caesar's crossing of the Rubicon is one such example, as is the story of the palace of destinies at the end of Leibniz's *Theodicy*.[15] There, Theodorus browses through the infinite array of possible worlds not at random, but through a specific character, Sextus, observing his many possible fates. Even though a possible world is complete, everything that remains outside the frame of the realisation of particular other possibilities remains completely out of focus, which makes the completeness of a possible world merely abstract. While the completeness of possible worlds is abstract, fictional worlds – incomplete by definition – are also not without an at least implied completion. When immersed into a fictional world, we are under the impression that it is not limited to the frame of our view.[16] While fiction thus becomes a dimension of possibility, there is no guarantee that the reverse is also true. As literary theorists make clear, fictional worlds are not necessarily consistent and can be contradictory – and therefore impossible in the strong sense of the term.

What interests us here are not so much the technical details of distinguishing between actual, possible and fictional worlds, but the blurring of these distinctions implied by the proliferation of actual worlds. If the multiplicity of worlds is actual – as is the premise of this book – what is the relation of the multiple actual worlds to possible and fictional ones? Are they to be understood as actualisations of possible or fictional worlds? I will try to answer these questions by revisiting two accounts of the multiplicity of worlds I have already presented, Deleuze's and Badiou's. In both accounts, the generation of actual worlds is not understood as a realisation of a pre-existent possibility, but as a contingency that demarcates a particular field of possibility. I will also argue that from both perspectives, the proliferation of worlds endows actuality with a fictional dimension.

According to Deleuze's subversion of Leibniz, as we have seen, the multiplicity of worlds is no longer possible, but becomes actual. Yet, the actualisation of worlds is not a realisation of a possibility. Rather, it is a realisation of what Leibniz called incompossibility. Caesar crosses the Rubicon *or* he does not: for Leibniz, both events are possible, but not compossible within the same world. The two opposite possibilities can only be parts of two different worlds. For Deleuze, on the contrary, the actualisation of worlds is not an actualisation of distinct worlds, but a becoming of incompossible singularities in bifurcating worlds: 'with its unfurling of divergent series in the same world, comes the irruption of incompossibilities on the same stage, [. . .] where Caesar crosses *and* does not cross the Rubicon'.[17] The ontological basis for the formation of worlds is a chaos of singularities, which is not a realm of predefined possibility, but a field of virtuality. The coexistence of incompossibilities is a consequence of a constant redistribution of singularities in the becoming of bifurcating and diverging worlds. This constitutes the chaosmos, the creative tension between virtuality and actuality, between the chaos of singularities and the multi-cosmos of worlds.

Deleuze's worlds, like Leibniz's, are differentiated by particular events and characters through which pre-individual singularities get determined in a particular world. Caesar crosses, Caesar does not cross: such variations determine different worlds. Although actualised, Deleuze's worlds are based on variation and derivation, which means that they are still essentially structured as possible worlds. Deleuze's multiplicity of worlds is thus a multiplicity of actualised possible worlds, where incompossibilities coexist.

The focus on events and characters, as we have seen, also gives possible worlds a fictional dimension. It is no wonder, then, that Deleuze resorts to literature to describe the multiplicity of diverging worlds as 'a "chaosmos" of the type found in Joyce, but also in Maurice Leblanc, Borges, or Gombrowicz'.[18] The term 'chaosmos' itself comes from Joyce's *Finnegans Wake*. Borges's 'The Garden of Forking Paths' seems to be Deleuze's favourite illustration, though, as it appears in many of Deleuze's texts, usually in the context of subverting Leibniz: 'This is Borges's reply to Leibniz: the straight line as force of time, as labyrinth of time, is also the line which forks and keeps on forking, passing through incompossible presents.'[19] A musical parallel is also proposed by Deleuze, contrasting Baroque harmony (Leibniz's own example) with the Neo-Baroque 'polyphony of polyphonies', a term he borrows from Pierre Boulez.[20] It is finally Nietzsche who, for Deleuze, reveals the aesthetics of 'real experience'. Nietzsche's will to power enables us to understand, 'in opposition to Leibniz', how incompossibilities may emerge together through an affirmation 'of the false and its artistic, creative power'.[21] With virtuality replacing possibility as the counterpoint of actuality, the actual world becomes pervaded with bifurcating world-fictions.

While Deleuze's multiple worlds are essentially structured as possible worlds (with all the annotations we have just described), Badiou's multiple worlds are structured as fictional worlds. This claim should immediately arouse suspicion in any reader of *Logics of Worlds*. Therein, Badiou clearly states that worlds are objective transcendental structures that can only be properly explained through mathematical logic. What, then, justifies the claim that Badiou's multiplicity of worlds is a multiplicity of actualised fictional worlds?

There is one aspect to the fictionality of worlds Badiou would agree to. In *Logics of Worlds*, he characterises world as fiction in relation to the ontological foundation of worlds. Compared to being-qua-being, worlds are shown to be mere appearances: 'The only inflexible truth regarding the intimate decomposition of the worldly fiction of being-there is that of being-qua-being. The object objects to the transcendental fiction, which it nevertheless is, the "fixion" of the One in being.'[22] This formulation, which is not further elaborated on anywhere else in the book, is a covert homage to Jacques Lacan. It refers to a passage from Lacan's text 'L'étourdit', in which he opposes the real to any 'fiction of Worldliness'.[23] Beyond 'the World' as a philosophical illusion, according to Lacan, there is a need to find other 'fixions' of the real, starting from the not-all and the impasses of logic. Combining 'fiction' and 'fixation', Lacan points out that our relation to the real as the impossible is fixated within the structure of language. Even though he generally rejects Lacan's focus on language, Badiou feels close to Lacan when he assigns to ontological multiplicity the role of the real as the impossible (or the impasse of logic), which can decompose the fiction of worlds. Still, transcendental fictions are the frames through which being appears. Transcendentals thus fixate being-qua-being as being-there, in a particular world.

My intention here, however, is to show that worlds are not merely fictional in relation to being but are also structurally fictional. There is no need to wait for the appearance of being-qua-being to expose worlds as fictions, since worlds are themselves immanently fictional. Returning one last time to the distinction between possible and fictional worlds, we have seen that while possible worlds are complete and generated by evoking divergent possibilities, fictional worlds are incomplete and generated as partial (framed) parallel realities, furnished with (imaginary) objects, characters, relations and events. Contrary to Deleuze, who focuses on divergent possibilities (that are no longer part of different possible worlds but emerge on the same stage), Badiou describes worlds as partial transcendental frames that single out fragments of the ontological multiplicity and give them an intensity of appearance.

Consider a couple of examples Badiou uses to explain his concept of the transcendental. The first example comes from the story of *Ariadne and Bluebeard*, Paul Dukas's opera whose libretto was adapted from a play by Maurice Maeterlinck, in which Ariadne, who marries Bluebeard, attempts to liberate his former five wives from their captivity. In contrast to what we can assume would be a Deleuzian take on the story, Badiou is not interested in alternative possibilities that could alter the course of events (for example, the five wives follow or do not follow Ariadne to freedom). Badiou is rather interested in the structural logic of appearance that regulates identities, differences and relations between the characters that constitute the world of this opera and the way this fictional world relates to the real world.[24] Badiou's interests thus coincide with the way the concept of world is used in literary theory.

The second example Badiou introduces is not taken from any work of fiction, even though it could be read as a passage of prose. The world in question is framed by an autumn evening at a country house grown over by ivy and involves the author himself as the main character: 'At the moment when I'm lost in the contemplation of the wall inundated by the autumnal red of the ivy, behind me, on the gravel of the path, a motorcycle is taking off.'[25] Badiou sets this world around an observer (himself) who first focuses on the redness of the ivy and is then distracted by the motorcycle. Despite the objectivity of worlds and their firm logical architecture Badiou develops, one could say that the framing of this world is dependent on narrative (the motorcycle interrupts the narrator's initial state) and style (the centre of this world is not simply ivy, but its 'blood-red leafage'[26]). In what way can it be said that the red leaves are what objectively appears most intensely in this world or that the motorcycle is objectively connected to the ivy growing on the walls of a nearby house? Is there not a necessary perspectivism involved, a subject for whom this world appears? Or – to get closer to Lacan, in fact – is this world not fixated by language that describes the scene? What else 'objectively' connects all these objects within a particular world?

Some of Badiou's examples are more 'realistic' in that they describe social and political realities rather than a personal experience. Yet, the point is not to cast doubt on the objective existence of worlds, but to show that this objectivity has a fictional structure. Badiou's worlds are limited in space (for example, a specific country house and its surroundings) and time (an autumn evening). They are furnished with characters (Bluebeard, Ariadne, Badiou himself), relations (the six wives), objects (the ivy, the house) and events (Ariadne's escape, the motorcycle taking off), which appear within their worlds with various degrees of intensity. As framed and furnished, these worlds are incomplete: within each world, only a section of the ontological multiplicity appears. These are parallel worlds not generated by ramification from the actual world but by framing a piece of ontological multiplicity.

To claim that the structure of such worlds is fictional is not to deny that there is a logic to its construction. Rather, it is to claim that there is a logic of fiction that supplements the mathematical logic Badiou uses to explain the construction of worlds. Without adding the fictional logic to the mathematical one, there is simply no way to explain the framing of worlds, that is, the perspective that defines the limits and unity of a given world as world. Worlds are generated by a frame that covers a part of the ontological multiplicity and singles out multiples as objects. As Jean-Jacques Lecercle puts it, 'a fictional world is constructed by a series of interpellations of entities into singularities, individual elements of the world'.[27] Badiou's logical apparatus might explain in detail the way the transcendental operates, once a world is given, but cannot on its own account for the very moment of setting a frame upon a selected piece of ontological multiplicity that 'interpellates' it into a world. Worlds are generated by this transcendental framing, which forms the fictional dimension of worlds.

To claim that the structure of such worlds is fictional is also not to deny that there is an objectivity to their existence. Even in a solitary evening at a country house, which is completely subjectively framed, the intrusion of the motorcycle is objective in the standard sense of the term. Social or political worlds are indeed objective in a much stronger sense, as they inevitably impact the lives of many people who have limited capacity to change them. Yet, as we saw with Rancière in Chapter 4, fictional constructions are present in a crucial way even in such objective worlds. The fall of the distinction between actual and non-actual worlds (be they possible or fictional or both) does not entail a denial of the existence of an ontological reality or a socio-economic totality. It just states that the concept of world is not designed to describe either of them. Worlds as overlapping transcendental frameworks with a fictional structure may not be real in an ontological sense, but they do affect reality.

Now that we have discussed the fictional structure of worlds, it is time to move forward to the problem of the interferences between them. As I announced above, I will address this problem through art.

Aesthetics as Monadology

The notion of transcendental framing seems to correspond well with the traditional conception of the artwork as a window to the world. The comparison between the artwork and the window, which has its origin in Leon Battista Alberti's *De pictura*, has since the Renaissance provided a fitting – if clichéd – metaphor for the basic structure of paintings (as framed representations) and artworks more generally.[28] While many modern and contemporary approaches to art and art theory have been based on transcending the basic structure of the frame, which they have considered too limiting, Adorno's *Aesthetic Theory* goes in the opposite direction by providing a theory of art based on its radical closure. To the metaphor of the artwork as a window, Adorno opposes the Leibnizian conceptual metaphor of the artwork as a windowless monad. By closing their windows, artworks break the representational relation between themselves and the world. It is 'by virtue of separation from empirical reality', Adorno claims, that artworks achieve their 'heightened order of existence'.[29] It is only on the condition of this separation that art develops its autonomy and the immanent principles according to which it is produced.

Art's separated existence behind closed windows seems to evoke another clichéd metaphor, the metaphor of art's closure within an ivory tower. Adorno, however, strongly opposes this conclusion: despite its windowless closure, which makes it an end in itself, art still expresses something about the world, and it is in this expression that its truth can be found.[30] This is why the metaphor of the monad is useful for Adorno. For Leibniz, monads are completely separated from their surroundings, yet reflect the harmony that makes a world out of their sheer multiplicity. Adorno applies this logic to artworks. Although artworks as monads are hermetically separated parts of the social whole, this whole is nevertheless inscribed in each of them: 'As an element of an overarching context of the spirit of an epoch, entwined with history and society, artworks go beyond their monadic limit even though they lack windows.'[31] It is this dialectic of separation and connection that serves Adorno as the foundation of his reflections on art.[32]

Adorno introduces the monadic relation between the interior structure of art and external reality in the following way:

> That artworks as windowless monads 'represent' what they themselves are not can scarcely be understood except in that their own dynamic, their immanent historicity as a dialectic of nature and its

domination, not only is of the same essence as the dialectic external to them but resembles it without imitating it.³³

With windows that framed the artistic view shut, art is no longer thought of primarily as representation. The identity of a monadic artwork depends on its immanent structure and dynamic. Nevertheless, Adorno still thinks of art in terms of a resemblance, which is independent of imitation, a resemblance not to empirical reality but to the principle of domination that governs society in the midst of which art – as autonomous as it may be – is produced. Art achieves its identity through dominating its own sensory material, just as society exists through the domination of nature. Despite its closure, therefore, the universal principle of its world is present in the monad. The Leibnizian concept of harmony is subjected by Adorno to a materialist reversal. As Adorno writes in *Negative Dialectics*, the social world is established according to 'a pre-established disharmony'.³⁴ If art has anything to say about the world it is separated from, but which it nevertheless resembles, it has to do with social disharmony rather than divine harmony.

The monadic logic allows Adorno to think of art both as autonomous (being produced of its own accord) and as a *fait social* (its production being subordinated to the general mode of production and subjected to social antagonisms), without subordinating one to the other.³⁵ But how should this double logic be understood? In what way does the artwork 'resemble' the social dialectic? First, the autonomy of art should itself be understood socially and historically, in terms of class relations. The autonomy of art is a 'sedimentation of a historical process', an invention linked to a specific historical moment and the interests of a particular class.³⁶ Art's 'autonomy, its growing independence from society, was a function of the bourgeois consciousness of freedom that was itself bound up with the social structure'.³⁷ Even at its most autonomous, art is nothing but a product of ideological and economic domination. Art can thus be subjected to a historical materialist analysis, although this is not what primarily interests Adorno. The heteronomy inscribed in art's very autonomy does not serve to subvert autonomy as merely apparent and thus to fully integrate art within the social totality. Instead, it is the social totality that is integrated in the immanence of art. As the object of aesthetic theory, art is not merely a product of external forces and relations, but is to be understood according to its own internal logic. In turn, this very internal logic resembles the external historical dialectic. To understand art as a social product aesthetically, one needs to understand in what way the social can be read within the immanent structure of artworks: 'The unsolved antagonisms of reality return in artworks as immanent problems of form.'[38] Artworks resemble society because its internal problems of form correspond to external social antagonisms. The point is not to view art as a part of the social totality (which it nevertheless is, but this is not the object of aesthetic theory), but to understand how social totality is inscribed in art's internal form. The logic of the monad is not the logic of the inclusion of a part within the whole but the inclusion of the whole within each separate part.

Monadic objects are separated from the world, but contain within them the (harmonious or disharmonious) principle that holds the world together. The moment of separation is crucial. Without it, the monad could not develop its own singularity and would merely be a part of the whole. Insistence on separation also distinguishes the monadic logic from other conceptions of the inclusion of the whole within each part. Ontological monism also lets us observe the whole in each part, but only because there effectively are no parts, since everything is a manifestation of the same substance. For Leibniz, however, each monad is its own substance, which sets up a stronger dialectic of separation and pre-established connection. The whole is present within the monad not despite but on the condition of its separation. Only as separated from the world can the monad testify to the harmony that makes the world.

According to Adorno, therefore, the proper way for art to interact with social reality is not by opening its windows or descending from its ivory tower, but by insisting on its separation: 'Only in the crystallization of its own formal law and not in a passive acceptance of objects does art converge with what is real.'[39] The real can be found in art not by means of representing or engaging with empirical or social reality but precisely by addressing its immanent formal problems. That being said, Adorno is well aware of the risk of fetishisation the monadic constitution of artworks entails in combination with its status within class society. Yet, this is a risk that art should fully embrace: 'The truth content of artworks, which is indeed their social truth, is predicated on their fetish character.'[40] This claim should be read in both ways. First, art's position within social antagonisms makes of it a fetish. Second, art is only capable of producing something true not despite but on the condition of its fetish character. Art's autonomous separation from society is at once a social product – a fetish – and that by which art can resist society:

> Art, however, is social not only because of its mode of production, in which the dialectic of the forces and relations of production is concentrated, nor simply because of the social derivation of its thematic material. Much more importantly, art becomes social by its opposition to society, and it occupies this position only as autonomous art. By crystallizing in itself as something unique to itself, rather than complying with existing social norms and qualifying as 'socially useful,' it criticizes society by merely existing, for which puritans of all stripes condemn it.[41]

Art's monadic separation is in itself the ultimate social statement of art, since it makes art opposed to society. According to Adorno, capitalism creates a society dominated by exchange value, a principle of generalised heteronomy. Everything exists for something else. This is what aesthetic autonomy opposes. For Adorno, political art that legitimately criticises artistic autonomy for its ideological role in a class society paradoxically falls victim to this very principle of heteronomous exchange as it renounces the only thing that makes art politically subversive:

> The principle of heteronomy, apparently the counterpart of fetishism, is the principle of exchange, and in it domination is masked. Only what does not submit to that principle acts as the plenipotentiary of what is free from domination; only what is useless can stand in for the stunted use value. Artworks are plenipotentiaries of things that are no longer distorted by exchange, profit, and the false needs of a degraded humanity. In the context of total semblance, art's semblance of being-in-itself is the mask of truth.[42]

The question if Adorno is still or ever was right in claiming that art is capable of resisting the world dictated by capitalism despite its embeddedness in class relations and the (art) market is a matter of discussion that exceeds the purpose of this chapter. What interests us here is the logic of aesthetical monadology. The artwork as a monadic object seems shaped by two transcendentals at once. On the one hand, the separated monad enables us to observe the disharmony of the (capitalist) world. On the other, another kind of harmony seems to be inscribed in the monad as a promise. Against the generalised exchange value, artworks as the ultimate useless objects keep the promise of the lost use value alive. By testifying to something that is not possible within the given social transcendental, artworks become 'plenipotentiaries' of another world no longer subjected to the disharmony of social antagonisms. While Deleuze and Badiou, as we have seen above, radicalise Leibniz by making the multiplicity of worlds actual, Adorno's aesthetical monadology radicalises the status of the monad. Artworks as monadic objects are not merely parts of the world that – in their separation from each other – convey the harmony of the whole. They become more radically separated, almost alien objects that not only testify to the world's disharmony, but offer a glimpse of the harmony of another world.

Windows to the Worlds

In order to complete the path from the window (as representation) to the windowless monad and then from the monad again to the window (as transcendental reframing), we have to take into consideration another aesthetic theory that connects art to a recalibration of the limits of possible experience. Namely, we have to return to Rancière and his conception of the distribution of the sensible from the aesthetical side.

Rancière is interested in the forms of sensible experience within which artworks and artistic practices are perceived and understood (what he calls the 'regimes of art') as well as in art's ability to recalibrate such forms (to redistribute the sensible). In order to trace the genealogy of a regime of art that puts this ability in the centre of how art is perceived and understood, Rancière outlines an aesthetic revolution that started at the end of the eighteenth century.[43] The new regime of art began to emerge at that time, which identified art in terms of 'a particular sensorium, foreign to the ordinary forms of sensory experience'.[44] The exceptionality of this sensorium lies in what Friedrich Schiller defined as 'free appearance'.[45] The beauty of an artwork as a free appearance is not measured according to the principles of representation or the perfection of a form imposed upon matter. Beauty now comes from the indeterminacy that radiates from the suspension of ordinary modes of experience and pre-established criteria of accomplishment.

Since art is now defined by a certain mode of sensible or sensory experience rather than a specific practice or mode of forming, its independence and separation coincides with an inability to clearly define its boundaries. What defines art as a specific mode of experience also makes it impossible to demarcate this specificity: 'Art exists as a separate world since anything whatsoever can belong to it.'[46] Any kind of object and any kind of practice can potentially enter this separated sphere. Art's closure within itself is also a form of radical openness, its autonomisation being a form of heteronomisation.

Rancière finds the model of this interplay of autonomy and heteronomy already in Schiller. Schiller praised a Greek statue of Juno due to its self-contained appearance, indifferent to the world around it. As such, it personified Schiller's ideal of play as the essence of humanity, which he directly related to the Kantian play of faculties as the crux of autonomous aesthetic experience. According to Rancière, Schiller viewed the statue as expressing a form of experience that 'suspends the ordinary connections not only between appearance and reality, but also between form and matter, activity and passivity, understanding and sensibility'.[47] Rancière also revisits Johann Joachim Winckelmann's reflections on another ancient statute, the Belvedere Torso (believed at the time to represent Hercules), as one of the origins of this new regime of thinking and perceiving art.[48] The pioneering art historian appreciated the statue with missing limbs and head in its very fragmentarity. The activity of the hero is suspended in the bent posture of a thinker, whose thoughts and actions can now only be admired as the curvy forms that shape his muscles. Separated from any ideal of an organic whole or an expression of a narrative, the beauty of the statue is in its indeterminacy, which implies 'the rupture of all specific relations between a sensible form and the expression of an exact meaning'.[49]

Even though the Schillerian aesthetic experience is indifferent to anything external to it, it also entails a new form of social coexistence. The elimination of aesthetic hierarchies and the rejection of domination of active form over passive matter occur in the domain that aesthetics shares with politics: the distribution of the sensible, whose political aspect I described in Chapter 4. For Schiller, Rancière emphasises, free appearance 'adheres to a sensorium different to that of domination'.[50] Contrary to Adorno, therefore, Rancière believes that the rise of artistic autonomy breaks with the principle of domination. However, he shares with Adorno the conviction that art can be considered political precisely through its separation from empirical and social reality: 'It is therefore as an autonomous form of experience that art concerns and infringes on the political division of the sensible.'[51] For Rancière, as for Adorno before him, aesthetic autonomy is not thinkable without a specific dialectic that links it to social heteronomy. Yet, whereas Adorno described the political role of aesthetic separation as a promise or a sanctuary of what is impossible to realise in the world as it is, Rancière considers art as already an intervention in the framework that makes a world out of sensory multiplicity. The aesthetic revolution

> links the autonomisation of the sphere of art to the reconfiguration of the common world in two ways. First, Art constructed and consolidated its sphere of existence through the inclusion of subjects, performances, objects or uses that were formerly held to belong to prosaic and non-artistic life. The development of the aesthetic regime coincided with a democratisation of sensible experience. Second, this democratisation of sensible experience fostered the project of an aesthetic revolution, in which the aim was to reshape the very forms of sensory experience. The existence of a sphere of Art in the aesthetic regime is part of a reconfiguration of the common, both a result and an agent.[52]

Art's separation thus makes possible a reconfiguration of sensible experience that is not limited to art as a separated sphere. It touches on the very fictional frameworks that constitute worlds according to Rancière.

Even though Rancière does not use the Leibnizian metaphor, we could say that the new form of experience introduced by the aesthetic revolution refers to its objects in a monadic fashion. Whatever such experience takes as its object, it experiences it as a fragment, separated from its surroundings, and thus as indeterminate and self-enclosed. In their separation, such objects are viewed as singularities in their own right, rather than from the perspective of the missing whole. Such parts thus metonymically take on the role of the whole. In a reflection on the poetry of Walt Whitman, which is indicative of Rancière's approach to the aesthetic regime of art more generally, he writes:

> It is the fragment detached from the whole that carries the potential of the whole, that bears it on the condition that one draw it out of

its solitude as a material thing, that one link it to other fragments and that one circulate air – which is the breath of the whole – in between these fragments.[53]

Since this mode of experience is exceptional, it does not reproduce the breath of a predetermined whole, but of a whole as it appears when the coordinates of experience are radically reframed.

While Adorno's windowless monads only offered a glimpse of the harmony of another world, Rancière's monads turn to windows, since they already enact a reframing of possible experience. The aesthetic revolution brings forth a new form of experience by constructing a sensorium consisting of a multitude of sensory singularities or micro-events. This new sensorium can be found not only in romantic observations on ancient statues but also in realist and modernist literature, where the Aristotelian primacy of the narrative – the political implications of which we observed in Chapter 4 – is replaced by a multiplicity of sensible events of equal importance. Whereas Georg Lukács, for example, pitted realism against modernism along the lines of the Aristotelian understanding of narrative construction as a means of adequate representation, Rancière refers to Gustave Flaubert to point out that realism paves the way for modernism by piercing the narrative structure with descriptions that produce a 'new real', a real that makes the representational re-creation of the world return to the 'dust of impersonal sensible micro-events'.[54] Plots and characters dissolve in Flaubert into 'unbound perceptions and affections'.[55] Rancière refers to Flaubert's declaration of a new literary ideal of 'a book about nothing', a book consisting of absolute style alone.[56] Realism is thus not, according to Rancière, defined by its representational narrative structure, but by its ability to give rise to the democratic coexistence of the unbound sensory events.

The aesthetic release of the flow of sensible singularities seems to bring Rancière close to what we earlier described as onto-poetics, the idea that art reveals the presence of the sensible in its being beyond the confines of representational construction of reality. Rancière does not develop an ontology *per se*, but often resorts to Deleuze to describe the sensible multiplicity of unbound perceptions and affections in an ontological way. The aesthetic regime of art and particularly modern literature unleashes the 'molecular equality of micro-events' as a world of 'becomings and haecceities', 'singular crystallisations of the great impersonal Life'.[57] Releasing the productivity of the fragmentary aesthetic object from Adornian monadic enclosure thus brings Rancière close to a Deleuzian understanding of ontology. The aesthetic monads are transformed into an undifferentiated flow of sensible singularities.

Despite these references to Deleuzian ontology, Rancière distances himself from Deleuze's ontologisation of art. What for Deleuze is an 'ontological difference' between the molar world of representation and the molecular world of becomings and singularities is for Rancière limited to a 'sensible difference [. . .] without ontological consistency, a difference remade each time in the singular work of impersonalization specific to a particular artistic procedure'.[58] According to Rancière, a sensible difference cannot be given the ontological gravity nor a direct political power as Deleuze imagines. What Deleuze considers to be an ontology is in fact 'only a fiction'.[59] The question remains, however, how this remark should be understood given that for Rancière, fictional frameworks constitute worlds. The sensible difference might be only a fiction, but precisely as such, it effects the distribution of the sensible that constitutes the aesthetic dimension of political realities.

Nevertheless, Rancière's aesthetic regime of art can also be understood as an alternative to onto-poetics. The subversion of representation carried out by the aesthetic revolution does not oppose representation in general but rather the 'rules of appropriateness between a particular subject and a particular form' that restricted and regulated it before the modern aesthetic revolution.[60] These rules were at the heart of what Rancière calls the representational regime of art against which the aesthetic regime can be seen as enacting a revolution.[61] Far from attempting to overcome representation in all of its forms, the aesthetic revolution declares 'a general availability of all subjects for any artistic form whatsoever', which means that there are 'no longer any inherent limits to representation, to its possibilities'.[62] Unlimited representation opens up the sphere of aisthesis as a sphere of sensible exceptions in which representations are a matter of singular invention. Rather than seeking a revelation of being beyond representation as such, it looks for surplus representations that undermine the given representational regime.

The two opposing views on Rancière in relation to onto-poetics can be rephrased in terms of the following question: is the relation of the sensible multiplicity to representational structures one of 'deframing' or one of 'reframing'? While the first view implies the onto-poetic deframing that unleashes the becoming of unbound singularities, the second view rather argues for a reframing based on an exceptional aesthetic experience. While the former subverts the representational distinction between active form and passive matter in the name of the immanent vitality of the sensible matter itself, the latter destabilises form from within with unbound representation. Such surplus representations rely on the productivity of the frame itself to recalibrate the transcendental coordinates of sensible experience.

It seems that Rancière opts for a model of permanent tension between both levels of the quasi-ontological difference, the level of sensible multiplicity and the level of representational construction. Rancière clearly formulates this in relation to modern literature: 'The ontology of the new fiction is monist, but its practice can only be dialectical: it can only subsist as a tension between the great lyricism of impersonal Life and the arrangements of the plot.'[63] The contradiction between narrative structure and its dissolution into the unbound multiplicity of sensible singularities is what drives, according to Rancière, different forms of modern literature since realism. The question is how this dialectic should be understood. Is it a static tension between two levels that might yield partial resolutions but leaves the initial terms of the contradiction intact, or is it a properly dialectical movement that can redefine the two terms of the contradiction that reappear each time in a different guise? If the former is true, then the tension between impersonal Life and narrative arrangements can provide a general framework for understanding all forms of modern literature. If the latter is true, however, then the relation between these two levels can evolve beyond their permanent tension in new narrative forms. From this perspective, Flaubert's absolutisation of style can be understood not only as a deframing of sensible singularities, but also as a new vision of connectivity between such singularities. Beyond the opposition between representational structure and unbound multiplicity, absolute style poses the question of how to connect micro-events in a way that disregards narrative conventions. Such understanding of style also opens the way for exploring the unbound representation of the aesthetic regime as a new kind of formalisation that no longer requires a reference to an anti-representational vitalist ontology. Any dialectical contradiction would now be completely internal to style itself as a radical reframing. This also opens the way for analysing – as Rancière himself already does – modern fiction in terms of its narrative inventions, that is, the different kinds of connectivity between micro-events that no longer follow the Aristotelian narrative form.[64]

Rancière thus offers a model for recomposing the contemporary aesthetical Leibnizianism, making it possible to bring its two poles – the proliferation of fictional worlds without proper objectivity and the monadic objects, separated from their worlds – back together. Monadic objects can now be put at the centre of the multiplicity of actualised fictional worlds as their specific aesthetic mode of objectivity. What is the relation between objectless worlds and worldless objects? The monadic object is a seemingly worldless object in which another transcendental is inscribed. Yet, the world inscribed therein still requires the development of new connections and formalisations through which transcendental reframing takes place.

Notes

1. Gilles Deleuze, *Difference and Repetition*, trans. Paul Patton (London: Continuum, 2001), 68.
2. Marcel Proust, *In the Shadow of Young Girls in Flower: In Search of Lost Time, Volume 2*, trans. James Grieve (London: Penguin Books, 2003), 414.
3. Deleuze, *Difference and Repetition*, 68–9.
4. Rok Benčin, 'Rethinking Representation in Ontology and Aesthetics via Badiou and Rancière', *Theory, Culture & Society* 36, no. 5 (2019): 95–112, https://doi.org/10.1177/0263276418806573.
5. Ruth Ronen, *Possible Worlds in Literary Theory* (Cambridge: Cambridge University Press, 1994), 96–107.
6. Ibid. 74–5, 229.
7. Ibid. 8.
8. Jean-Jacques Lecercle, *Interpretation as Pragmatics* (New York: St. Martin's Press, 1999), 186.
9. Jean-Jacques Lecercle, 'Error/Mirror: How to Generate Fiction', in *Literature and Error: A Literary Take on Mistakes and Errors*, ed. Marc Porée and Isabelle Alfandary (New York: Peter Lang, 2018), 109–22.
10. G. W. Leibniz, 'The Philosopher's Confession', trans. Lloyd Strickland, Leibniz Translations, accessed 13 September 2019, http://www.leibniz-translations.com/confession.htm.
11. Ibid.
12. Ibid.
13. G. W. Leibniz, *Philosophical Papers and Letters*, trans. Leroy E. Loemker (Dordrecht: Kluwer, 1989), 661.
14. Ibid. 661.

15. G. W. Leibniz, *Theodicy: Essays on the Goodness of God, the Freedom of Man and the Origin of Evil*, trans. E. M. Huggard, Project Gutenberg, 2005, § 414–16, https://www.gutenberg.org/files/17147/17147-h/17147-h.htm.
16. This implied completion of the incomplete could be the basis for a redefinition of what Roland Barthes called the reality effect in literature: all the surplus details in literary description serve to imply that there is a world (if unknowable) outside the frame. See Roland Barthes, 'The Reality Effect', in *The Rustle of Language*, trans. Richard Howard (Berkeley: University of California Press, 1989), 141–8.
17. Gilles Deleuze, *The Fold: Leibniz and the Baroque*, trans. Tom Colney (London: Athlone Press, 1993), 82. My emphasis.
18. Ibid. 81.
19. Gilles Deleuze, *Cinema 2: The Time-Image*, trans. Hugh Tomlinson and Robert Galeta (Minneapolis: University of Minnesota Press, 1989), 131. See also Gilles Deleuze, *The Logic of Sense*, trans. Mark Lester and Charles Stivale (London: Athlone Press, 1990), 114–15, and Deleuze, *The Fold*, 82. In this story from Borges's *Ficciones* appears a fictional novel by a writer called Ts'ui Pên, in which all possible outcomes of an event involving the character Fang take place simultaneously. See Jorge Luis Borges, 'The Garden of Forking Paths', in *Labyrinths: Selected Stories and Other Writings*, ed. Donald A. Yates and James E. Irby (New York: New Directions Publishing, 1962), 34–42.
20. Deleuze, *The Fold*, 82.
21. Deleuze, *Cinema 2*, 131.
22. Alain Badiou, *Logics of Worlds: Being and Event, 2*, trans. Alberto Toscano (London: Continuum, 2009), 221.
23. 'Recourir au pastout, à l'hommoinzun, soit aux impasses de la logique, c'est, à montrer l'issue hors des fictions de la Mondanité, faire fixion autre du réel: soit de l'impossible qui le fixe de la structure du langage.' Jacques Lacan, 'L'étourdit', in *Autres Écrits* (Paris: Seuil, 2001), 479.
24. Badiou, *Logics of Worlds*, 115–25.
25. Ibid. 128.
26. Ibid. 126.
27. Lecercle, *Interpretation as Pragmatics*, 186.
28. Leon Battista Alberti, *On Painting*, trans. Rocco Sinisgalli (Cambridge: Cambridge University Press, 2011), 39. In a book-length study on this conception from a Lacanian perspective, Gérard Wajcman claims that Alberti's comparison marks the creation of world as representation and of modern subjectivity, whose relation to the world is structured as a window frame. See *Fenêtre. Chroniques du regard et de l'intime* (Paris: Verdier, 2004).
29. Theodor W. Adorno, *Aesthetic Theory*, trans. Robert Hullot-Kentor (London: Continuum, 1997), 4.

30. 'The cliché about the ivory tower no longer applies to the windowless monadic works.' Ibid. 321–2.
31. Ibid. 179–80.
32. Adorno's use of Leibniz's concept owes a great deal to Walter Benjamin. In the 'Prologue' to *The Origin of German Tragic Drama*, Benjamin claims that every philosophical idea is like a monad: it contains all other ideas and an image of the world as a whole. Walter Benjamin, *The Origin of German Tragic Drama*, trans. John Osborne (London: Verso, 1998), 47–8. In the 'Theses on the Philosophy of History', Benjamin returns to the conceptual metaphor of the monad, this time discussing the method of historical materialism: 'A historical materialist approaches a historical subject only where he encounters it as a monad.' Unlike 'universal history', which looks at the course of history as a homogeneous entity, the materialist historiographer looks for monads in which the course of history is crystallised as 'pregnant with tensions'. Such monadic fragments of history are 'blasted out' of the historical continuum. Yet, it is through these fragments that the 'entire course of history' is accessible to a historical materialist. Such monadic fragments are endowed with a messianic character that opens 'a revolutionary chance in the fight for the oppressed past'. Walter Benjamin, 'Theses on the Philosophy of History', in *Illuminations*, ed. Hannah Arendt, trans. Harry Zohn (New York: Schocken Books, 1969), 262–3. The necessity to single out a separated part in which the tensions of the whole can be observed is adopted by Adorno, as well as the promise of redemption that artworks as monads provide.
33. Adorno, *Aesthetic Theory*, 5.
34. Theodor W. Adorno, *Negative Dialectics*, trans. E. B. Ashton (London: Routledge, 1973), 14.
35. Adorno, *Aesthetic Theory*, 5, 225.
36. Ibid. 17.
37. Ibid. 225.
38. Ibid. 6.
39. Theodor W. Adorno, 'Extorted Reconciliation: On Georg Lukács' Realism in Our Time', in *Notes to Literature, Vol. 1*, trans. Shierry Weber Nicholsen (New York: Columbia University Press, 1991), 224.
40. Adorno, *Aesthetic Theory*, 227.
41. Ibid. 225–6.
42. Ibid. 227.
43. Jacques Rancière, *Aisthesis: Scenes from the Aesthetic Regime of Art*, trans. Zakir Paul (London: Verso, 2013), x.
44. Jacques Rancière, *Aesthetics and its Discontents*, trans. Steven Corcoran (Cambridge: Polity, 2009), 27.
45. Ibid. 27–8. See also Friedrich von Schiller, *Letters on the Aesthetic Education of Man*, trans. Elizabeth M. Wilkinson and L. A. Willoughby (Oxford: Clarendon Press, 1967).

46. Rancière, *Aisthesis*, x.
47. Rancière, *Aesthetics and its Discontents*, 30.
48. Rancière, *Aisthesis*, 1–20. See also Johann Joachim Winckelmann, *The History of Ancient Art, Vol. II*, trans. G. Henry Lodge (Boston: James R. Osgood and Company, 1880), 264–5.
49. Rancière, *Aisthesis*, 18.
50. Rancière, *Aesthetics and its Discontents*, 30–1.
51. Ibid. 32.
52. Jacques Rancière, 'The Aesthetic Revolution', *Maska* 32, nos. 185–6 (2017): 25.
53. Rancière, *Aisthesis*, 64. Rancière's political thought also includes such fragments that take on the role of the whole: 'On the one side, there is the inegalitarian logic – the police logic – in which the part can only be understood in relation to the whole, according to a process whose steps must be followed in a determined order with a learned guide. On the other side, there is the emancipatory logic according to which "everything is in everything", which means that it is possible, from any point of departure to find a path making it possible to link this particularity to other ones and to invent, step by step, a still unknown method of linkage.' Jacques Rancière, 'Re-politicizing 68', *Crisis and Critique* 5, no. 2 (2018): 291, https://www.crisiscritique.org/storage/app/media/2018-11-29/ranciere.pdf.
54. Jacques Rancière, *The Lost Thread: The Democracy of Modern Fiction*, trans. Steven Corcoran (London: Bloomsbury, 2017), 15, 21. See also Georg Lukács, 'Narrate or Describe?', in *Writer & Critic and Other Essays*, ed. and trans. Arthur D. Kahn (New York: Grosset & Dunlap, 1971), 110–48.
55. Jacques Rancière, *Mute Speech: Literature, Critical Theory, and Politics*, trans. James Swenson (New York: Columbia University Press, 2011), 118.
56. Ibid. 115–17. See also Gustave Flaubert, *The Letters of Gustave Flaubert: 1830–1857*, ed. and trans. Francis Steegmuller (Cambridge, MA: Belknap Press, 1980), 154.
57. Jacques Rancière, *The Flesh of Words: The Politics of Writing*, trans. Charlotte Mandell (Stanford: Stanford University Press, 2004), 150. Jacques Rancière, *Politique de la littérature* (Paris: Galilée, 2007), 35. Rancière, *The Lost Thread*, 22.
58. Jacques Rancière, 'The Monument and its Confidences; or Deleuze and Art's Capacity of "Resistance"', in *Dissensus: On Politics and Aesthetics*, ed. and trans. Steven Corcoran (London: Continuum, 2010), 182.
59. Jacques Rancière, 'A Politics of Aesthetic Indetermination: An Interview with Frank Ruda and Jan Voelker', in *Everything Is in Everything: Jacques Rancière between Intellectual Emancipation and Aesthetic Education*, ed. Jason E. Smith and Annette Weisser (Pasadena: Art Center Graduate Press/JRP, 2011), 27.

60. Jacques Rancière, *The Future of the Image*, trans. Gregory Elliott (London: Verso, 2007), 118.
61. Rancière, *Aesthetics and its Discontents*, 29.
62. Rancière, *The Future of the Image*, 118, 137.
63. Ibid. 62.
64. Bruno Besana claims that creating new kinds of fiction entails 'identifying the narrative strategies by which one can connect together different moments of dissensual interruption'. Bruno Besana, 'Fictioning Disagreement: The Construction of Separation in the Work of Jacques Rancière', *Maska* 32, nos. 185–6 (2017): 81, https://doi.org/10.1386/maska.32.185-186.64_1.

6 Proust's Worlds: From Logic to Prose

THROUGHOUT THE BOOK WE have been expanding the notion of fiction in order to show how constitutive it is for any construction of a world. In the previous chapter, however, we returned to fiction in the narrower sense in order to explore the importance of the Leibnizian concept of world for understanding literature and art. In this chapter I would like to integrate the two perspectives by proposing a literary model for thinking the concept of world as I have been developing it so far, a model based on Marcel Proust's *In Search of Lost Time*.

This requires a philosophical reading of a particular work of literature, which is hardly a procedure that can rely on a reliable methodology. Such readings often merely use works of literature to illustrate a philosophical point or demonstrate the wide applicability of pre-defined philosophically forged concepts. Despite a good measure of interpretative violence, however, such conceptual impositions are not necessarily incompatible with close reading. As Jean-Jacques Lecercle has demonstrated, a strong philosophical reading of literature can enable us to discover previously inaccessible dimensions of the literary text, which, in turn, has a transformative effect on the philosophical concepts deployed.[1]

My take on Proust in this chapter is an exercise in this manner of reading. According to Lecercle, philosophical reading requires the 'extraction of a problem which pervades the [literary] text but is not explicitly formulated' as well as 'the construction of the [philosophical] concept that grasps it'.[2] The legitimacy of my attempt is based on two assumptions. First, that the problem of the multiplicity of worlds can be shown to be a problem for Proust himself. I will demonstrate that his novel not only contains the problem of world in terms of its fictional construction and multiplicity, but also proposes a specific solution to this problem, a kind of aesthetic cosmogony. The second assumption is that Proust's treatment of the problem of world does not just bring us close to how some contemporary philosophers have posed the problem, but also provides solutions to some of the puzzles the philosophers we have been dealing with have left us with.

More specifically, I will return to Chapter 3 and the problems of Alain Badiou's concept of world. I thus intend to read Proust's 'prose of worlds' and Badiou's 'logics of worlds' as complementing each other. Reading Proust with Badiou will allow us to see the problem of world in Proust's novel more clearly. Yet, a demonstration of the applicability of Badiou's concepts to Proust's novel on its own would not be worthwhile. This is why it will be necessary to supplement it with reading Badiou with Proust: can the encounter between Badiou's philosophy and Proust's literature provide solutions to the problems of Badiou's conceptualisation of the multiplicity of worlds?

Lecercle shows that philosophers often work with a limited set of works that constitute their unique literary canon.[3] The choice of one novel to provide a model for thinking the concept of world can thus be considered to be consistent with standard philosophical reading practice. Literary theory, in contrast, usually aims for its concepts to be applicable to a wide variety of literary phenomena, although we could take Gérard Genette's narratology as an example of a general theory explicitly developed around one sole example: his *Narrative Discourse* develops a theory based on Proust's great novel.[4]

The choice of Proust in particular should not be surprising in our philosophical context, especially if we take into consideration that most of the philosophers we have been discussing in this book are devoted readers of Proust: most obviously Gilles Deleuze, but also Jacques Rancière and Theodor W. Adorno.[5] Badiou, however, is not a reader of Proust in any significant way. Apart from an unpublished lecture, to which we will return later,[6] mentions of Proust in Badiou's work are mostly intended to disqualify Proust's portrayal of jealousy in contrast to the proper understanding of love as a truth procedure that Badiou himself offers.[7] Yet, the absence of Proust from Badiou's distinctive literary canon may not be solely down to a lack of philosophical interest in his works. One could also see it as a symptom of a more interesting and far-reaching omission that characterises Badiou's dealings with literature. As Lecercle suggests, Badiou is primarily a reader of poetry and does not engage philosophically with prose. Beckett is the exception here, although – as Lecercle emphasises – Badiou reads 'avant-garde prose for its latent *poem*: something which cannot easily be done with prose narratives, with novels and tales'.[8] Even though Badiou sometimes references examples from novels to illustrate philosophical points (for example, the love story in Rousseau's *Nouvelle Héloïse* as an example used for the theory of change in *Logics of Worlds*[9]), prose writings do not provide the material for proper 'inaesthetic' practice.[10]

The question here is not so much why Badiou does not read prose or Proust, but rather if this constitutes a significant lack within his philosophical system, or if a Badiousian reading of a novel like Proust's corresponds to a need within this system. My answer to this question is yes. Stéphane Mallarmé, the central figure of Badiou's canon of poets, has an important role in *Being and Event*. The chapter ('meditation') on Mallarmé's *A Cast of Dice* is placed at the crucial point of the book that marks the passage from the discussion of being to the discussion of the event.[11] It is also clear from Badiou's other writings on Mallarmé that, for him, he is indeed the poet of being and event.[12] But what happens when Badiou moves from being to appearance in the second instalment of his system? No such prime literary example can be found in *Logics of Worlds*, the sequel to *Being and Event*. But what kind of an example should we be looking for? Does the philosophical passage from being to world, from ontology to phenomenology, not correspond, in terms of literature, to the passage from poetry to prose? What I want to show in this chapter is that Proust can provide this missing example, the prose of worlds.

Proust with Badiou

There is an obvious way to demonstrate the existence of the problem of world in Proust through his conception of artistic cosmogony revealed in the final volume of the novel:

> It is only through art that we can escape from ourselves and know how another person sees a universe which is not the same as our own and whose landscapes would otherwise have remained as

unknown as any there may be on the moon. Thanks to art, instead of seeing only a single world, our own, we see it multiplied, and have at our disposal as many worlds as there are original artists, all more different one from another than those which revolve in infinity and which, centuries after the fire from which their rays emanated has gone out, whether it was called Rembrandt or Vermeer, still send us their special light.[13]

Artists thus have the power to multiply the world, that is, to present reality through different transcendental frameworks defined by their singular artistic style. The narrator comes to this insight after experiencing a series of sensations (tripping up on uneven paving-stones, the knock of a spoon against a plate, noises coming out of the plumbing) that trigger involuntary memories similar to the initial one experienced in the first volume thanks to the famous madeleine.[14] Only this time the narrator not only sees a past world re-emerging, but also understands the artistic procedure that can restore such worlds through fiction. Deleuze noticed that Proust's problem was not how to adequately represent a past world, but how to reinvent it through a style of writing that creates its own individuating world.[15] As we will see below in more detail, the correspondence between the present sensation and the past sensation provides the model for the metaphoric analogy between different objects which constitutes a singular artistic style as the basis of aesthetic world-creation.

However, the problem of world first appears in the first pages of the novel, even before the taste of the madeleine returns the narrator to Combray, the town of his youth, and sets him on the path toward the final revelations on artistic cosmogony. Even though involuntary memory and the way it regains lost time is usually considered to be the central topic of the novel, the narrator's first return to the town of Combray actually happens before the madeleine scene.

At the beginning of the novel, the narrator is faced with another kind of multiplicity of worlds, a deeply disorienting one. The text opens with the fleeting moments just before falling asleep and just after waking up. These moments serve to introduce the reader to the temporal and spatial displacements and discontinuities around which the narrative will be organised. Sleep itself appears in Proust as an equivalent of the ideal time before creation in which the Leibnizian God pondered over all the possible worlds. Awakening, then, occurs as the moment of contingency that places the person within a particular time and space:

> A sleeping man holds in a circle around him the sequence of the hours, the order of the years and worlds. He consults them instinctively as he wakes and reads in them in a second the point on the earth he occupies, the time that has elapsed up to his waking.[16]

Normally, one can orient oneself quickly in space and time, just as Leibniz's God has calculated which world is the best possible one. But there is still a discontinuity at the moment of awakening, a moment of disorientation among the possible worlds, a moment that requires a process of 'consultation'.

What Proust is interested in here is precisely this initial moment of disorientation, which possesses the capacity to temporarily tear the continuity of time and space. Such occurrences are particularly evident when one wakes up unexpectedly in the middle of the night, faced with the surrounding darkness:

> immediately I recovered my sight and I was amazed to find a darkness around me soft and restful for my eyes, but perhaps even more so for my mind, to which it appeared a thing without cause, incomprehensible, a thing truly dark.[17]

This '*chose obscure*' persists upon awakening and eliminates the rationality of orientation among worlds. The novel thus opens with the narrator waking up to the disorder of worlds:

> their ranks [the sequence of the hours, the order of the years and worlds] can be mixed up, broken. If toward morning, after a bout of insomnia, sleep overcomes him as he is reading, in a position quite different from the one in which he usually sleeps, his raised arm alone is enough to stop the sun and make it retreat, and, in the first minute of his waking, he will no longer know what time it is, he will think he has only just gone to bed. If he dozes off in a position still more displaced and divergent, for instance after dinner sitting in an armchair, then the confusion among the disordered worlds will be complete.[18]

Faced with this disorder in the middle of the night, the narrator reports that he 'did not even understand in the first moment who [he] was; all [he] had, in its original simplicity, was the sense of existence as it may quiver in the depths of an animal'.[19] Just as the ideal time of sleep corresponds to the neutral coexistence of all possible worlds, the initial moment of awakening exposes the quiver of being itself before it appears in a particular world. After waking up, we have to rebuild the world we find ourselves in. The beginning of the novel can thus be read as a description of what Badiou theorises as the contingency of appearing in relation to being. It is always contingent that a being (in its multiple-composition) appears in a given world in the way that it does.[20]

The effect of this moment of discontinuity, of the simple quivering of being, is that it pushes the multiplicity of possible worlds out of their ideal coexistence towards the vertigo of actuality: 'when I woke thus, my mind restlessly attempting, without success, to discover where I was, everything revolved around me in the darkness, things, countries, years'.[21] What Proust presents here is not a spiritual exercise, nor a metaphysical treatise. The mind presents to us the multiplicity of worlds, yet it is the body that is thrown in the midst of these worlds, which are no longer only possible, but already actual. Badiou insists that even though appearance is contingent in relation to being and therefore independent to a certain extent, appearance retroactively affects being, which means that 'no multiple comes out unscathed from its appearance in a world'.[22] We can see that in Proust. The times and places where the narrator has fallen asleep in the past are imprinted on parts of his body, which thus contains the memorial traces of different worlds:

> My body, too benumbed to move, would try to locate, according to the form of its fatigue, the position of its limbs in order to deduce from this the direction of the wall, the placement of the furniture, in order to reconstruct and name the dwelling in which it found itself. Its memory, the memory of its ribs, its knees, its shoulders, offered in succession several of the rooms where it had slept, while around it the invisible walls, changing place according to the shape of the imagined room, spun through the shadows. And even before my mind, which hesitated on the thresholds of times and shapes, had identified the house by reassembling the circumstances, it – my body – would recall the kind of bed in each one, the location of the doors, the angle at which the light came in through the windows, the existence of a hallway.[23]

This drama ends happily with 'the good angel of certainty' that arranges the furniture around the room back to its proper place.[24] Yet, waiting for the angel, the spinning succession of possible rooms sometimes temporarily delivers us to the wrong one. Proust presents us with a sci-fi image of a man simply dozing off on an armchair, only to find himself in the moment of awakening on 'the magic armchair' that 'will send him travelling at top speed through time and space, and, at the moment of opening his eyelids, he will believe he went to bed several months earlier in another country'.[25] It is such an involuntary voyage through time and space among the disordered worlds – and not the specific sensation of reminiscence that comes later – that first leads the narrator to the town of Combray and thus the world of his youth. Trying to guess the room he is waking up in, his body returns to his childhood bed, where he waited for his mother to come and kiss him goodnight: 'So it was that, for a long time, when, awakened at night, I remembered Combray again.'[26]

The confusion of spinning furniture from different rooms and different times reveals the novel's model of world-construction, based on a moment of discontinuity, of disorder. Such disorder, however, is not entirely negative. The moment of discontinuity that exposes the contingency of appearing is not, for Proust, a moment of anxious revelation of worldlessness. As we have seen, the affect that the dark thing stimulates in the narrator is rather one of amazement, *étonnement*.[27] The suspension of the actual world brings about a piece of another world that is thus resurrected. Yet, the resurrection is only fragmentary: 'always seen at the same hour, isolated from everything that might surround it, standing out alone against the darkness, the bare minimum of scenery', it was 'as though Combray had consisted only of two floors connected by a slender staircase and as though it had always been seven o'clock in the evening there'.[28] The world around the staircase is yet to be (re)created. At the very beginning of the novel, before the reminiscence and the artistic recovery of the multiplicity of worlds, we thus find the moment of the proliferation and actualisation of the multiplicity of singular worlds, as well as a model of constructing them: from an initial fragment of space and time, to which other objects and moments are still to be added.

Now that we have discovered the multiplicity of worlds in Proust, the question arises how the Proustian fictional construction of worlds compares to the logical construction of worlds theorised by Badiou.

We have already seen in Chapter 5 how, despite Badiou's insistence on the objective nature of logical procedures that constitute worlds, the way a certain world is framed by Badiou seems very literary, even fictional.

To demonstrate that the principles of Badiou's logics of worlds can be applied to the novel, we will take as our point of departure the four worlds of *In Search of Lost Time* as described by Deleuze in his book on Proust. Deleuze distinguishes four 'different worlds of signs' in which the narrator participates:[29]

1. the world of worldliness or high society with its codes of behaviour and the complicated rules and dynamics that determine the inclusion and exclusion of persons from a given salon and its social circle;
2. the world of love: the loved person inhabits their own world, which is inaccessible to us and which we can only know through partial and limited signs that require incessant work of interpretation fuelled by jealousy;
3. the world of sensuous impressions or qualities, the exceptional sensitive experiences attached to everyday objects that, in a certain moment, amaze or affect us;
4. the world of art, which is exceptional since it allows us to discover the very principles of world-construction and thus to regain the lost time.

Instead of studying the logic of signs in each of the four worlds, as Deleuze does, I will present them as corresponding to the fundamental concepts of Badiou's phenomenology. I will use the first three worlds to describe the three central concepts of Badiou's logics of worlds: the transcendental, object and relation. I will address the fourth world, the world of art, in relation to the fourth major topic of Badiou's objective phenomenology: the appearance of truths.

The first world, the world of worldliness, can serve as an example of the Badiousian concept of the transcendental. As we saw in more detail in Chapter 3, the transcendental of a given world attributes the degrees of intensity to ontological multiples, thereby determining their appearance in this world. To simplify, it is the principle of order and hierarchy that determines what can appear in a specific world and how it appears therein as more or less visible, more or less important. One could say that Proust examines social life precisely from the point of view of its transcendental. The centres of the worlds of worldliness are the salons that form their own rules of acceptance and codes of behaviour. Being invited to a certain salon is equivalent to being accepted into a social circle and determines one's position on the social ladder. One's social existence, that is, one's appearance in these worlds, is completely determined by the transcendental of a given salon and has nothing to do with the supposed 'intrinsic' characteristics of the person:

> The Prince d'Agrigente passed for a foreign vulgarian in the eyes of a club *chasseur* to whom he owed twenty-five *louis*, and resumed his importance only in the Faubourg Saint-Germain, where he had three sisters who were duchesses, for the great nobleman has some effect, not on people of modest means, in the eyes of whom he counts for little, but on the brilliant ones, well informed as to his status.[30]

Individual salons could be said to constitute a larger world of Parisian worldliness, with a transcendental that determines the degrees of prestige associated with each one. Proust's novel records the modifications of this transcendental, the situation of rivalry between the fading aristocratic salons (represented by the Guermanteses) and their ascending *nouveaux riches* counterparts (represented by the Verdurins). More importantly, though, we can observe that there are no general rules of acceptance and behaviour as each salon develops its own criteria of evaluation of one's worth, of different tastes, opinions and behaviours:

> To belong to the 'little set', the 'little circle', the 'little clan' attached to the Verdurins, one condition was sufficient but necessary: you had to abide tacitly by a Credo one of whose articles was that the young pianist patronized by Mme Verdurin that year, of whom she would say: 'It ought to be against the law to be able to play Wagner like that!', 'was miles above' both Planté and Rubinstein and that Doctor Cottard was a better diagnostician than Potain. Any 'new recruit' who could not be persuaded by the Verdurins that the soirées given by people who did not come to the Verdurins' house were as tedious as a rainy day was immediately excluded.[31]

The salons thus offer a perfect opportunity to study the way human multiples appear within a multiplicity of worlds determined by particular transcendentals.

The second world is the world of love. What is at stake from our point of view here is the second fundamental concept of Badiou's logics, namely the object. The question for Badiou is how the ontological multiples are constituted as objects on the level of appearing within a world: 'by "object" we must understand that which counts as one within appearing, or that which authorises us to speak of this being-there as inflexibly being "itself"', relative to the transcendental of a given world.[32] In Proust, the constitution of an object can best be observed in love-worlds. For Proust, examining love is first a question of how, among the multiplicity of people or, more precisely, the multiplicity of bodies and their parts, an individual becomes an object of amorous affection. The famous scene on the beach in Balbec in which the narrator sees 'a gang of girls' approaching presents the original multiplicity out of which Albertine will eventually be constituted as the narrator's primary love interest:

> I had been looking at them for so few moments, and was so far from daring to stare at them, that I had not yet been able to individualize any of them. [...] they were knowable only as a pair of hard, stubborn, laughing eyes in one of the faces; as two cheeks of that pink touched by coppery tones suggesting geraniums in another; and none of even these features had I yet inseparably attached to any particular girl rather than to some other. [...] The fact that my view of them was devoid of demarcations, which I was soon to draw among them, sent a ripple of harmonious imprecision through their group, the uninterrupted flow of a shared, unstable and elusive beauty.[33]

The second volume of the *Search* spends many pages on the way Albertine is slowly constituted as the object of the narrator's love-world out of this dispersed, libidinally invested multiplicity.[34] Yet, the way the object of love is constituted is even more apparent in the way it is dissolved once the fixation ceases. Such is Swann's amazement at his own obsession with Odette: 'To think that I wasted years of my life, that I wanted to die, that I felt my deepest love, for a woman who did not appeal to me, who was not my type!'[35]

The final of the central concepts of Badiou's logics is relation. Relations between objects complete the continuity, coherence and completeness of a world. Badiou insists that relations do not have an effect on the existence of objects, but rather concern their coexistence within the same world.[36] In order to illustrate this, we can use the third

Proustian world, the world of sensible impressions. As we have already seen, relations are essential to the way Proust describes sensible experience. An impression is immediately connected to another, to the extent that impressions become but a sign of other impressions. As Deleuze observed, 'thus experienced, the quality no longer appears as a property of the object that now possesses it, but as the sign of an *altogether different* object that we must try to decipher'.[37] This is clearest in the case of the reminiscences, the secret of which is revealed in the final volume not only as the possibility to regain time but also as a principle of artistic style. The relations between impressions can also be observed in Proust's regular metaphoric descriptions of events and surroundings, where there is no great temporal mystery to decipher. A famous example of this is the analogy between the homosexual encounter of Charlus and Jupien and a bumblebee's fertilisation of the Duchesse's orchid, both of which the narrator happens to observe from a window at the same time.[38]

It thus seems that the ultimate relation that establishes the coherence of a world in Proust is the relation of analogy. Metaphors, however, seem too subjective to provide the coherence of a world as an objective structure as required by Badiou's phenomenology. At this point I will rely on the analysis of Proust's style given by Genette, for whom the fundamental importance of metaphor in Proust has led us 'to overestimate its action to the detriment of other semantic relations'.[39] Genette emphasises the overlooked importance of metonymy for Proust and with it the relation of spatio-temporal contiguity, which, as we have known since Roman Jakobson, is dominant in prose as opposed to the metaphoric analogy dominant in poetry.[40] According to Genette, it is in fact the intertwinement of metaphor and metonymy that is the defining characteristic of Proust's style. He shows that out of the variety of possible analogies, 'Proust chooses in each case the one that best adapts to the situation or context'.[41] The relation of contiguity – the objective spatial and temporal proximity – directs Proust's choice of analogy. In the aforementioned case of the homosexual encounter and the fertilisation of the orchid, Genette observes, analogy is merely a side-effect of simultaneity.[42] To further prove his point, Genette compares two descriptions of bell towers in the novel. When the narrator sees a pair of bell towers over a wheat field, they appear to him to be like two ears of wheat, but when he sees a similar pair of bell towers near the seaside, he compares them to fish rising in the water.[43]

The primacy of contiguity is what places figurative relations within the objectivity of the surrounding world. To conclude our comparison, relations between objects are figurative in Proust, which makes them secondary to the existence of objects, just as relations are supposed to be according to Badiou. Furthermore, Proust's figuration remains prosaic and objective due to the primacy of contiguity. The metonymic foundation of analogy guarantees the coherence of appearance in a given world.

We have therefore derived from Proust the three central components of the logical constitution of worlds according to Badiou: the transcendental of the salon, the object of love and the figurative relation. Badiou's logics, however, are not only a theory of the construction of worlds, but also a theory of their transformation. We should thus explore the figures of change in Proust and how they correspond to Badiou's distinction between real change, instigated by an event and developed subjectively in a truth procedure, and milder modifications that in the end only serve to reaffirm the transcendental principles of a given world.[44]

To a certain extent, modifications in the intensity of appearing are allowed for or even encouraged by the transcendental of a world. This is the case with the constant modifications that are crucial for the transcendental of a salon. The Proustian worlds of worldliness change constantly due to fluctuations of fashion, falls from grace, shifting political allegiances and so forth. But all this change changes nothing: the logic of these worlds is the logic of hypocrisy, which the narrator slowly unravels.

This can be expanded to all three Proustian worlds we have already analysed. Therein, change can be reduced to repetition, albeit a creative one. Through such repetition, the transcendental remains essentially the same, as can best be observed in the world of love. Marcel's love for Albertine follows the pattern set up by his earlier love for Swann's daughter Gilberte and can be traced all the way back to the initial scene from Combray, where the child narrator waits for his mother's kiss. But the mother is not presented as some primal origin. The detailed model of Proustian love is already set in the first volume with Swann's relationship with Odette. As the narrator himself reflects:

> A novelist could shape the whole life of his hero by depicting his consecutive loves in more or less the same terms, giving thereby

the impression, not of being self-repetitive, but of being creative, there being less power in an artificial innovation than in a reiteration designed to convey a hitherto unrevealed truth.[45]

The objects of libidinal interest change, but the logic of their constitution remains the same. The importance of creative repetition reaches its peak in the world of the sensible, where it is no longer merely a modification, but an opening that can lead to the re-creation of a world through art, where the properly Proustian truth procedure takes place.

For Badiou, the possibility of real change is linked to the 'subversion of appearing by being'.[46] This happens when something in being bypasses the given transcendental and forces its way to appearance. Some part of the multiple constituting an object may not be able to appear in a given world, even though it is ontologically a part of it. This is what Badiou calls 'the inexistent'. The inexistent shows that there is more to being than can appear in a world: 'There is a reserve of being which, subtracted from appearance, traces within this appearance the fact that it is always contingent for such a being to appear there.'[47] The excess of being over appearing marks the point where the contingency of appearance can be seen in objects themselves. The actual appearance of the inexistent breaks the transcendental principles of a given world and thus implies real change.

Such 'sites', as Badiou calls them,[48] of being forcing its way to appearance can be seen regularly in the *Search*. In the worlds of worldliness and love it often becomes clear that a person is more in their being than what appears of them in a given world. Swann's social position as an art connoisseur in the salon of the Duchesse de Guermantes is contrasted to her complete indifference to his condition when he tells her that he will not be able to accompany her on a trip to Italy because his illness will most likely have taken his life by the time of departure.[49] The transcendental of the salon cannot assign any degree of appearance to his personal problems, however grave they may be. While the inexistent of the social persona is something completely antithetical to the transcendental of its world, the inexistent of the love object is much more constitutively ingrained in the object. The narrator is under no illusions that his object of desire corresponds to the other person's being: he reflects how his love for Albertine is 'enveloping her without taking any heed of her, like a tide engulfing a fragile reef'.[50] For

Proust, love is nothing but an obsessive yet paradoxical task to know and conquer the love object's inexistent part:

> I could feel that part of Albertine's life escaped me. Love, in painful anxiety as in happy desire, is the need for complete possession. It is born, it lives only for so long as there is something left to conquer. We love only that which we do not wholly possess.[51]

The unknown and unpossessed being of the love object is what makes jealousy such an important factor in Proust's depiction of love; it is the reaction to constant but obscure appearances of the inexistent that the transcendental cannot account for.

It is important to note that the inexistent is not an absolute state, but rather is relative to a given world. What is inexistent within one world can have a perfectly clear degree of existence assigned in another world. Swann's illness surely has an important place in the world of his family, for example, while Albertine's great secrets only exist for the narrator. The inexistent could therefore also be described as a consequence of the divergence between multiple worlds. Albertine exists simultaneously in several worlds, many of which remain obscure, undevelopable to the narrator:

> We imagine that love has for its object a being which can lie down before us, enclosed in a body. Alas! It is the extension of that body to every point in space and time which that being has occupied or will occupy.[52]

It could be argued that the excess of appearance over being is just as defining for the inexistent as is the excess of being over appearance.

The appearances of being that bypass the transcendental do not necessarily lead to a proper event. If the consequences of such appearances are not far-reaching enough, the world can carry on as before.[53] Salons can simply exclude and replace the people who break the spell of their social personas, while the jealous lover's affection actually feeds off the inexistent of its object. What such weak appearances of the inexistent do enable is the knowledge that the narrator gains about each of these worlds, that is, the general laws of human social and libidinal behaviour that he manages to deduce from them. This is what strengthens the narrator's ability to read the signs of these worlds, which is the true aim of his *recherche*, according to Deleuze. As Malcolm Bowie points out, jealousy is not only the condition of love in Proust, but also the condition of how he sees science – as a specific form of jealousy.[54] Proust uses many scientific metaphors to describe his investigations of Albertine's other relationships, showing that the unknown in the object of desire is what drives our quest for knowledge in general: 'The unknown element in the lives of human beings is like that of nature, which every new scientific discovery diminishes but does not eliminate.'[55]

However, knowledge does not equal truth. The regaining of time is based on the sensation of reminiscence as a strong appearance of the inexistent that makes a world appear within another world through a specific kind of object. Developing the consequences of such events takes place in art. While art as a separate world in Proust could also be analysed in terms of its constitution (the changing transcendental conditions of what counts as art and what does not and according to whom, the constitution of the artwork as an object of perception, the relations between artworks and so on), it is more important to see art in terms of Proust's own conception of truth.

The Laboratory of Creation

How, then, does Proust articulate truth as a procedure in relation to the multiplicity of worlds and how does this reflect back on Badiou's *Logics of Worlds*? The appearance of the inexistent that leads the narrator on the path to truth happens in the world of the sensible. This is how the narrator recalls experiences he had on his childhood walks, experiences of pure aesthetic appearance that gave him 'unreasoning pleasure' but also seemed to reveal something yet to be discovered:

> suddenly a roof, a glimmer of sun on a stone, the smell of the road would stop me because of a particular pleasure they gave me, and also because they seemed to be concealing, beyond what I could see, something which they were inviting me to come take and which despite my efforts I could not manage to discover.[56]

An object reduced to its pure appearance that brings a specific kind of pleasure also points to something beyond itself, something that remains unclear to the narrator. The pure sensible events that the narrator enjoys are detached from the surrounding world: it seems like they arrive without a proper transcendental, as pure contingent emergences. Their mystery, however, nevertheless implies a relation, a connection that leads to some sort of world-building. We have already seen how Proust's metonymically based metaphoric descriptions establish relations between sensible experiences within the surrounding world. But the exceptional experiences first encountered on childhood walks do not form relations in the same way. Their connectivity seems interrupted, marked by a discontinuity. They still seem to imply a contiguity or an analogy but it remains unclear what they are close or similar to. Different from ordinary figurative relations, they seem to unearth an inexistent that troubles the narrator.

Such appearances announce the experience of reminiscence that comes with the same type of curious pleasure. After tasting the madeleine dipped in tea, the narrator reports: 'A delicious pleasure had invaded me, isolated me, without my having any notion as to its cause.'[57] The pleasure that the madeleine provides has nothing to do with the degree of culinary delight that could be assigned to it by the transcendental of the narrator's taste. The sensation seems without cause, isolated from the world it appears in. The experience first appears as a pure event, but nevertheless implies a connection that remains obscure:

> Where could it have come to me from – this powerful joy? I sensed that it was connected to the taste of the tea and the cake, but that it went infinitely far beyond it, could not be of the same nature. Where did it come from? What did it mean? How could I grasp it?[58]

The answer to this question is what eventually – after the experience of reminiscence is repeated several times in the final volume – reveals the secret of lost time.

Yet, the fact that the experience of reminiscence has a predecessor in the sensations experienced by the narrator on his childhood walks tells us that the dimensions of time and memory might be overemphasised. In the case of a child having a similar type of experience, what lost time could the enigma of the sensation possibly refer to? Can it simply be said that what is at stake here is an event that implies no greater mystery than that of a contingent discontinuity in experience? And when such discontinuity is encountered, it may not point only to the presence of another timeline in the present moment but, more generally, to the presence of another world within this one. The isolated sensible event that leads the narrator to investigate the connection it implies but obscures may also suggest a different kind of transcendental, a different type of connectivity between sensible experiences. The ephemeral appearance points to the contingent formation of any world and the divergences between multiple worlds. But it also implies something else: the formation of a world based on this very discontinuity, a world that comes into being with an event.

We should now recall the narrator's awakenings at night, when he first catches a glimpse of a resurrected Combray, seen always as merely a fragment, 'isolated from everything that might surround it, standing out alone against the darkness, the bare minimum of scenery'.[59] Resurfacing as a result of the confusion of worlds upon awakening, the fragment of a past world first appears as a ruin of something possibly dead forever. In order to truly regain the past, to resurrect the world of Combray, the traces of contingency of world-formation are not enough. Another experience is needed: the reminiscence that comes from an encounter with a specific kind of object. This is how the madeleine enters the picture:

> The past is hidden outside the realm of our intelligence and beyond its reach, in some material object (in the sensation that this material object would give us) which we do not suspect. It depends on chance whether we encounter this object before we die, or do not encounter it.[60]

The madeleine is thus what in the previous chapter we called a monadic object: an object that becomes isolated from the world but which through this very isolation contains the design of another world that can be developed from it.

After the narrator tastes the madeleine, the initial minimal scenery consisting of two floors and a staircase expands, object by object:

> And as soon as I had recognized the taste of the piece of madeleine dipped in lime-blossom tea that my aunt used to give me (though I did not yet know and had to put off to much later discovering why this memory made me so happy), immediately the old grey house on the street, where her bedroom was, came like a stage-set to attach

itself to the little wing opening on to the garden that had been built for my parents behind it (that truncated section which was all I had seen before then); and with the house the town, from morning to night and in all weathers, the Square, where they sent me before lunch, the streets where I went on errands, the paths we took if the weather was fine. And as in that game enjoyed by the Japanese in which they fill a porcelain bowl with water and steep in it little pieces of paper until then indistinct, which, the moment they are immersed in it, stretch and shape themselves, colour and differentiate, become flowers, houses, human figures, firm and recognizable, so now all the flowers in our garden and in M. Swann's park, and the water lilies on the Vivonne, and the good people of the village and their little dwellings and the church and all of Combray and its surroundings, all of this which is assuming form and substance, emerged, town and gardens alike, from my cup of tea.[61]

This is how a world is reconstructed from the monadic object, like the construction of a stage set. Again, it is not only remembering that is at stake. Combray is not to be found again but created: 'Seek? Not only that: create.'[62] The madeleine has put the narrator 'face to face with something that does not yet exist'.[63] Making it exist will depend on developing the event's consequences, on exploring the transcendental inscribed in the monadic object.

At this point we have to revisit Genette's analysis of Proust's style. We have already seen how contiguity and simultaneity metonymically dictate Proust's choice of metaphor. But what happens when both contiguity and simultaneity are lost? What is the difference between the figurative sensible relations that make the surrounding world cohere in Proust's descriptions and the exceptional sensible events? While the former are based on continuity, in the latter the figural connection is interrupted by discontinuity. The analogy is implied but cannot find its other term as there is no guidance of contiguity. The experience isolates an object from its surrounding world, but only to point to another world that remains obscure. Thus, the connection to Combray was interrupted by the lost time. As Proust writes: 'the memory, thanks to forgetfulness, has not been able to make a single connection, to throw up a single link between it and the present moment'.[64] Memory on its own, as Proust emphasises, is powerless when it comes to resurrecting a lost world.

To make up for the absence of contiguity, 'the miracle of an analogy' is needed: the world of Combray can only be resurrected if a contingent metaphoric event takes place.[65] The analogy between the present and the past moment is established in the event of involuntary memory that makes up for lost time, but beyond the initial joy that disperses quickly, the event – as Badiou himself often emphasises – only exists in its consequences.[66] Genette writes that

> the true Proustian miracle is not that a madeleine dipped in tea has the same taste as another madeleine dipped in tea and recalls the memory of it; it is rather that this second madeleine brings to life a room, a house, an entire town, and that for a second, this old place can 'rattle the solidity' of the current place, break down the doors and shake the furniture.[67]

The event that for a moment forced the entry of another world into the present one continues to exist through the further building of the world that fragmentarily emerged from it. Genette thus claims that the overall architecture of Proust's novel rests on a mode of interlacing metaphor and metonymy that inverts the relation of both figures. While Proustian description is based on metonymy, which determines the metaphor, Proust's overall narrative edifice is built on initial metaphoric events that establish the spatiality and temporality in which metonymy then operates. It is now metonymy that is dependent on the metaphor, but the miraculous analogy can only rebuild the world it brings back to life through the work of contiguity that builds the entire town based on the re-emergence of a single staircase. The initial metaphor would amount to nothing without the metonymic work that continues to add new parts to the fragment of the world initially recovered. Genette concludes:

> Without metaphor, says (roughly) Proust, no real memories; we add for him (and for everyone): without metonymy, no chain of memories, no *story*, no novel. It is the metaphor that finds the Lost Time, but it is metonymy that brings it to life, and makes it work.[68]

The Proustian truth procedure, therefore, is the making of the novel itself: the subjective procedure of metonymic work, the work of building the fictional world that first emerged fragmentarily through a metaphoric event. But should the Proustian truth procedure be seen as merely individual or as subjective in the Badiousian sense? Is the regaining of lost time not a matter of the finite 'human animal' that has nothing to do with the collective, generic and eternal dimension of Badiou's understanding of subjectivity? In fact, Proust's presentation of regaining time is not a meditation on human finitude, but a discovery of a true life outside of time. The experience of reminiscence makes of the narrator a witness of another 'being which had now been resuscitated in me', a being that appears in 'these moments of identity between the present and the past', in 'the only milieu in which it could live and enjoy the essence of things, that is to say outside of time'.[69] While the narrator's movement through the worlds of worldliness and love made him desperate, even to the point of giving up on his artistic ideals, the exceptional sensible experiences finally reveal the idea that allows him to live a true life (an ideal that Badiou describes in the conclusion to *Logics of Worlds* as a life that defies human finitude[70]):

> Yet a single sound, a single scent, already heard or breathed long ago, may once again, both in the present and the past, be real without being present, ideal without being abstract, as soon as the permanent and habitually hidden essence of things is liberated, and our true self, which may sometimes have seemed to be long dead, but never was entirely, is re-awoken and re-animated when it receives the heavenly food that is brought to it. One minute freed from the order of time has recreated in us, in order to feel it, the man freed from the order of time. And because of that we can understand why he trusts his joy, and even if the simple taste of a madeleine does not seem logically to contain reasons for this joy, we can understand how the word 'death' has no meaning for him; situated outside time, what should we fear from the future?[71]

This kind of experience is not arbitrary and individual but rather contingent and subjective. It is only contingently that such experiences occur, but when they do, they occur as a necessity that unravels the truth of one's life. The narrator reflects that many die 'before the truth made for them can be revealed to them'.[72] Such experiences, as Pierre Macherey argues, function for Proust like an interpellation of individuals into subjects, although considering the true life to which it delivers the subject, the Badiousian concept of subjectivation might be closer to Proust's than the Althusserian one employed by Macherey.[73] It also seems that Badiou himself – at least for a moment – was willing to see in Proust's novel a process of subjectivation. Peter Hallward's summary of Badiou's unpublished lecture on Proust shows that Badiou sees the narrator's search for lost time as a path towards truth.[74]

We have seen the world of Combray emerge from the monadic object, that is, the madeleine as the initial fragment of another world, but this does not in itself solve the mystery that the childhood walks first unearthed. It is not until the final volume, when a series of reminiscences strike the narrator again, that the mystery is revealed not only as the principle of regaining the past on the basis of an involuntary memory but as the principle of aesthetic cosmogony. It is at this point, the point of the imperative to write, to build fictionally the world that emerged through the metaphoric event, that the personal experience becomes a subjective task. As Macherey observes, the subjectivation of Proust's narrator is a process of depersonalisation that transforms the narrative subject from an 'I' to a 'we': the experience now no longer belongs only to the individual, but can be transmitted and shared by others.[75]

We should be careful not to presume that the creation of a fictional world through style entails an idealistic detachment from reality. The process of subjectivation does not release the narrator from his ordinary existence and from the multiplicity of worlds in which he previously erred. Just as in Badiou, events can only occur at specific places, in the lacunae between being and appearing. As Genette argues – in a statement that could also be read as a quote from *Logics of Worlds* – truth is encountered where the 'incompatibility between being and appearance' is revealed.[76] In order for the narrator to be subjectivised as a writer, a series of such incompatibilities had first to be revealed: the disappointments of social life, the double life of Albertine, the mystery of sensible events and the hollowness of the artistic ideals he believed in.[77] These sites determine the possibility of an event, but do not bring it about. It is only after tripping on an uneven pavement and hearing strange sounds coming from the plumbing that the narrator finally understands the mystery of the reminiscence as the principle of aesthetic cosmogony. Yet, this does not entail an escape into the world of art but the creation of a world that will consist of nothing but tracing the incompatibilities between being and appearance in all the worlds he was previously engaged in. The final revelations provide orientation among the multiplicity of worlds by presenting them from the point of view of the inexistent within them, the inexistent that not only reveals the real but also points to divergences between various coexisting worlds. Artistic world-creation in Proust is by no means a path to a transcendent aesthetic ideal that allows for an escape from the individual and social disturbances that constitute the reality of existence. On the contrary, it is through the fictional world based on the necessity of style imposed by a contingent event that such disturbances can finally be presented for what they are.

According to Hallward's summary of Badiou's lecture, Proust's novel makes it 'possible to see how true reality can be grasped through the strictly formal operations of "thought" and "style"'.[78] So how is this formal operation achieved in Proust? Offering his reflection on artistic truth, Proust shows how style emerges as a strict procedure, comparable to science, as opposed to the false literary ideal of comprehensive description:

> One can list indefinitely in a description all the objects that figured in the place described, but the truth will begin only when the writer takes two different objects, establishes their relationship, the analogue in the world of art of the unique relation created in the world of science by the laws of causality, and encloses them within the necessary armature of a beautiful style. Indeed, just as in life, it begins at the moment when, by bringing together a quality shared by two sensations, he draws out their common essence by uniting them with each other, in order to protect them from the contingencies of time, in a metaphor. Had not nature herself, from this point of view, set me on the way to art, wasn't she herself the beginning of art, she who made it possible for me, often after a long interval, to recognise the beauty of one thing only in another, noon at Combray only in the sound of its bells, mornings at Doncières only in the hiccupping of our water-heater? The relationship may not be very interesting, the objects ordinary, the style bad, but if no relationship has been established, there is nothing.[79]

Amidst the arbitrariness of description thus arises the contingent event that introduces necessity – *'les anneaux nécessaires d'un beau style'* – into the singular way of connecting objects and experiences into a world. What makes style beautiful is not the predefined aesthetic value of the represented objects, the significance of discovered analogies, or the criteria for good writing. What matters is the contingency of the event and the necessity of enchainment that follows from it and produces a singularity of style that is completely indifferent to any predefined evaluations.

Proust's reflections on style should not be reduced to mere aestheticism. Instead, we should recall Proust's comments on Gustave Flaubert in response to a contemporary literary critic who dismissed Flaubert's literary legacy simply as one of a bad style of writing. Proust does not claim that Flaubert's style is actually good according to some universal criteria (in fact, he admits that he himself does not consider it good in this sense), but that it is singular in a way that makes the criteria for good and bad irrelevant. Flaubert's 'grammatical singularities', as Proust calls them, achieved a stylistic revolution that can be compared to Immanuel Kant's revolution in philosophy.[80] For Proust, Flaubert is a writer who,

> by the entirely novel and personal use which he made of the past definite, the past indefinite, the present participle, and of certain pronouns and prepositions, has renewed our vision of things almost to the same extent as Kant, with his Categories, renewed our theories of knowledge and of the reality of the external world.[81]

The renewal of 'our vision of things' could also be read in a post-Kantian way as resetting the parameters of transcendental aesthetics. Macherey comments that through his remarks on Flaubert and Kant, Proust implies that the *a priori* transcendental forms are not unchangeable, which renders an artistic reframing of the world possible.[82] In the *Search*, the narrator reflects on such artistic reframings especially in relation to the work of Elstir, the novel's imaginary painter. The narrator perceives the painter's studio as a 'laboratory of a new creation of the world: from the chaos made of all things we see'.[83] The material for artistic creation is thus the sensible multiplicity as such, before the categories of reason manage to enforce clear distinctions between objects.[84]

Proust's aesthetic cosmogony does not entail the creation of a distant aesthetic world that would provide a redemption from this one. The fictional world created by art remains fully immanent to the multiplicity of worlds. In fact, it opens up this multiplicity by shifting the limits of possible experience. Proust decomposes the metaphor of the cosmological multiplicity of worlds in order to reveal this multiplicity as transcendental:

> Wings, another repertory system which allowed us to cross the immensity of space, would not help us. For if we went to Mars or Venus while keeping the same senses, everything we might see there would take on the same aspect as the things we know on Earth. The only real journey, the only Fountain of Youth, would be to travel not towards new landscapes, but with new eyes, to see the universe through the eyes of another, of a hundred others, to see the hundred universes that each of them can see, or can be; and we can do that with the help of an Elstir, a Vinteuil; with them and their like we can truly fly from star to star.[85]

It is not other worlds that we see thanks to art; it is this world that we can see through different transcendental frames. The transcendental reframing of ontological multiplicity based on an encounter with a monadic object is thus the final mystery revealed in the *Search*.

Badiou with Proust

Now that we have an understanding of the Proustian truth procedure and its relation to the multiplicity of worlds, we can take it as a standpoint from which to take a look back at the problems of Badiou's *Logics of Worlds* that we detected in previous chapters. The first problem is the fictional character of worlds that was largely unaccounted for by Badiou with his insistence on the objectivity of worlds and the whole mathematical apparatus that supports the presentation of their logical structure. At one point in his book, as we have seen, Badiou does mention that the transcendental can be considered as a fiction, although he does not elaborate on this claim. Even if we fully accept the mathematical explanation of world-construction, the way ontological multiplicity gets framed as a world (a battle, the history of a territory, an evening at a country house, to use some of Badiou's own examples of worlds) remains purely fictional, that is, dependent on framing and narrative.

Nevertheless, fiction should not be understood in this context as something that undermines the objective nature of the world. It in no way implies that, say, a battle and its aftermath or an evening at a Parisian salon are not real. From the beginning, my transcendental approach to the concept of world as mediating between fiction and reality was an attempt to present the dilemma between realism and correlationism as something of a false problem. In addition, fiction should not be understood as something arbitrary in contrast to the rigour of logic. Narrative construction has its own structure that can be studied in detail – as we did following Genette.

The second problem we encountered in Badiou was the articulation of truth to a specific world, on the one hand, and the multiplicity of worlds, on the other. We have seen that Badiou insists that a truth has its origin in a specific world and is the truth of that world, even though it has a universal or 'trans-worldly' value. But if a human being – as Badiou also claims – simultaneously exists in a virtually unlimited number of overlapping worlds, how can we confine an event and the subsequent truth procedure to one specific world? Is the world in which truth appears really given objectively, beforehand? Or should we rather, as I have tried to show, see this world as a retroactive effect of the truth procedure itself? Is the struggle of the subject of truth not in the first place the struggle to define the world to be changed in the light of the event?

I have shown that the inexistent should not only be understood as a consequence of the excess of being over appearance, but also as the excess of appearance over being. The inexistent is relative to specific worlds: what is inexistent in one world can have a strong existence in another one. This means that the starting point of a truth procedure should not only be understood as the subversion of appearance by being, but also by gaps within appearance itself, that is, gaps, conflicts and interferences between worlds. After such gaps appear, the indifferent coexistence of worlds is disturbed.

This brings me to the third and final problem, the 'worldly' nature of the truth procedure itself. Badiou emphasises the 'bodily' nature of the subject of truth's existence in a world, while truth itself is 'trans-worldly', that is, a singular universality or a temporary instance of eternity. Yet, beyond the appearance of the subject as a body in a world and the trans-worldly nature of the truth it develops in that world, should we not also consider the truth procedure itself as a becoming of a singular world? And if that is the case, how does this new world impose itself upon the indifferent or hostile multiplicity of worlds?

Finally, I can attempt to give an answer to these questions with Proust. First, the *Search* has provided us with a model for examining the logics of the fictional construction of worlds. Above, we have observed how all the fundamental concepts of Badiou's logics can be redefined in terms of prose: the transcendental of social circles, the object of love and the relation that connects sensible experiences into a coherent world. Genette's study of the narrative structure of the novel in terms of the intertwining of metaphor and metonymy has given us additional tools to understand the logics of Proust's worlds.

Proust's novel has allowed us to see the relative nature of the inexistent as dependent on the intersections in the multiplicity of worlds: people in relation to the various worlds they inhabit, the dispersal of the loved object in times and spaces the lover has no access to, the exceptional sensible experiences that point to another experience in an unclear time and space. Such appearances of the inexistent not only as an irruption of being within appearance but also as the overlapping of different worlds disturb the indifferent coexistence of worlds. They mark the sites of an interference or even a conflict of worlds that has real consequences for the beings that appear in them.

It is only with the reminiscences, however, that strong appearances of the inexistent emerge as the true Proustian events. Even though such events emerge in a specific world – exceptional experiences in the world of the sensible – they are related to several other worlds. They directly entail a principle of artistic creation, which means that the truth procedure based on these events is established as an artistic world. Moreover, this world – the world of the novel – provides a specific perspective on social, amorous and sensible worlds. This does not, however, imply that the world-construction in the novel is a process of totalisation, where presented worlds would be subordinated to the *telos* of the mystery revealed by the reminiscence. These worlds provide most of the content of time regained and thus hold a degree of independence from the truth revealed by the reminiscence, although they are also conditioned by it: without it, they would be lost in time and could not be reconstructed.

Due to the correspondence between the beginning and the end of the novel – the initial reminiscence and the final resolution of its mystery – the world of the novel might indeed be considered to be closed and circular since the end returns to the beginning.[86] We now know that Proust wrote the ending at approximately the same time as the beginning, but after the publication of further volumes was interrupted by the Great War, Proust started to add new episodes, producing several additional volumes that were not part of the original plan. For Badiou, the truth procedure might have its limits as a sequence in time and space, but remains in itself 'the infinite result of a risky supplementation'.[87] It goes the same for the world of the novel. Even though the novel's ending was clearly defined at the start, it created a world opened to infinite supplementation, as evidenced by Proust, who kept adding new episodes and sentences even on his deathbed.

The reading of Proust I have been developing here aims to surpass the traditional division in Proustian scholarship between those who interpret the final revelations of the novel as redemption from time and those who insist on deconstructing such trans-temporal metaphysics from within by emphasising passages of the novel that are at odds with the redemptive declarations of time regained.[88] Time regained is not a discovery of a redemptive essence outside time, but an opening of a delicate subjective procedure, the process of building a world based on a discontinuity in the experience of time and space. The parts of the novel that present seemingly unredeemable social, amorous or existential afflictions are not opposed to the truth revealed in the final volume. It is this truth as a development of the supplementary world of the novel that gives rise to these incompatibilities between being and appearance.

Where the inexistent appears strongly, it appears not only as an event, but also as a monadic object: an object that first appears worldless, isolated from the world in which it is encountered, but is then revealed as a fragment of another world that can be further developed from it. In Proust, the truth procedure is, in the final instance, the world of the novel as unfolded from the encountered monadic object. The novel's narrative metonymically builds its own world based on this encounter as a metaphoric event. Even though the full significance of the event is only revealed at the end, everything we have been reading from the start is a consequence of the event. The multiplicity of worlds that the novel enables us to observe – the worlds of high society, of love affairs and so on – are only retroactively constituted and made relevant from the perspective of the supplementary world developed by the novel. The world constructed by the truth procedure thus draws the multiple worlds around it in a state of becoming.

Notes

1. Discussing the interpretative practices of Deleuze and Badiou, Lecercle concludes that 'both philosophers really engage with literature and its texts, which gives their readings an urgency and depth that are characteristics of a strong reading, at the cost of rediscovering in literature the concepts independently elaborated by their philosophies, but with the benefit of new insights into the literary texts thus "exploited": the strong reading submits the literary text to the rule of the concept, but it does not kill it, it makes it alive – it reaches parts of the text that ordinary literary criticism cannot reach.' Jean-Jacques Lecercle, *Badiou and Deleuze Read Literature* (Edinburgh: Edinburgh University Press, 2010), 202.
2. Ibid. 69.
3. Ibid. 105.
4. Genette explains this procedure in the Preface to *Narrative Discourse: An Essay in Method*, trans. Jane E. Lewin (Ithaca, NY: Cornell University Press, 1980), 21–3.
5. See Gilles Deleuze, *Proust and Signs*, trans. Richard Howard (Minneapolis: University of Minnesota Press, 2000); Jacques Rancière, *Mute Speech: Literature, Critical Theory, and Politics*, trans. James Swenson (New York: Columbia University Press, 2011), 145–66; Theodor W. Adorno, 'Short Commentaries on Proust', in *Notes to Literature, Vol. 1*, trans. Shierry Weber Nicholsen (New York: Columbia University Press, 1991), 174–84.
6. The unpublished lecture 'Proust et la vérité', given at Maison Française, Oxford, on 14 October 2000, is summarised by Peter Hallward in *Badiou: A Subject to Truth* (Minneapolis: University of Minnesota Press, 2003), 203–5.
7. Alain Badiou and Nicolas Truong, *In Praise of Love*, trans. Peter Bush (London: Serpent's Tail, 2012), 59–60.
8. Lecercle, *Badiou and Deleuze Read Literature*, 158.
9. Alain Badiou, *Logics of Worlds: Being and Event, 2*, trans. Alberto Toscano (London: Continuum, 2009), 367–80.
10. 'Inaesthetics' is Badiou's term for a proper philosophical reading of artworks. See *Handbook of Inaesthetics*, trans. Alberto Toscano (Stanford: Stanford University Press, 2005). With the already discussed exception of Beckett, no prose writings feature as examples in the book.
11. Alain Badiou, *Being and Event*, trans. Oliver Feltham (London: Continuum, 2005), 191–8.
12. See Alain Badiou, 'Mallarmé's Method: Subtraction and Isolation', in *Conditions*, trans. Steven Corcoran (London: Continuum, 2008), 49–67.
13. Marcel Proust, *Finding Time Again: In Search of Lost Time, Volume 6*, trans. Ian Patterson (London: Penguin Books, 2003), 204.
14. Ibid. 174–82.

15. 'Precisely because reminiscence proceeds from subjective associations to an originating viewpoint, objectivity can no longer exist except in the work of art; it no longer exists in significant content as states of the world, nor in ideal signification as stable essence, but solely in the signifying formal structure of the work, in its style. It is no longer a matter of saying: to create is to remember – but rather, to remember is to create, is *to reach that point where the associative chain breaks, leaps over the constituted individual, is transferred to the birth of an individuating world.*' Deleuze, *Proust and Signs*, 111.
16. Marcel Proust, *The Way by Swann's: In Search of Lost Time, Volume 1*, trans. Lydia Davis (London: Penguin Books, 2003), 9.
17. Ibid. 7.
18. Ibid. 9.
19. Ibid. 9.
20. Badiou, *Logics of Worlds*, 146, 322.
21. Proust, *The Way by Swann's*, 10.
22. Badiou, *Logics of Worlds*, 259, 196.
23. Proust, *The Way by Swann's*, 10.
24. Ibid. 12.
25. Ibid. 9.
26. Ibid. 46.
27. I explore the affects in Proust in my article '"Sans cause": Affect and Truth in Marcel Proust', *Filozofski vestnik* 38, no. 3 (2017): 53–66, https://ojs.zrc-sazu.si/filozofski-vestnik/article/view/6693.
28. Proust, *The Way by Swann's*, 46.
29. Deleuze, *Proust and Signs*, 4–14.
30. Marcel Proust, *Sodom and Gomorrah: In Search of Lost Time, Volume 4*, trans. John Sturrock (London: Penguin Books, 2003), 301.
31. Proust, *The Way by Swann's*, 191.
32. Badiou, *Logics of Worlds*, 193.
33. Marcel Proust, *In the Shadow of Young Girls in Flower: In Search of Lost Time, Volume 2*, trans. James Grieve (London: Penguin Books, 2003), 370–1.
34. The individuation of Albertine from the gang of girls also interested Deleuze and Guattari: 'Albertine is slowly extracted from a group of girls with its own number, organization, code, and hierarchy; and not only is this group or restricted mass suffused by an unconscious, but Albertine has her own multiplicities that the narrator, once he has isolated her, discovers on her body and in her lies—until the end of their love returns her to the indiscernible.' Gilles Deleuze and Félix Guattari, *A Thousand Plateaus: Capitalism and Schizophrenia*, trans. Brian Massumi (Minneapolis: University of Minnesota Press, 1987), 36. Rancière also comments on

this passage from Proust, exploring the split between the level of the plot with individualised characters and their affairs, on the one hand, and the level of writing which captures the gang as an impersonal multiplicity of sensible events, on the other. Jacques Rancière, *Politique de la littérature* (Paris: Galilée, 2007), 75–6.
35. Proust, *The Way by Swann's*, 383.
36. Badiou, *Logics of Worlds*, 300–1.
37. Deleuze, *Proust and Signs*, 11.
38. Proust, *Sodom and Gomorrah*, 5–36.
39. Gérard Genette, 'Métonymie chez Proust', in *Figures III* (Paris: Éditions du Seuil, 1972), 43.
40. Roman Jakobson, 'Two Aspects of Language and Two Types of Aphasic Disturbances', in *On Language*, ed. Linda R. Waugh and Monique Monville-Burston (Cambridge, MA: Harvard University Press, 1990), 115–33.
41. Genette, 'Métonymie chez Proust', 44.
42. Ibid. 49–50.
43. Ibid. 42–4.
44. See Badiou, *Logics of Worlds*, 355–96.
45. Proust, *In the Shadow*, 472.
46. Badiou, *Logics of Worlds*, 363.
47. Ibid. 322.
48. Ibid. 363–80.
49. Marcel Proust, *The Guermantes Way: In Search of Lost Time, Volume 3*, trans. Mark Treharne (London: Penguin Books, 2003), 594–7.
50. Marcel Proust, *The Fugitive*, trans. Peter Collier, in *The Prisoner and The Fugitive: In Search of Lost Time, Volume 5* (London: Penguin Books, 2003), 470.
51. Marcel Proust, *The Prisoner*, trans. Carol Clark, in *The Prisoner and The Fugitive*, 94.
52. Ibid. 88. See also Deleuze's analysis: 'the beloved's gestures, at the very moment they are addressed to us, still express that unknown world that excludes us. The beloved gives us signs of preference; but because these signs are the same as those that express worlds to which we do not belong, each preference by which we profit draws the image of the *possible world* in which others might be or are preferred.' Deleuze, *Proust and Signs*, 6.
53. Badiou, *Logics of Worlds*, 371–6.
54. Malcolm Bowie, *Freud, Proust and Lacan: Theory as Fiction* (Cambridge: Cambridge University Press, 1988), 55.
55. Proust, *The Prisoner*, 362.
56. Proust, *The Way by Swann's*, 179.
57. Ibid. 47.
58. Ibid. 47–8.
59. Ibid. 46.

60. Ibid. 47.
61. Ibid. 50.
62. Ibid. 48.
63. Ibid. 48.
64. Proust, *Finding Time Again*, 178.
65. Ibid. 180.
66. Badiou, *Being and Event*, 207, 211.
67. Genette, 'Métonymie chez Proust', 57–8.
68. Ibid. 63.
69. Proust, *Finding Time Again*, 183, 179.
70. Badiou, *Logics of Worlds*, 507–14.
71. Proust, *Finding Time Again*, 181.
72. Ibid. 186.
73. Pierre Macherey, *Proust entre littérature et philosophie* (Paris: Éditions Amsterdam, 2013), 191.
74. Hallward, *Badiou: A Subject to Truth*, 203–5.
75. Macherey, *Proust*, 195.
76. Gérard Genette, 'Proust et le langage indirect', in *Figures II* (Paris: Éditions du Seuil, 1969), 266.
77. 'During the train journey, when I eventually did return to Paris, the thought of my lack of literary talent, which, as I believed, I had discovered long ago on the Guermantes way [. . .] and which I had almost identified, the night before I left that house, as I read those pages of the Goncourts' journal, with the pointlessness and falsity of literature, this thought, perhaps less painful now but more dismaying than ever, its subject being not an infirmity peculiar to myself alone, but the non-existence of the ideal in which I had for so long believed, this thought which for so long had not troubled my mind, struck me once again with a more lamentable force than ever.' Proust, *Finding Time Again*, 162–3.
78. Hallward, *Badiou: A Subject to Truth*, 205.
79. Proust, *Finding Time Again*, 198.
80. Marcel Proust, 'About Flaubert's Style', in *A Selection from his Miscellaneous Writings*, ed. and trans. Gerard Hopkins (London: Allan Wingate, 1948), 231.
81. Ibid. 224.
82. Macherey, *Proust*, 134. We should also recall here Deleuze's distinction (to which I referred in Chapter 5) between the limits of possible experience defined by Kant and the real experience beyond such limits made possible by art. Gilles Deleuze, *Difference and Repetition*, trans. Paul Patton (London: Continuum, 2001), 68–9.
83. Proust, *In the Shadow*, 414.
84. Ibid. 415.

85. Proust, *The Prisoner*, 236–7.
86. Yet, this was not the impression that some contemporary critics had before the final volumes were published. For some, the novel's construction seemed far too chaotic to be able to lead to any kind of proper conclusion. See Malcolm Bowie, *Proust Among the Stars* (New York: Columbia University Press, 1998), 189.
87. Alain Badiou, *Manifesto for Philosophy*, trans. Norman Madarasz (Albany: State University of New York Press, 1999), 106–7.
88. The need to surpass this dichotomy was suggested by Martin Hägglund. His 'counter-reading of the aesthetic-philosophical program' emphasises the temporal dimension of the supposedly trans-temporal regaining of time. See *Dying for Time: Proust, Woolf, Nabokov* (Cambridge, MA: Harvard University Press, 2012), 52. This differs from my own approach, which sees the Proustian trans-worldly regaining of time as a development of a singular world based on an encounter with a monadic object.

Conclusion: The Multiplicity of Worlds and Inter-Worldly Phenomena

ON A TRAJECTORY SPANNING from Leibniz to contemporary philosophers, particularly Gilles Deleuze, Alain Badiou and Jacques Rancière, I have presented in the preceding chapters a rethinking of the concept of world through the lens of transcendental multiplicity. This approach, which I propose to designate as hypercorrelationism, refuses to reduce the concept of world to an obsolete metaphysical notion of totality. Also casting aside the phenomenological ideal of worldliness as a horizon of meaningful experience, I examined worlds as divergent transcendental structures that frame the appearance of ontological multiplicity. I have argued that the modern destruction of the cosmos does not result in the loss of world or its obsoleteness as a concept, but in its irreversible and irreducible multiplication.

I have proposed to think of worlds as both actual and fictional. Actual, because other worlds are not to be sought in the spatial, temporal or hypothetical distance, but are everywhere around us, here and now. Fictional, not because they would be imaginary, but due to their structure as fragmentary framings of ontological multiplicity, which set the parameters of what can appear within a particular transcendental framework. As both actual and fictional, worlds can be analysed in political and aesthetical terms, as I have done in the second half of the book. Political, because the divergent coexistence of worlds leads to conflicts between them. Aesthetical, because transcendental multiplicity reconfigures the coordinates of sensible experience.

I offer below a set of concluding remarks on some of the questions that might arise from the hypercorrelationist hypothesis. If the multiplicity of worlds is irreducible to any one universe, what connects these worlds in their multiplicity and guarantees contact between them? If worlds as transcendental frameworks are fictional, in what sense can anything real or objective be encountered within them? In what way does the social totality established by the world system of global capitalism limit, frame or produce the perception that we are living in multiple worlds? I conclude by arguing that the multiplicity of actual worlds is experienced at points of juncture between worlds (a conflict of worlds; interference between worlds) through encounters with inter-worldly phenomena, that is, objects defined by their divergent and incompossible coexistence in multiple worlds (contested and monadic objects).

*

If no all-encompassing world can be established, what prevents worlds from drifting apart from each other in total seclusion? Does the multiplicity of worlds not entail total dispersion? As I have stated several times in the book, the transcendental multiplicity of worlds should be understood through its interplay with ontological multiplicity. What connects different worlds together are the ontological multiples they share. A transcendental shapes ontological multiples into an object within a particular world, but this does not mean that the same ontological multiples do not form objects in other worlds as well. This is one of the aspects in which the assertion that there is an excess of being over any world can be understood. Different transcendental frameworks are thus grounded in being, which connects worlds and makes the objects that appear within them real. The fictional structure of the frameworks does not mean that the reality of objects they give rise to can be avoided. The transcendentalist perspective developed here is not an anti-realist position in any strong sense.

Ontological multiplicity, however, should not be considered as the ultimate totality that unites different worlds. In the ontologies we have looked closely at in the previous chapters, no such ontological totality exists and therefore it cannot constitute a universal world of all worlds. The sharing of ontological multiplicity among different transcendental frameworks is always partial. An ontological multiple may coexist in many different worlds, but might never have any relation to an infinity of others. Badiou's thesis that worlds are local and partial appearances of ontological multiplicity should also be applied to interactions between worlds: such interactions are always local and partial. Multiple worlds can thus be said to be divergent and overlapping at the same time. Divergent, since they form separate spheres, defined by their transcendental frameworks. Overlapping, because several worlds can involve the same ontological multiples that are then shaped into objects according to a different transcendental framework within each of these worlds.

Such ontological multiples can coexist within several worlds indifferently, but can also cause conflicts or interferences between them. A tree in a forest, for example, can exist in many different worlds, such as the worlds of the many animals that inhabit it, the world of a hiker and the world of a forester, even though its objective reality is not quite the same in each of these worlds. However, obviously, if a forester takes the tree down, this impacts all the other worlds in which the tree existed. In this respect, worlds can have a stronger or weaker impact on their objects as well as on other worlds with which they share ontological multiples. The problem thus shifts from the excess of being over worlds to the excess of worlds over being. Instead of total dispersion, the prose of worlds reveals locally connected worlds around inter-worldly phenomena. Yet, there is no ultimate world that would frame them all.

*

How, then, is the hypothesis of transcendental multiplicity to be understood in the face of global capitalism? Is capitalism not precisely the system that frames the social totality as the world of all worlds? From this perspective, the multiplicity of worlds itself could be seen merely as an effect of the excessive nature of capitalism itself and thus as a distraction from looking for new representations of the social totality constructed by capitalism. What use is the theory of multiple worlds, if capital as the one thing that most determines our lives is both global and worldless? This question demands a political perspective on the concept of world. In Chapter 4, we saw how Hannah Arendt and Jean-Luc Nancy oppose the worldlessness of globalist totalisation to a reaffirmation of a plural worldliness. In this sense, the multiplicity of worlds does not amount to total dispersion but constitutes a harmonic plurality through political action. For some, however, even plurality cannot redeem the concept of world for contemporary political use. The problem, it is claimed, is that global capitalism does not rob us of the sense of worldliness, but is – on the contrary – precisely what drives the proliferation of worlds and our desire for it. According to Roland Végső,

> it is no longer self-evident that the phenomenological critique of worldlessness still applies in a post-Fordist age, when neoliberal finance capital appears to run on the very values of phenomenological world-formation: it presents constantly renewed risk and uncertainty as the projections of authentic possibilities of subjective self-creation and world-construction.[1]

Instead of depriving us of the world, late capitalism produces 'an excess of worlds' and the 'extreme fantasy [...] that every individual will become the sovereign creator of their own private world'.[2] According to Végső, therefore, capitalism is at once worldless and world-producing. To be fair, Nancy already admits that the plurality of worldliness is alienated – and perhaps even originally produced as alienated – by capitalism. Still, while Nancy believes that the plurality of worlds can be reappropriated in a meaningful way, Végső draws the conclusion that the only way to counter capitalist worldlessness is by also countering its excessive production of worlds. What we should be striving for is not a renewal of worldliness, but 'the invention of new forms of worldlessness'.[3]

The absence of a satisfactory analysis of capitalism has also been one of the primary objections commentators have raised to Badiou's theory of worlds. In an early commentary, Alberto Toscano attempted to correct this perceived lack and suggested a conception of globalised capitalism as 'a *world-less transcendental*', that is,

> a kind of transcendental regime devoid of totalisation, [...] not a world, in Badiou's technical vocabulary, [...] but rather an operational principle which, whilst abstractly identifiable, resists localisation, relentlessly generating and exploiting worlds (worlds of labour, intellect, culture, matter, and so on).[4]

Toscano's assertion here is close to Végső's. From this perspective, the worldlessness imposed by capitalism is nothing but an appropriation of plural worldliness. In their eyes, capitalism is a worldless machine that produces worlds for consumption and exploitation. Contrary to Badiou, who (as we saw in Chapter 1) bemoans the contemporary lack of a clearly defined world that would ascribe a set of political names and therefore establish the basic orientation for political struggles, both Toscano and Végső are sceptical that striving for a 'world' can reignite emancipatory politics in the face of the world-producing capitalist machine.[5]

The problem of worldlessness, however, goes even deeper than lacking a shared horizon of meaningful experience or a common set of political names. Although capitalism is 'global, encompassing all worlds', as Slavoj Žižek neatly summarises, 'it sustains a *stricto sensu* "worldless" ideological constellation, depriving the great majority of people of any meaningful "cognitive mapping"'.[6] In this sense, worldlessness implies a profound sense of disorientation.[7] The conception of capitalism as a problem for our capacities of cognitive mapping was developed by Fredric Jameson, for whom the social totality constructed by capitalism is overwhelming for our transcendental and representative frameworks: capitalism forms 'a system so vast that it cannot be encompassed by the natural and historically developed categories of perception with which human beings normally orient themselves'.[8] From this perspective, global capitalism cannot be said to form a fictionally structured world not because it is too objective, but because it is not clearly and distinctly imaginable (which was one of Leibniz's conditions for imagining other possible worlds). What makes capital an aesthetic problem is precisely that it does not constitute a representable totality that we could call a world. As Toscano and Jeff Kinkle claim, what is at stake in the issue of the cognitive mapping of capitalism 'is the figurability or representability of our present and its shaping effect on political action'.[9] What we thus lack today is not a common world, but clear and politically useful representations of social totality. The presupposition here is that clearer forms of capital's presence in the collective imaginary would lead the way to a stronger struggle against it.

Such discussions on the worldless and world-producing character of capitalism, I argue, use the concept of world in an essentially phenomenological way as a horizon of meaningful (authentic or ideologically produced) experience that provides a sense of belonging and orientation for the people who share it. This is the world that capitalism destroys and replaces with an excess of non-authentic simulacra. If the multiple-world perspective can provide something other than this diagnosis, it is on the basis of switching to a different understanding of what a world is altogether.

From a hypercorrelationist perspective, capitalism might actually constitute a world. In a recent article, Nick Nesbitt provides a fresh reading of Badiou's concept of world in relation to capitalism. Nesbitt first highlights the complete absence of any consideration of capitalism in *Logics of Worlds*, which he finds perplexing given the magnitude of its influence on the global social world(s) today. Yet, instead of stopping at his shortcomings, Nesbitt claims that Badiou's objective phenomenology can be read as an advanced formalisation of Marx's logical procedure in *Capital*:

> while it is true that *Logics of Worlds* never discusses the logic of appearance that governs all *capitalist* things (i.e., commodities), we should nonetheless read *Logics* in a quite specific sense as the (objective, likely unintentional) abstract translation and formalization of Marx's *Capital*. In this view, *Capital* should quite simply be read as the systematic demonstration of the logic of what Marx calls the *capitalist social form*, which is to say in Badiou's jargon, as the logic of the appearance of things in the *capitalist world*.[10]

While I cannot go here into the details of Nesbitt's precise and insightful elaboration of this thesis, one general observation stands out: capitalism can indeed be considered as forming a world with its own specific logic. As soon as the phenomenological perspective on the concept of world as providing a horizon of meaningful experience, centred around the Dasein, is put aside and the novelty of the transcendentalist approach is taken up in all of its implications, there is no longer any need to regard capitalism as worldless. It constitutes a particular world with an identifiable transcendental, which indeed has the power to subordinate most of the worlds relevant to the existence of humans and the natural environment of our planet.

The problem of climate change and the discourse on the Anthropocene comes into view here as another kind of totalisation that seems to demand the abandonment of the apparently all-too-human concept of world. From the perspective I am developing here, however, the Anthropocene amounts to the fact that the transcendentals of human worlds have a major impact on natural processes through the way nature is perceived and acted upon within these frameworks. In this sense, the Anthropocene names a specific singularisation of the world in which the planet itself becomes an object moulded by such transcendentals. My wager here is that instead of abandoning the concept of world in order to situate politics within a social or natural totality, we have to grasp politics through the junctures between worlds and their dissensual bifurcation.[11]

If the transcendental specific to capitalism (or, for that matter, the Anthropocene) falls outside the ordinary frameworks of experience and representation, this is precisely what the notion of transcendental multiplicity developed in this book tries to capture. The challenge capitalism poses to the aesthetic coordinates of everyday imagination is part of the wider challenge of the historisation and multiplication of the supposedly *a priori* transcendental frameworks. The problem, I argue, is not how to represent capital as the structuring principle of the social totality, the problem is how to capture the junctures at which the world of capitalism crosses or interrupts other worlds. Despite the difficulty of forming a clear picture of the global social reality, local encounters with contested objects, through which the capitalist transcendental cuts across worlds of labour, culture, nature and so on, are proliferating. In a realm of multiple worlds, cognitive mapping would thus constitute a mapping of local conflicts and interferences between worlds. Following Rancière, we could say the crucial political problem is not one of inventing new forms of representation, which would supposedly lead to an increase in political action, but one of redistributing subjective capacities for both perception and action, which, in turn, produce new mappings and representations. This is to say that capitalism can only be counteracted from the position of intervals and interruptions between such worlds and not from the position of a world picture that represents capitalism as the ultimate real world in which human existence takes place.

Apart from the problem of representation, the problematic nature of capital in relation to the experience of worldliness thus also impacts the internal structures of emancipatory politics itself. If political emancipation is thought of as an excess rising against a stable system, what to do when we are up against a system that, in Žižek's words, 'no longer excludes the excess, but directly posits it as its driving force'?[12] In other words, if capitalism constitutes no stable symbolic order, it is because there is no symbolic Other at its centre, either as the addressee of political demands or as the target of a political subject's subversion. Drawing from Jacques Lacan, Jelica Šumič describes the non-world of capitalism in which the Other no longer exists as 'a universe without a beyond, an infinite or not-all universe' in which emancipatory politics – aimed at subverting a limit, imposed by the Other – finds itself at a deadlock.[13] The question, then, is how emancipatory politics can orient itself today, considering that capitalism offers no stable symbolic limit to transgress.

This constitutes a problem for emancipatory politics only if it is defined in an intra-worldly manner, as we have seen is the case with Badiou's truth procedures. If truth is defined by a break with the transcendental of a world, how can it possibly occur in a world not defined by a clear limit? As I have tried to show, however, the capitalist social reality in which the Other does not exist can also be presented as one of a diverging and overlapping multiplicity of worlds. From this perspective, the inherent excess of a 'not-all' universe can be understood not as a sign of worldlessness, but as an excess of proliferating worlds. Either way, the task of emancipatory politics, as Šumič proposes, is to reinvent its trajectory as one moving from the 'not-all' to the 'for all'.[14] From the perspective developed here, this would translate to the trajectory from an indifferent multiplicity of worlds to the emergence of a new world with a particular universalist transcendental.

Discussing Badiou, I have insisted that his definition of a truth procedure as intra-worldly and trans-worldly comes up short, since it skips the inter-worldly dimension, which alone can inscribe truth into the realm of a multiplicity of worlds. Such procedures should rather be defined as emerging from the junctures and discontinuities between worlds. This inter-worldly dimension is what defines a truth procedure's singularity. Its universalism, on the other hand, is never trans-worldly in a general sense. From the beginning, the new transcendental developed within the truth procedure is faced with a number of other worlds with which it shares ontological multiples. Some of these worlds may be indifferent or even hostile to its existence. Its growth is dependent on how it will engage with other worlds, which can be a question of force, but also of expansion by connectivity.

The practice of constructing new transcendentals and striving for their expansion in a way that bends the arrangement of other worlds around it no longer has anything to do with the phenomenological ideal of worldliness. Its aim is not to provide a meaningful sense of coexistence (which exclusive, anti-universalist worlds can also provide) but to redistribute subjective capacities and, through this, dissensually reframe the coordinates of experience and understanding. Following Rancière, I discussed such world-building principles in the conclusion of Chapter 4. On the one hand, the political subject establishes a world of its own by way of connecting equals in a collective effort in which any issue takes the role of the whole, immediately enacting the principles it strives for in its practice. On the other hand, this transcendental is dissensually projected beyond itself as an alternative framing of the common world.

Badiou's principal political example of changing the world in *Logics of Worlds* is the Paris Commune. Badiou defines the event of this political sequence as the historic appearance of workers as beings with political capacity.[15] Even though the Commune as a truth procedure did not manage to completely subvert the world in which the workers' political capacity is subdued, it did manage to create a reference and inspiration for the subsequent workers' struggle and thereby a blueprint of another world in which political capacity in general would be radically transformed. Badiou quotes a line from the Internationale, '*Le monde va changer de base*' (the world will change its foundations), as a suggestion that the transcendental of the world is what is at stake.[16] The Commune can also be seen from an inter-worldly perspective as the emergence of a new, supplementary world on a background of a multiplicity of overlapping worlds in conflict ranging from the Franco-Prussian War to the internal social and political tensions in France, and in particular Paris, at the time. The emergence of the Commune as a surplus world completely rearranged the relations among pre-existing worlds. Its transcendental was developed in a truly universalist spirit through the split in the distribution of social identities introduced by the new collective political subject. As a 'Universal Republic', Kristin Ross explains, the Commune saw itself as a singular universality, 'an autonomous collective in a universal federation of peoples', to which anyone could belong.[17] Its transcendental was constructed through introductions of all kinds of social and political measures, which connected to and transformed a variety of other worlds within which the Communards coexisted. The internal forming of the Commune's transcendental is thus not a matter of closure but of its power to connect to other worlds and transform them. The new transcendental is also faced with other worlds externally, in a conflictual manner, as testified by the brutal suppression of the Commune. The question of the new world's relation to other worlds is thus a question of both (internal) connectivity and (external) force. Emancipatory politics thus depends on a bifurcation of worlds, the forging of new dissensual transcendentals and their expansion.

*

The bifurcation of worlds coincides with the occurrence of incompossibilities, which disturb the indifferent coexistence of worlds. In general, multiples form objects belonging to multiple worlds at once all the time, without this fact interfering with their existence in any one of them. At certain points, however, the existence of these multiples within one world becomes incompossible with their existence in another, triggering a conflict of worlds. As we have learned from Rancière, a factory on strike or an occupied square, for example, becomes an object that exists in two worlds at once, not indifferently, but through a political dissensus regarding the delimitations between the public and the private, between political capacity and incapacity. The factory or the square does not constitute the same object in different worlds – say, the worlds of factory owners or real-estate developers, the worlds of workers or city dwellers – even though they are the same ontologically. I propose to call contested objects the objects that share ontological multiples that can no longer indifferently coexist in a certain number of worlds. Their existence in one world contradicts their existence in another following the emergence of a dissensus in which a political subject provokes a bifurcation of worlds around those objects.

Contested objects are a sign of both a proliferation and a reduction of worlds. With the occurrence of contested objects, the surplus of worlds, which is otherwise not necessarily noticed by the inhabitants of separate worlds that share the same ontological multiples, becomes apparent. Suddenly, incompossible worlds start to proliferate around the object. Yet, this also reduces the multiplicity of worlds, since the further existence of the object in one world demands its non-existence in another, which means that one world may seek to dominate or eliminate another. Such objects are not sufficiently explained by the gap between being and appearance, since they are dependent on the way different worlds shape ontological multiples into specific objects.

They do not merely mark the presence of inconsistent being within a world, but also a conflict of worlds. The surplus of worlds, which otherwise coexists indifferently and abstractly, is thus objectivised.

*

The conflict of worlds involving contested objects is not the only form of objectivation that the multiplicity of worlds can take. Another type of objectivity caught between worlds corresponds to interference between worlds, that is, the appearance of one world within another. In the last two chapters of the book, I proposed to call monadic the objects that appear within one world but carry within them the inscription of another transcendental. The monadic object appears as windowless – in the sense of being foreign to the world we encounter it in. On the other hand, it seems to contain a harmony of another world, a transcendental that is there in partial or condensed form, which requires a subject's effort to be unfolded or developed. Paradoxically, the windowless monad itself appears as a window upon another world.

Throughout the book, I have avoided references to science fiction (apart from evoking sci-fi elements in Proust), since I wanted to present multiple worlds not as parallel realities in some other, imagined time or space, but as an actual divergent multiplicity of the here and now. I will nevertheless conclude with one that, in my view, provides a vivid demonstration of how a monadic object bifurcates worlds.

In Denis Villeneuve's 2016 film *Arrival*, based on a novella by Ted Chiang,[18] twelve alien spaceships descend upon the earth. Throughout the film, the expectation that the extraterrestrials' arrival will culminate in an invasion, following the well-worn scenario of a war of worlds, provides the tension on the background of which a different kind of story unfolds. Slowly, we begin to realise that the film stages not the cosmic collision of two separate worlds, but two different transcendental framings of the same ontological reality.

The aliens do not leave the ship and their intentions are unknown. Their spaceships constitute a visual enigma, standing still in the air, seemingly violating the basic laws of physics. The vertical oval monolithic structure of the vessels resembles a kind of modernist sculpture and displays no visible doors or windows. It could thus be seen as a monad in the Adornian sense, an alien object, separated from the world. Yet, contact is established and Dr Louise Banks (played by

Amy Adams), a professor of linguistics, enters one of the alien vessels through a hidden opening in an attempt to translate the extraterrestrial language. Within the windowless monad, a window is found, as behind a glass-like screen, the aliens appear. After attempts to understand their spoken language fail, Banks makes the breakthrough by analysing their writing. The circle-shaped logograms list words in a non-linear way. As Banks begins to understand the writing, she begins to have unfamiliar recollections of time spent with her daughter – a daughter she does not actually have. Along with Banks, we slowly realise that the images she is seeing are memories from her own future.

Arrival thus presents an image of transcendental reframing through a subjectivised encounter with a monadic object. The alien language Banks acquires through writing completely subverts – for her, at first, but also for others as she shares her experience – the coordinates of possible experience. It brings with it not only another perception of time, but a complete transformation of the transcendental arrangement of reality. Despite her not leaving the planet, it allows her to inhabit a different world. The monad turns into a window that reframes ontological multiplicity.

Notes

1. Roland Végső, *Worldlessness After Heidegger: Phenomenology, Psychoanalysis, Deconstruction* (Edinburgh: Edinburgh University Press, 2020), 9.
2. Ibid. 299.
3. Ibid. 20.
4. Alberto Toscano, 'From the State to the World: Badiou and Anti-Capitalism', *Communication & Cognition* 37, nos. 3–4 (2004): 199–224.
5. Ibid.; Végső, *Worldlessness After Heidegger*, 288.
6. Slavoj Žižek, *The Parallax View* (Cambridge, MA: MIT Press, 2006), 318.
7. Ruth Ronen, drawing from Nancy and Lacan, proposes an interesting view on contemporary disorientation among multiple worlds as the inability to contingently actualise possible worlds. When the ability to actualise worlds is lost, all possibilities acquire equal weight, which allows everyone to inhabit a world of their own choosing, leading to the collapse of commonly shared truths. Ruth Ronen, 'The Actuality of a World: What Ceases Not to Be Written', in 'The Concept of World in Contemporary Philosophy', ed. Rok Benčin, special issue, *Filozofski Vestnik* 42, no. 2 (2021): 93–112, https://doi.org/10.3986/fv.42.2.05.
8. Fredric Jameson, *The Geopolitical Aesthetic: Cinema and Space in the World System* (Bloomington: Indiana University Press, 1995), 2.

9. Alberto Toscano and Jeff Kinkle, *Cartographies of the Absolute* (Winchester: Zero Books, 2015), 15.
10. Nick Nesbitt, 'Capital, Logic of the World', *Filozofski Vestnik* 42, no. 2 (2021): 162, https://doi.org/10.3986/fv.42.2.08.
11. I leave for another occasion a more detailed discussion of these issues. The question remains how this view compares to the positions that understand the Anthropocene from the perspective of the end (as the ultimate loss) of the world and the necessity to shift our ethical and political commitments from world to the earth (which makes the concept of world more or less obsolete). From these other perspectives, the multiplicity of worlds nevertheless again comes to the fore, as the multiplicity of worlds that are either ending (and thus the multiplicity of these ends themselves) or share the same earth that provides them with an unstable unity. See in particular Kelly Oliver, *Earth and World: Philosophy after the Apollo Missions* (New York: Columbia University Press, 2015); Déborah Danowski and Eduardo Viveiros de Castro, *The Ends of the World*, trans. Rodrigo Guimaraes Nunes (Cambridge: Polity Press, 2017); and Pablo Servigne, Raphaël Stevens and Gauthier Chapelle, *Another End of the World Is Possible: Living the Collapse (and Not Merely Surviving It)*, trans. Geoffrey Samuel (Cambridge: Polity Press, 2021).
12. Žižek, *The Parallax View*, 318.
13. Jelica Šumič, 'Politics and Psychoanalysis in the Times of the Inexistent Other', in *Jacques Lacan between Psychoanalysis and Politics*, ed. Samo Tomšič and Andreja Zevnik (London: Routledge, 2016), 30.
14. Ibid. 30.
15. Alain Badiou, *Logics of Worlds: Being and Event, 2*, trans. Alberto Toscano (London: Continuum, 2009), 365.
16. Ibid. 380.
17. Kristin Ross, *Communal Luxury: The Political Imaginary of the Paris Commune* (London: Verso, 2015), 23. See the whole of chapter 1 of Ross's book for a discussion on the universalist dimension of the Commune.
18. Ted Chiang, 'Story of Your Life', in *Stories of Your Life and Others* (London: Picador, 2015), 109–72.

Bibliography

Adorno, Theodor W. *Aesthetic Theory*. Translated by Robert Hullot-Kentor. London: Continuum, 1997.

Adorno, Theodor W. 'Extorted Reconciliation: On Georg Lukács' Realism in Our Time.' In *Notes to Literature, Vol. 1*, 216–40.

Adorno, Theodor W. *Negative Dialectics*. Translated by E. B. Ashton. London: Routledge, 1973.

Adorno, Theodor W. *Notes to Literature, Vol. 1*. Translated by Shierry Weber Nicholsen. New York: Columbia University Press, 1991.

Adorno, Theodor W. 'Short Commentaries on Proust.' In *Notes to Literature, Vol. 1*, 174–84.

Alberti, Leon Battista. *On Painting*. Translated by Rocco Sinisgalli. Cambridge: Cambridge University Press, 2011.

Appiah, Kwame Anthony. *The Ethics of Identity*. Princeton: Princeton University Press, 2005.

Arendt, Hannah. *The Human Condition*. Chicago: University of Chicago Press, 1958.

Arendt, Hannah. *The Origins of Totalitarianism*. San Diego: Harcourt Brace & Co., 1979.

Arthur, Richard. 'Infinite Number and the World Soul; in Defence of Carlin and Leibniz.' *Leibniz Society Review* 9 (1999): 105–16.

Arthur, Richard T. W. 'Leibniz's Actual Infinite in Relation to his Analysis of Matter.' In *G. W. Leibniz, Interrelations between Mathematics and Philosophy*, edited by Norma B. Goethe, Philip Beeley and David Rabouin, 137–56. Dordrecht: Springer, 2015. https://doi.org/10.1007/978-94-017-9664-4_7

Badiou, Alain. *The Adventure of French Philosophy*. Edited and translated by Bruno Bosteels. London: Verso, 2012.

Badiou, Alain. *Being and Event*. Translated by Oliver Feltham. London: Continuum, 2005.

Badiou, Alain. 'The Caesura of Nihilism.' In *The Adventure of French Philosophy*, 53–66.

Badiou, Alain. *Conditions*. Translated by Steven Corcoran. London: Continuum, 2008.

Badiou, Alain. *Deleuze: The Clamor of Being*. Translated by Louise Burchill. Minneapolis: University of Minnesota Press, 2000.

Badiou, Alain. 'Gilles Deleuze, *The Fold: Leibniz and the Baroque*.' In *The Adventure of French Philosophy*, 241–67.

Badiou, Alain. *Handbook of Inaesthetics*. Translated by Alberto Toscano. Stanford: Stanford University Press, 2005.

Badiou, Alain. *The Immanence of Truths: Being and Event III*. Translated by Susan Spitzer and Kenneth Reinhard. London: Bloomsbury, 2022.

Badiou, Alain. *Logics of Worlds: Being and Event, 2*. Translated by Alberto Toscano. London: Continuum, 2009.

Badiou, Alain. *Logiques des mondes. L'être et l'événement 2*. Paris: Seuil, 2006.

Badiou, Alain. 'Logology Against Ontology.' In *The Adventure of French Philosophy*, 309–20.

Badiou, Alain. 'Mallarmé's Method: Subtraction and Isolation.' In *Conditions*, 49–67.

Badiou, Alain. *Manifesto for Philosophy*. Translated by Norman Madarasz. Albany: State University of New York Press, 1999.

Badiou, Alain. *Mathematics of the Transcendental*. Translated by A. J. Bartlett and Alex Ling. London: Bloomsbury, 2014.

Badiou, Alain. *The Meaning of Sarkozy*. Translated by David Fernbach. London: Verso, 2008.

Badiou, Alain. *Saint Paul: The Foundation of Universalism*. Translated by Ray Brassier. Stanford: Stanford University Press, 2003.

Badiou, Alain, and Nicolas Truong. *In Praise of Love*. Translated by Peter Bush. London: Serpent's Tail, 2012.

Balibar, Étienne. 'Cosmopolitisme et internationalisme: deux modèles, deux héritages.' In *Philosophie politique et horizon cosmopolitique*, edited by Moufida Goucha, 37–64. Paris: UNESCO, 2006.

Barthes, Roland. 'The Reality Effect.' In *The Rustle of Language*, 141–8. Translated by Richard Howard. Berkeley: University of California Press, 1989.

Beck, Ulrich. 'Cosmopolitanism as Imagined Communities of Global Risk.' *American Behavioral Scientist* 55, no. 10 (2011): 1,346–61. https://doi.org/10.1177/0002764211409739

Benčin, Rok, ed. 'The Concept of World in Contemporary Philosophy.' Special issue, *Filozofski vestnik* 42, no. 2 (2021). https://ojs.zrc-sazu.si/filozofski-vestnik/issue/view/849

Benčin, Rok. 'Rethinking Representation in Ontology and Aesthetics via Badiou and Rancière.' *Theory, Culture & Society* 36, no. 5 (2019): 95–112. https://doi.org/10.1177/0263276418806573

Benčin, Rok. '"Sans cause": Affect and Truth in Marcel Proust.' *Filozofski vestnik* 38, no. 3 (2017): 53–66. https://ojs.zrc-sazu.si/filozofski-vestnik/article/view/6693

Benjamin, Walter. *The Origin of German Tragic Drama*. Translated by John Osborne. London: Verso, 1998.

Benjamin, Walter. 'Theses on the Philosophy of History.' In *Illuminations*, 253–64. Edited by Hannah Arendt. Translated by Harry Zohn. New York: Schocken Books, 1969.

Besana, Bruno. 'Fictioning Disagreement: The Construction of Separation in the Work of Jacques Rancière.' *Maska* 32, nos. 185–6 (2017): 74–85. https://doi.org/10.1386/maska.32.185-186.64_1

Bhabha, Homi K. 'Unsatisfied: Notes on Vernacular Cosmopolitanism.' In *Text and Nation: Cross-Disciplinary Essays on Cultural and National Identities*, edited by Laura Garcia-Morena and Peter C. Pfeifer, 191–207. London: Camden House, 1996.

Bhambra, Gurminder K. 'Whither Europe? Postcolonial versus Neocolonial Cosmopolitanism.' *Interventions: International Journal of Postcolonial Studies* 18, no. 2 (2016): 187–202. https://doi.org/10.1080/1369801X.2015.1106964

Birnbaum, Antonia. *Égalité radicale. Diviser Rancière*. Paris: Amsterdam, 2018.

Birnbaum, Antonia. *Trajectoires obliques*. Paris: Sens & Tonka, 2013.

Borges, Jorge Luis. 'The Garden of Forking Paths.' In *Labyrinths: Selected Stories and Other Writings*, 34–42. Edited by Donald A. Yates and James E. Irby. New York: New Directions Publishing, 1962.

Bowie, Malcolm. *Freud, Proust and Lacan: Theory as Fiction*. Cambridge: Cambridge University Press, 1988.

Bowie, Malcolm. *Proust Among the Stars*. New York: Columbia University Press, 1998.

Braidotti, Rosi, Patrick Hanafin and Bolette Blaagaard, eds. *After Cosmopolitanism*. Abingdon: Routledge, 2013.

Bryant, Levi R. *The Democracy of Objects*. Ann Arbor: Open Humanities Press, 2011.

Carlin, Laurence. 'Infinite Accumulations and Pantheistic Implications: Leibniz and the *Anima Mundi*.' *Leibniz Society Review* 7 (1997): 1–24.

Celan, Paul. *Atemwende*. Frankfurt: Suhrkamp, 1967.

Celan, Paul. *Poems of Paul Celan*. Translated by Michael Hamburger. New York: Persea Books, 1988.

Cheah, Pheng. 'Cosmopolitanism.' *Theory, Culture & Society* 23, nos. 2–3 (2006): 486–96. https://doi.org/10.1177/026327640602300290

Chiang, Ted. 'Story of Your Life.' In *Stories of Your Life and Others*, 109–72. London: Picador, 2015.

Clavier, Paul. *Le concept du monde*. Paris: PUF, 2000.

Crockett, Clayton. *Deleuze Beyond Badiou: Ontology, Multiplicity, and Event*. New York: Columbia University Press, 2013.

Danowski, Déborah, and Eduardo Viveiros de Castro. *The Ends of the World*. Translated by Rodrigo Guimaraes Nunes. Cambridge: Polity Press, 2017.

Deleuze, Gilles. *Cinema 2: The Time-Image*. Translated by Hugh Tomlinson and Robert Galeta. Minneapolis: University of Minnesota Press, 1989.

Deleuze, Gilles. *Difference and Repetition*. Translated by Paul Patton. London: Continuum, 2001.

Deleuze, Gilles. *Essays Critical and Clinical*. Translated by Daniel W. Smith and Michael A. Greco. Minneapolis: University of Minnesota Press, 1997.

Deleuze, Gilles. *The Fold: Leibniz and the Baroque*. Translated by Tom Colney. London: Athlone Press, 1993.

Deleuze, Gilles. *The Logic of Sense*. Translated by Mark Lester and Charles Stivale. London: Athlone Press, 1990.

Deleuze, Gilles. *Proust and Signs*. Translated by Richard Howard. Minneapolis: University of Minnesota Press, 2000.

Deleuze, Gilles, and Félix Guattari. *A Thousand Plateaus: Capitalism and Schizophrenia*. Translated by Brian Massumi. Minneapolis: University of Minnesota Press, 1987.

Deleuze, Gilles, and Félix Guattari. *What Is Philosophy?* Translated by Hugh Tomlinson and Graham Burchell. New York: Columbia University Press, 1996.

Deranty, Jean-Philippe, and Emmanuel Renault. 'Democratic Agon: Striving for Distinction or Struggle against Domination and Injustice?' In *Law and Agonistic Politics*, edited by Andrew Schaap, 43–56. Farnham: Ashgate, 2009.

Derrida, Jacques. *The Beast and the Sovereign, Volume II*. Translated by Geoffrey Bennington. Chicago: University of Chicago Press, 2011.

Derrida, Jacques. 'Rams: Uninterrupted Dialogue – Between Two Infinities, the Poem.' In *Sovereignties in Question: The Poetics of Paul Celan*, 35–163. Edited by Thomas Dutoit and Outi Pasanen. New York: Fordham University Press, 2005.

Dick, Steven J. *Plurality of Worlds: The Origins of the Extraterrestrial Life Debate from Democritus to Kant*. Cambridge: Cambridge University Press, 1982.

Divers, John. *Possible Worlds*. London: Routledge, 2002.

Douzinas, Costas. 'The Metaphysics of Cosmopolitanism.' In *After Cosmopolitanism*, edited by Braidotti, Hanafin and Blaagaard, 57–76.

Fischbach, Frank. *Sans objet. Capitalisme, subjectivité, aliénation*. Paris: Vrin, 2009.

Flaubert, Gustave. *The Letters of Gustave Flaubert: 1830–1857*. Edited and translated by Francis Steegmuller. Cambridge, MA: Belknap Press, 1980.

Foucault, Michel. *The Government of Self and Others: Lectures at the Collège de France 1982–1983*. Translated by Graham Burchell. New York: Palgrave Macmillan, 2010.

Freud, Sigmund. *New Introductory Lectures on Psycho-Analysis and Other Works*. Translated by James Strachey. In *The Standard Edition of the Complete Psychological Works of Sigmund Freud, Vol. 22 (1932–1936)*, 5–182. Edited by James Strachey and Anna Freud. London: Hogarth Press, 1964.

Gabriel, Markus. *Fields of Sense*. Edinburgh: Edinburgh University Press, 2015.

Gabriel, Markus. *Why the World Does Not Exist*. Translated by Gregory S. Moss. Cambridge: Polity Press, 2015.

Garber, Daniel. *Leibniz: Body, Substance, Monad*. Oxford: Oxford University Press, 2009.

Gaston, Sean. *The Concept of World from Kant to Derrida*. London: Rowman & Littlefield, 2013.

Genette, Gérard. 'Métonymie chez Proust.' In *Figures III*, 41–63. Paris: Éditions du Seuil, 1972.

Genette, Gérard. *Narrative Discourse: An Essay in Method.* Translated by Jane E. Lewin. Ithaca, NY: Cornell University Press, 1980.

Genette, Gérard. 'Proust et le langage indirect.' In *Figures II*, 223–94. Paris: Éditions du Seuil, 1969.

Germek, Magdalena. 'The Dialectic of Formalization.' *Filozofski vestnik* 42, no. 1 (2021): 25–47. https://doi.org/10.3986/fv.42.1.02

Glissant, Édouard. *Treatise on the Whole-World.* Translated by Celia Britton. Liverpool: Liverpool University Press, 2020.

Goodman, Nelson. *Ways of Worldmaking.* Indianapolis: Hackett, 1978.

Habermas, Jürgen. *The Philosophical Discourse of Modernity.* Translated by Frederick G. Lawrence. Cambridge: Polity Press, 1987.

Hägglund, Martin. *Dying for Time: Proust, Woolf, Nabokov.* Cambridge, MA: Harvard University Press, 2012.

Hallward, Peter. *Badiou: A Subject to Truth.* Minneapolis: University of Minnesota Press, 2003.

Hallward, Peter. 'Staging Equality: Rancière's Theatrocracy and the Limits of Anarchic Equality.' In *Jacques Rancière: History, Politics, Aesthetics*, edited by Gabriel Rockhill and Philip Watts, 140–57. Durham, NC: Duke University Press, 2009.

Harvey, David. *Cosmopolitanism and the Geographies of Freedom.* New York: Columbia University Press, 2009.

Heidegger, Martin. 'The Age of the World Picture.' In *Off the Beaten Track*, 57–85. Edited and translated by Julian Young and Kenneth Haynes. Cambridge: Cambridge University Press, 2002.

Heidegger, Martin. *Basic Writings.* Edited by David Farrell Krell. San Francisco: Harper, 1993.

Heidegger, Martin. *Being and Time.* Translated by Joan Stambaugh. Albany: State University of New York Press, 2010.

Heidegger, Martin. *The Fundamental Concepts of Metaphysics: World, Finitude, Solitude.* Translated by William McNeill and Nicholas Walker. Bloomington: Indiana University Press, 1995.

Heidegger, Martin. *Introduction to Metaphysics.* Translated by Gregory Fried and Richard Polt. New Haven: Yale University Press, 2014.

Heidegger, Martin. 'Letter on Humanism.' In *Basic Writings*, 213–65.

Heidegger, Martin. 'The Origin of the Work of Art.' In *Basic Writings*, 139–212.

Held, David. 'Cosmopolitanism in a Multipolar World.' In *After Cosmopolitanism*, edited by Braidotti, Hanafin and Blaagaard, 28–39.

Husserl, Edmund. *The Crisis of European Sciences and Transcendental Phenomenology*. Translated by David Carr. Evanston: Northwestern University Press, 1970.

Husserl, Edmund. *Ideas Pertaining to a Pure Phenomenology and to a Phenomenological Philosophy, Second Book: Studies in the Phenomenology of Constitution*. Translated by Richard Rojcewicz and Andre Schuwer. Dordrecht: Kluwer Academic Publishers, 1989.

Ingram, James D. *Radical Cosmopolitics: The Ethics and Politics of Democratic Universalism*. New York: Columbia University Press, 2013.

Jakobson, Roman. 'Two Aspects of Language and Two Types of Aphasic Disturbances.' In *On Language*, 115–33. Edited by Linda R. Waugh and Monique Monville-Burston. Cambridge, MA: Harvard University Press, 1990.

Jameson, Fredric. *The Geopolitical Aesthetic: Cinema and Space in the World System*. Bloomington: Indiana University Press, 1995.

Johnston, Adrian. '"Naturalism or Anti-Naturalism? No, Thanks – Both Are Worse!": Science, Materialism, and Slavoj Žižek.' *Revue internationale de philosophie* 261, no. 3 (2012): 321–46.

Kant, Immanuel. 'An Answer to the Question What Is Enlightenment?' In *Toward Perpetual Peace*, 17–23.

Kant, Immanuel. 'The Contest of the Faculties, Part 2.' In *Toward Perpetual Peace*, 150–63.

Kant, Immanuel. *Critique of Pure Reason*. Translated by Paul Guyer. Cambridge: Cambridge University Press, 1998.

Kant, Immanuel. 'Idea for a Universal History from a Cosmopolitan Perspective.' In *Toward Perpetual Peace*, 3–16.

Kant, Immanuel. 'Toward Perpetual Peace: A Philosophical Sketch.' In *Toward Perpetual Peace*, 67–109.

Kant, Immanuel. *Toward Perpetual Peace and Other Writings on Politics, Peace, and History*. Edited by Pauline Kleingeld. Translated by David L. Colclasure. New Haven: Yale University Press, 2006.

Koyré, Alexandre. *From the Closed World to the Infinite Universe*. Baltimore: Johns Hopkins University Press, 1957.

Lacan, Jacques. *Anxiety: The Seminar of Jacques Lacan, Book X*. Translated by A. R. Price. Cambridge: Polity, 2014.

Lacan, Jacques. 'L'étourdit.' In *Autres Écrits*, 449–95. Paris: Seuil, 2001.

Lacan, Jacques. *The Four Fundamental Concepts of Psychoanalysis: The Seminar of Jacques Lacan, Book XI.* Translated by Alan Sheridan. New York: W. W. Norton, 1981.
Lacan, Jacques. *On Feminine Sexuality: The Limits of Love and Knowledge: The Seminar of Jacques Lacan, Book XX: Encore.* Translated by Bruce Fink. New York: W. W. Norton, 1998.
Lacan, Jacques. *Television: A Challenge to Psychoanalytic Establishment.* Translated by Denis Hollier, Rosalind Krauss, Annette Michelson and Jeffrey Mehlman. New York: W. W. Norton, 1990.
Lacan, Jacques. 'The Third.' Translated by Philip Oravers. *The Lacanian Review: Hurly-Burly* 7 (2019): 83–108.
Lacan, Jacques. *The Triumph of Religion, Preceded by Discourse to Catholics.* Translated by Bruce Fink. Cambridge: Polity, 2013.
Lecercle, Jean-Jacques. *Badiou and Deleuze Read Literature.* Edinburgh: Edinburgh University Press, 2010.
Lecercle, Jean-Jacques. 'Error/Mirror: How to Generate Fiction.' In *Literature and Error: A Literary Take on Mistakes and Errors*, edited by Marc Porée and Isabelle Alfandary, 109–22. New York: Peter Lang, 2018.
Lecercle, Jean-Jacques. *Interpretation as Pragmatics.* New York: St. Martin's Press, 1999.
Leibniz, G. W. 'Discourse on Metaphysics.' In *Philosophical Essays*, 35–69.
Leibniz, G. W. *The Leibniz-Arnauld Correspondence.* Edited and translated by H. T. Mason. Manchester: Manchester University Press, 1967.
Leibniz, G. W. *The Leibniz-Clarke Correspondence.* Edited by H. G. Alexander. Manchester: Manchester University Press, 1956.
Leibniz, G. W. 'A New System of the Nature and Communication of Substances, and of the Union of the Soul and Body.' In *Philosophical Essays*, 138–45.
Leibniz, G. W. 'The Philosopher's Confession.' Translated by Lloyd Strickland. Leibniz Translations. Accessed 13 September 2019. http://www.leibniz-translations.com/confession.htm
Leibniz, G. W. *Philosophical Essays.* Translated by Roger Ariew and Daniel Garber. Indianapolis: Hackett, 1989.
Leibniz, G. W. *Philosophical Papers and Letters.* Translated by Leroy E. Loemker. Dordrecht: Kluwer, 1989.

Leibniz, G. W. 'The Principles of Philosophy, or, the Monadology.' In *Philosophical Essays*, 213–25.

Leibniz, G. W. *Theodicy: Essays on the Goodness of God, the Freedom of Man and the Origin of Evil*. Translated by E. M. Huggard. Project Gutenberg, 2005. https://www.gutenberg.org/files/17147/17147-h/17147-h.htm

Longo, Anna. 'Virtual Time and Possible Worlds: The Madness of the Real.' *Scenari* 8 (2018): 116–25.

Lukács, Georg. 'Narrate or Describe?' In *Writer & Critic and Other Essays*, 110–48. Edited and translated by Arthur D. Kahn. New York: Grosset & Dunlap, 1971.

Macherey, Pierre. *Proust entre littérature et philosophie*. Paris: Éditions Amsterdam, 2013.

Martin, Jean-Clet. *Plurivers. Essai sur la fin du monde*. Paris: PUF, 2010.

Marx, Karl. 'Letter from Marx to Arnold Ruge, September 1843.' Marxists Internet Archives. Accessed 13 September 2019. https://www.marxists.org/archive/marx/works/1843/letters/43_09-alt.htm

Mbembe, Achille. 'Afropolitanism.' In *Cosmopolitanisms*, edited by Bruce Robbins and Paulo Lemos Horta, 102–7. New York: New York University Press, 2017.

Mbembe, Achille. *Critique of Black Reason*. Translated by Laurent Dubois. Durham, NC: Duke University Press, 2017.

Meillassoux, Quentin. *After Finitude: An Essay on the Necessity of Contingency*. Translated by Ray Brassier. London: Continuum, 2008.

Nancy, Jean-Luc. *Being Singular Plural*. Translated by Robert D. Richardson and Anne E. O'Byrne. Stanford: Stanford University Press, 2000.

Nancy, Jean-Luc. *The Creation of the World, or Globalization*. Translated by François Raffoul and David Pettigrew. Albany: State University of New York Press, 2007.

Nancy, Jean-Luc. *The Possibility of a World: Conversations with Pierre-Philippe Jandin*. Translated by Travis Holloway and Flor Méchain. New York: Fordham University Press, 2017.

Nancy, Jean-Luc. *The Sense of the World*. Translated by Jeffrey S. Librett. Minneapolis: University of Minnesota Press, 1997.

Nesbitt, Nick. 'Capital, Logic of the World.' In 'The Concept of World in Contemporary Philosophy', edited by Rok Benčin, special issue, *Filozofski Vestnik* 42, no. 2 (2021): 159–91. https://doi.org/10.3986/fv.42.2.08

Nussbaum, Martha C. 'Kant and Cosmopolitanism.' In *Perpetual Peace: Essays on Kant's Cosmopolitan Ideal*, edited by James Bohman and Matthias Lutz-Bachmann, 25–57. Cambridge, MA: MIT Press, 1997.

Oliver, Kelly. *Earth and World: Philosophy after the Apollo Missions*. New York: Columbia University Press, 2015.

Pinker, Steven. *Enlightenment Now: The Case for Reason, Science, Humanism, and Progress*. New York: Viking, 2018.

Pollock, Sheldon, Homi K. Bhabha, Carol A. Breckenridge and Dipesh Chakrabarty. 'Cosmopolitanisms.' In *Cosmopolitanism*, edited by Carol A. Breckenridge, Sheldon Pollock, Homi K. Bhabha and Dipesh Chakrabarty, 1–14. Durham, NC: Duke University Press, 2002.

Proust, Marcel. 'About Flaubert's Style.' In *A Selection from his Miscellaneous Writings*, 224–40. Edited and translated by Gerard Hopkins. London: Allan Wingate, 1948.

Proust, Marcel. *Finding Time Again: In Search of Lost Time, Volume 6*. Translated by Ian Patterson. London: Penguin Books, 2003.

Proust, Marcel. *The Guermantes Way: In Search of Lost Time, Volume 3*. Translated by Mark Treharne. London: Penguin Books, 2003.

Proust, Marcel. *In the Shadow of Young Girls in Flower: In Search of Lost Time, Volume 2*. Translated by James Grieve. London: Penguin Books, 2003.

Proust, Marcel. *The Prisoner and The Fugitive: In Search of Lost Time, Volume 5*. Translated by Carol Clark and Peter Collier. London: Penguin Books, 2003.

Proust, Marcel. *Sodom and Gomorrah: In Search of Lost Time, Volume 4*. Translated by John Sturrock. London: Penguin Books, 2003.

Proust, Marcel. *The Way by Swann's: In Search of Lost Time, Volume 1*. Translated by Lydia Davis. London: Penguin Books, 2003.

Rabachou, Julien. *Qu'est-ce qu'un monde?* Paris: Vrin, 2016.

Rancière, Jacques. 'The Aesthetic Revolution.' *Maska* 32, nos. 185–6 (2017): 24–31.

Rancière, Jacques. *Aesthetics and its Discontents*. Translated by Steven Corcoran. Cambridge: Polity, 2009.

Rancière, Jacques. *The Aesthetics of Politics*. Translated by Gabriel Rockhill. London: Continuum, 2006.

Rancière, Jacques. *Aisthesis: Scenes from the Aesthetic Regime of Art*. Translated by Zakir Paul. London: Verso, 2013.

Rancière, Jacques. 'Communists Without Communism?' In *The Idea of Communism*, edited by Costas Douzinas and Slavoj Žižek, 167–77. London: Verso, 2010.

Rancière, Jacques. *Disagreement: Politics and Philosophy*. Translated by Julie Rose. Minneapolis: University of Minnesota Press, 1999.

Rancière, Jacques. *Dissensus: On Politics and Aesthetics*. Edited and translated by Steven Corcoran. London: Continuum, 2010.

Rancière, Jacques. *The Flesh of Words: The Politics of Writing*. Translated by Charlotte Mandell. Stanford: Stanford University Press, 2004.

Rancière, Jacques. *The Future of the Image*. Translated by Gregory Elliott. London: Verso, 2007.

Rancière, Jacques. *The Lost Thread: The Democracy of Modern Fiction*. Translated by Steven Corcoran. London: Bloomsbury, 2017.

Rancière, Jacques. *Modern Times: Essays on Temporality in Art and Politics*. Zagreb: Multimedijalni institut, 2017.

Rancière, Jacques. 'The Monument and its Confidences; or Deleuze and Art's Capacity of "Resistance".' In *Dissensus*, 169–83.

Rancière, Jacques. *Mute Speech: Literature, Critical Theory, and Politics*. Translated by James Swenson. New York: Columbia University Press, 2011.

Rancière, Jacques. 'The People or the Multitudes.' In *Dissensus*, 84–90.

Rancière, Jacques. 'A Politics of Aesthetic Indetermination: An Interview with Frank Ruda and Jan Voelker.' In *Everything Is in Everything: Jacques Rancière between Intellectual Emancipation and Aesthetic Education*, edited by Jason E. Smith and Annette Weisser, 10–33. Pasadena: Art Center Graduate Press/JRP, 2011.

Rancière, Jacques. *Politique de la littérature*. Paris: Galilée, 2007.

Rancière, Jacques. 'Re-politicizing 68.' *Crisis and Critique* 5, no. 2 (2018): 285–99. https://www.crisiscritique.org/storage/app/media/2018-11-29/ranciere.pdf

Rancière, Jacques. 'Ten Theses on Politics.' In *Dissensus*, 27–44.

Rescher, Nicholas. 'Leibniz on Possible Worlds.' *Studia Leibnitiana* 28, no. 2 (1996): 129–62. http://www.jstor.org/stable/40694300

Rescher, Nicholas. *G. W. Leibniz's Monadology: An Edition for Students*. Pittsburgh: University of Pittsburgh Press, 1991.

Roffe, Jon. *Badiou's Deleuze*. London: Routledge, 2014.

Ronen, Ruth. 'The Actuality of a World: What Ceases Not to Be Written.' In 'The Concept of World in Contemporary Philosophy', edited by Rok Benčin, special issue, *Filozofski Vestnik* 42, no. 2 (2021): 93–112. https://doi.org/10.3986/fv.42.2.05

Ronen, Ruth. *Possible Worlds in Literary Theory*. Cambridge: Cambridge University Press, 1994.
Ross, Kristin. *Communal Luxury: The Political Imaginary of the Paris Commune*. London: Verso, 2015.
Rubenstein, Mary-Jane. *Worlds Without End: The Many Lives of the Multiverse*. New York: Columbia University Press, 2014.
Schaap, Andrew. 'Enacting the Right to Have Rights: Jacques Rancière's Critique of Hannah Arendt.' *European Journal of Political Theory* 10, no. 1 (2011): 22–45. https://doi.org/10.1177/1474885110386004
Schiller, Friedrich von. *Letters on the Aesthetic Education of Man*. Translated by Elizabeth M. Wilkinson and L. A. Willoughby. Oxford: Clarendon Press, 1967.
Selasi, Taiye. 'Bye-Bye Babar.' *Callaloo* 36, no. 3 (2013): 529.
Serres, Michel. *Le système de Leibniz et ses modèles mathématiques*. Paris: PUF, 1968.
Servigne, Pablo, Raphaël Stevens and Gauthier Chapelle. *Another End of the World Is Possible: Living the Collapse (and Not Merely Surviving It)*. Translated by Geoffrey Samuel. Cambridge: Polity Press, 2021.
Simont, Juliette. 'Critique de la représentation et ontologie chez Deleuze et Badiou (Autour du "virtuel").' In *Alain Badiou: Penser le multiple*, edited by Charles Ramond, 457–76. Paris: L'Harmattan, 2002.
Smith, James A. 'Steven Pinker and Jordan Peterson: The Missing Link between Neoliberalism and the Radical Right.' *Open Democracy*, 1 November 2018. https://www.opendemocracy.net/en/steven-pinker-jordan-peterson-neoliberalism-radical-right
Sousa Santos, Boaventura de. 'Beyond Neoliberal Governance: The World Social Forum as Subaltern Cosmopolitan Politics and Legality.' In *Law and Globalization from Below: Towards a Cosmopolitan Legality*, edited by Boaventura de Sousa Santos and César A. Rodríguez-Garavito, 29–63. Cambridge: Cambridge University Press, 2005.
Šumič, Jelica. 'The For-All: Grappling with the Real of the Group.' *Crisis and Critique* 6, no. 1 (2019): 313–39. https://www.crisiscritique.org/storage/app/media/2019-04-02/jsumic.pdf
Šumič, Jelica. 'Politics and Psychoanalysis in the Times of the Inexistent Other.' In *Jacques Lacan between Psychoanalysis and Politics*, edited by Samo Tomšič and Andreja Zevnik, 28–42. London: Routledge, 2016.
Tassin, Étienne. *Un monde commun. Pour une cosmo-politique des conflits*. Paris: Seuil, 2003.

Tho, Tzuchien. 'The Void Just Ain't (What It Used to Be): Void, Infinity, and the Indeterminate.' In 'The Structure of the Void', edited by Mladen Dolar et al., special issue, *Filozofski vestnik* 34, no. 2 (2013): 27–48. https://ojs.zrc-sazu.si/filozofski-vestnik/article/view/3252/2969

Thomas, Allan James. *Deleuze, Cinema and the Thought of the World*. Edinburgh: Edinburgh University Press, 2018.

Tomšič, Samo. 'From the Orderly World to the Polluted Unworld.' In *Objective Fictions: Philosophy, Psychoanalysis, Marxism*, edited by Adrian Johnston, Boštjan Nedoh and Alenka Zupančič, 65–84. Edinburgh: Edinburgh University Press, 2022.

Toscano, Alberto. 'From the State to the World: Badiou and Anti-Capitalism.' *Communication & Cognition* 37, nos. 3–4 (2004): 199–224.

Toscano, Alberto, and Jeff Kinkle. *Cartographies of the Absolute*. Winchester: Zero Books, 2015.

Vartabedian, Becky. *Multiplicity and Ontology in Deleuze and Badiou*. London: Palgrave Macmillan, 2018.

Végső, Roland. 'On Acosmic Realism.' In 'The Concept of World in Contemporary Philosophy', edited by Rok Benčin, special issue, *Filozofski vestnik* 42, no. 2 (2021): 71–92. https://doi.org/10.3986/fv.42.2.04

Végső, Roland. *Worldlessness After Heidegger: Phenomenology, Psychoanalysis, Deconstruction*. Edinburgh: Edinburgh University Press, 2020.

Wajcman, Gérard. *Fenêtre. Chroniques du regard et de l'intime*. Paris: Verdier, 2004.

Winckelmann, Johann Joachim. *The History of Ancient Art, Vol. II*. Translated by G. Henry Lodge. Boston: James R. Osgood and Company, 1880.

Wittgenstein, Ludwig. *Tractatus Logico-Philosophicus*. Translated by D. F. Pears and B. F. McGuinness. London: Routledge, 2002.

Žižek, Slavoj. *In Defense of Lost Causes*. London: Verso, 2008.

Žižek, Slavoj. *Less Than Nothing: Hegel and the Shadow of Dialectical Materialism*. London: Verso, 2012.

Žižek, Slavoj. *The Parallax View*. Cambridge, MA: MIT Press, 2006.

Žižek, Slavoj, and Glyn Daly. *Conversations with Žižek*. Cambridge: Polity Press, 2004.

Zupančič, Alenka. *What Is Sex?* Cambridge, MA: MIT Press, 2017.

Index

action, 3, 5, 24, 81, 105–6, 115–19, 122–3, 125–6, 129–30, 198–9, 201
actualisation, 10, 40, 50, 61, 63, 71, 73–4, 76, 78, 80, 83, 97, 143
  counteractualisation, 73, 83
Adorno, Theodor W., 6, 12, 114, 132n, 139, 148–54, 164
aesthetics, 6, 12–13, 98, 137–9, 144, 148–58, 195, 199, 201
  inaesthetics, 165, 190n
  transcendental, 41, 185
  see also art, aesthetic regime of
Alberti, Leon Battista, 148, 159n
animal, 28, 31–2, 58, 63, 117, 125, 168, 182, 197
Anthropocene, 200–1, 207n
appearance, 1, 21–2, 35, 38–9, 43, 64, 74, 76, 91–7, 119, 138, 145–6, 152–3, 165, 168, 170–1, 174–9, 183, 187–9, 195, 197, 200, 203–5

Appiah, Kwame Anthony, 114
Arendt, Hannah, 2, 5, 9, 30, 36, 81, 105–6, 116–23, 125, 197
Aristotle, 125, 129, 155, 158
Arrival, 205–6
art, 6, 12, 21, 39, 96, 137–9, 144, 148–56
  aesthetic regime of, 12, 154–7
  autonomy of, 139, 148, 151, 153–4
  representational regime of, 156
Arthur, Richard T. W., 67n

Badiou, Alain, 4–13, 19–20, 22–3, 35, 38–40, 42–3, 52, 59–60, 62–5, 69–77, 84–98, 114, 138–9, 143–7, 152, 164–5, 168–70, 172–5, 177, 181–4, 186–9, 195, 197–200, 202–3
Balibar, Étienne, 134n
Barthes, Roland, 159n
Beck, Ulrich, 112

becoming, 73, 76, 83, 97–8, 121, 143–4, 155–7, 187, 189
being, 3, 18–9, 26–31, 38–9, 43, 69, 71–4, 76, 82, 84–98, 119–20, 138, 145, 156, 165, 168, 175–6, 183, 187–8, 196–7, 204–5
  being-in-the-world, 2–4, 23, 26–7, 30, 36, 78, 105–6, 118, 124
  being-there, 26, 30, 36, 91–2, 145, 172; see also Dasein
  being-with, 30, 36, 39, 120, 122
  univocity of, 10, 71–2, 74, 78, 80, 83
  see also difference, ontological; multiplicity, ontological; ontology
Benjamin, Walter, 160n
Besana, Bruno, 162n
Bhabha, Homi K., 114
Birnbaum, Antonia, 121, 131
Borges, Jorge Luis, 78–9, 82, 144, 159n
Bowie, Malcolm, 177
Breckenridge, Carol A., 114
Bryant, Levi R., 21, 23, 42, 45n

capitalism, 5, 11, 30, 34, 43, 96, 105–6, 114–15, 119–20, 151, 196–202
Celan, Paul, 33, 48n
Chakrabarty, Dipesh, 144
chaosmos, 6, 10–11, 76, 78–83, 97–8, 144
Chiang, Ted, 205
compossibility, 20, 36, 40, 55, 60–1, 77, 121, 141–3; see also incompossibility

contingency, 38–9, 50, 52, 54, 59, 73–4, 89, 92–3, 97, 123, 128, 141–3, 167–9, 175, 178–9, 181–2, 184–5, 206n
correlationism, 3, 14n, 187
  hypercorrelationism, 3, 195–6, 200
cosmogony, aesthetic, 12, 164–6, 183, 185
cosmopolitanism, 5, 11–12, 104–16, 119, 122, 125–6, 128
  Kantian, 105, 107–12, 128
  postcolonial critique of, 112–15
  stoic, 104, 107
cosmos, 10, 16–17, 19–20, 40–4, 61, 76–7, 80, 112–4, 205
  destruction of, 1, 5, 8, 15n, 16–17, 24, 35, 104, 111, 195
count-as-one, 10, 84–90
creation, 36, 54–5, 57, 59–60, 63, 78, 82, 121, 127, 138, 155, 159n, 166, 175, 183–5, 188

Dasein, 3, 26–30, 34, 36, 39, 44, 78, 200
Descartes, René, 53
Deleuze, Gilles, 4, 6–7, 9–10, 12, 35, 39–40, 43, 52, 59–65, 69–84, 87, 97–8, 137–9, 143–5, 152, 155–6, 164, 166, 170, 173, 177, 190–3n
Derrida, Jacques, 9, 30–4, 36, 39
difference, 61, 64, 75–6, 82–3
  ontological, 29, 31, 71–2, 75, 86–7, 156–7
  sensible, 156

Diogenes the Cynic, 104
dissensus, 5, 107, 124–8, 131, 162n, 201, 204
distribution of the sensible, 6, 124, 127–30, 152–3, 156
divergence, 3–4, 7, 17, 36, 40–1, 43–4, 60, 62–4, 71, 75, 77–83, 97–8, 107, 143, 145, 176, 179, 184, 195–7, 205
Douzinas, Costas, 112

Enlightenment, 108–14, 128, 132n
enthusiasm, 110–11, 130
equality, 5, 7, 89, 125, 128–30, 155; see also inequality
event, 63–4, 70–1, 73–4, 77–8, 80, 82, 86, 89–90, 92–7, 100n, 103n, 108, 110–11, 124, 129–30, 140–4, 155, 157–8, 159n, 165, 174, 176–9, 203
experience, 1–2, 4, 7, 19, 23–8, 30, 32, 34, 36, 44, 85, 98, 105, 107–110, 115, 118–20, 123, 127, 132n, 138–9, 155, 170, 177, 180, 183, 189, 196, 201
  existential, 2–3, 39, 42, 82, 115, 117, 121
  horizon of, 2, 7–8, 17, 26, 44, 82, 105, 115, 119, 121, 195, 199–200
  possible, 12, 137, 152, 155, 185, 193n, 206
  real, 137–8, 144, 193n
  sensible, 124, 137, 152–4, 157, 173, 178–9, 182, 188, 195
  shared, 5, 7, 17, 32, 105, 116

fiction, category of, 6–7, 11–12, 34, 43, 98, 105, 107–12, 119, 124, 128–31, 137–47, 154, 156, 162n, 163–4, 169–70, 186–7, 195–6; see also world(s), fictional
fiction, literary see literature
Fischbach, Frank, 101n
Flaubert, Gustave, 155, 157, 185
Foucault, Michel, 109, 112, 114, 124–5, 132n
Freud, Sigmund, 18

Gabriel, Markus, 2, 8, 21–4, 42
Garber, Daniel, 66n
Gaston, Sean, 14n, 31
Genette, Gérard, 164, 173, 180–1, 183, 187–8
Germek, Magdalena, 90
Glissant, Édouard, 114
globalisation, 4–5, 30, 34–5, 37, 105–6, 112, 115–16, 119–20, 123; see also capitalism
Goodman, Nelson, 14n
Guattari, Félix, 70, 83, 191n

Habermas, Jürgen, 112–13, 126
Hägglund, Martin, 194n
Hallward, Peter, 85, 183–4
harmony
  pre-established, 6, 9, 20, 56–7, 64, 92, 141, 148–52, 155, 205
  pre-established disharmony, 149
Harvey, David, 113
Heidegger, Martin, 2–3, 9, 23, 26–35, 38, 44, 73, 78, 84, 118–19, 138

history, 4, 11, 40–1, 105, 107–14, 119–20, 128–30, 148–9, 160n; *see also* narrative, history as
Husserl, Edmund, 2–3, 9, 23–7, 30, 34, 44, 75

incompossibility, 10, 13, 40, 43, 51, 60, 62–3, 71, 75, 77–82, 97, 127, 143–4, 196, 204
inexistent, the, 93–6, 175–8, 184, 187–9
inequality, 5, 35, 41, 128–9, 161n

Jakobson, Roman, 173
Jameson, Fredric, 199
Johnston, Adrian, 20, 45n
Joyce, James, 19, 76, 144

Kant, Immanuel, 1, 3, 11, 34, 61, 75, 77, 92, 104–5, 107–14, 116, 124, 128, 130, 132–3n, 138, 153, 185
Kinkle, Jeff, 199
Koyré, Alexandre, 1, 15n, 16–17, 105

Lacan, Jacques, 2, 8, 18–20, 22–4, 40–1, 43, 49n, 90, 102n, 145–6, 202, 206n
Lecercle, Jean-Jacques, 141, 147, 163–5, 190n
Leibniz, G. W., 3–4, 6, 9–10, 20, 35–6, 38, 40, 44, 50–65, 65–7n, 69–70, 75, 77–82, 84–5, 91–2, 138–44, 148–50, 152, 166–7, 195, 199
literary theory, 6, 12, 138–40, 143, 146, 164

literature, 6, 12, 19, 78, 107–8, 137, 139–42, 144, 155, 157, 159n, 163–6, 190n
Longo, Anna, 100n
Lukács, Georg, 155

Macherey, Pierre, 182–3, 185
Marx, Karl, 89–90, 114–5, 119–20, 200
Mbembe, Achille, 88n, 114
Meillassoux, Quentin, 14n, 100n
metaphor, 131, 166, 173, 178, 180–4, 188–9
metonymy, 130–1, 134, 173–4, 178, 180–1, 188–9
modernism, 155
modernity, 8, 10, 16–17, 29, 37, 81, 104–5, 115–16, 118–19, 121
monad, 3–4, 9, 35–6, 40, 49n, 52, 55–61, 64, 66–7n, 77–9, 87, 160n
  artwork as, 6, 12, 139, 148–52, 154–6, 205–6
  see also object, monadic
multiplicity
  consistent, 84–90
  inconsistent, 38, 74, 84–93
  ontological, 3–4, 9–11, 13, 35, 38–40, 52–4, 58–65, 69–98, 106, 131, 145, 147, 170, 172, 186, 195–7, 202, 204, 206
  sensible, 6, 128, 131, 154–7, 185, 192n
  transcendental, 3, 10, 40, 69–98, 195, 197, 201
  see also world(s), multiplicity of

Nancy, Jean-Luc, 4–5, 7, 9, 11, 30, 36–9, 43–4, 106, 120–1, 123, 197–8, 206n
narrative, 138–9, 146, 153, 157–8, 162n, 166, 181, 186–9
  history as, 105, 108, 111, 113–4, 119, 121, 128–31, 134n
narratology, 6, 164
negativity, 90–1
Nesbitt, Nick, 200
Nietzsche, Friedrich, 78, 82, 144
Nussbaum, Martha C., 112–13

object
  contested, 13, 127, 196, 201, 204–5
  of desire, 41, 175, 177
  of love, 13, 172–6, 188
  monadic, 12–13, 139, 150–2, 158, 179–80, 183, 186, 189, 194n, 196, 205–6
ontology, 18–22, 45n, 58, 63, 70, 72, 76, 84–92, 140, 155–6, 157, 165
  poetic, 38, 72, 84–6, 90, 138
  of the present, 103n, 109
  subtractive, 58, 72–3, 84, 98, 138
  vitalist, 63, 70, 84, 138, 157
  see also being; difference, ontological; multiplicity, ontological
onto-poetics, 138, 155–7

Paris Commune, 93, 130, 203–4
perception, 5, 11, 23, 41, 106, 124, 137–8, 155, 199, 201, 206
  of the monads, 55–7

phenomena, inter-worldly, 7, 13, 80, 94, 96–8, 103n, 196–7, 202–6; *see also* object, contested, monadic
phenomenology, 2–3, 5, 8–9, 14, 23–31, 34–6, 38, 41, 44, 82, 101n, 105–6, 117–24, 195, 198–200, 202
  Badiou's objective, 91–2, 165, 170, 200
Pinker, Steven, 132–3n
Plato, 38, 49n, 75–6
plurality, 7, 36, 43–4, 106, 117–21, 198; *see also*, world(s), plurality of
politics, 4–5, 11–12, 29–30, 35, 38–9, 41–3, 73, 88–9, 93, 104–6, 111, 113–31, 136, 138, 153–4, 156, 161n, 195, 197–9, 201–4
  as a conflict of worlds, 5, 11, 41, 106, 126; *see also* world(s), conflict of
  emancipatory, 5, 12, 35, 89, 103n, 106, 113, 122, 125, 128, 161n, 199, 201–2, 204
  political conflict, 7, 98, 122, 126
  see also subject, political subjectivation
Pollock, Sheldon, 114
progress, 105, 108–11, 113–15, 119, 128–30, 132–4n
prose, 146, 165, 173, 188, 190n; *see also* world(s), prose of
Proust, Marcel, 12–13, 137–8, 163–89, 205
psychoanalysis, 8, 14n, 18–19, 22, 40–1

Rancière, Jacques, 4–6, 9, 11–12, 41, 43, 106, 122–31, 135n, 147, 152–8, 161–2n
real, the, 7, 18–23, 43, 71, 145, 150, 184
realism
  in literature, 130, 155, 157
  in philosophy, 3, 6, 8, 14n, 18, 21–3, 45n, 187
reality
  and appearance, 153; *see also* appearance
  of appearances, 22; *see also* appearance
  artistic presentation of, 166; *see also* art
  chaosmotic, 80; *see also* chaosmos
  common, 5, 11, 41, 106, 124
  constitution of, 4, 184
  cosmological, 65n
  detachment from, 183
  empirical, 148–9
  existence of, 1, 18
  experience of, 2, 7, 36; *see also* experience
  explored by science, 119; *see also* science
  external, 1–2, 140, 148, 185
  and fiction, 187; *see also* fiction
  fictional, 140–1; *see also* fiction
  global, 4, 11; *see also* globalisation
  incompleteness of, 20
  inter-worldly, 97; *see also* phenomena, inter-worldly
  levels of, 52
  material, 9, 58–9
  natural, 24, 107
  nature of, 17–18, 23
  non-totalisable, 22
  objective, 24, 107
  of objects, 196; *see also* object
  ontological, 4, 42, 61, 106, 147, 205; *see also* ontology
  parallel, 3
  perception of, 3
  physical, 18
  possible, 77
  reality effect, 159n
  representational construction of, 71, 155; *see also* representation
  sense of, 124
  sensible, 126; *see also* multiplicity, sensible
  social, 103n, 106–7, 116, 150, 154, 201–2; *see also* society
  submission to, 82
  transcendental arrangement of, 147, 206; *see also* transcendental
  as whole, 18
representation, 71–6, 82–4, 87–91, 94, 128, 138, 148–9, 152, 155–7, 159n, 197, 199, 201; *see also* art, representational regime of
Rescher, Nicholas, 66n
revolution, 109–12, 185
  aesthetic, 152, 154–6; *see also* art, aesthetic regime of
  French, 110–11, 130
  scientific, 1, 3, 15n, 18–19, 117; *see also* science
Ronen, Ruth, 139–40, 206n
Ross, Kristin, 203

Schiller, Friedrich von, 152–3
science, 1–2, 8, 11, 15n, 18–20, 22, 24–6, 29–30, 34, 39, 42, 73, 105, 107–8, 117, 119, 177, 184; *see also* revolution, scientific
Selasi, Taiye, 114
sense, 3, 30, 37–9, 43–4, 49n, 71
  field of, 21–3, 42
Serres, Michel, 58
Simont, Juliette, 73
singularity, 4, 7, 9–10, 36, 39–40, 60–1, 63, 71–2, 74–80, 83, 88, 97, 100n, 106, 114–16, 119–22, 125, 128, 142–4, 147, 154–7, 185
society, 2, 5–6, 11, 24–5, 89, 103n, 106–7, 110–12, 115, 122, 127–31, 137, 148–54, 196–203
Sousa Santos, Boaventura de, 114
Spinoza, 53, 55
style, 146, 155, 157, 166, 173, 180, 183–5, 191n
subject, 14n, 24, 26, 29, 41, 49n, 102, 113, 115, 119, 124–5, 146, 159, 182–3, 189, 201, 205–6
  political subjectivation, 5, 12, 41–3, 106, 111, 114, 123, 127–31, 134, 202–4
  subjectivation of reason, 109, 111, 114, 128
  of truth, 39, 73, 88–9, 93–7, 174, 182–3, 187, 189
substance, 3–4, 9, 51–9, 66n, 85, 150; *see also* monad
Šumič, Jelica, 89, 202

Tassin, Étienne, 118, 121–3
technology, 2, 4, 14, 15n, 24, 29–30, 34, 44, 117
temporality, 6, 12, 40, 51–2, 65n, 80, 129–30, 144, 146, 166–70, 173, 176–8, 180–4, 188–9, 194n, 195, 206
Tho, Tzuchien, 85–6, 90
Thomas, Allan James, 82
time *see* temporality
Tomšič, Samo, 19
Toscano, Alberto, 103n, 198–9
totality, 1–5, 7, 13–15, 16–17, 19, 21–4, 26, 29, 32–3, 36–7, 42–4, 50–3, 55, 63, 78–80, 82, 97, 100n, 106, 115–16, 121, 130–1, 147, 149–50, 195–7, 199, 201
transcendental, the, 3, 6–7, 11–13, 61, 74, 92–6, 103n, 126–8, 130–1, 139, 145, 147, 151, 170–2, 174–80, 186, 196, 198, 200–6
transcendental field, 10, 40, 61–2, 74, 76–7, 83, 97
transcendental folding, 10, 74, 97, 99n
transcendental framework, 3, 7, 36, 39–40, 92–3, 99n, 137–8, 145, 147, 166, 186, 195–7, 199, 201
transcendental (re)framing, 10, 41, 74, 97–8, 99n, 126, 147–8, 152, 158, 186, 205–6

truth, 7, 11, 13, 21, 29, 38–9, 43, 54, 64, 70, 73, 82, 84, 86, 88–90, 92–8, 103n, 114, 139, 142, 145, 148, 150–1, 164, 170, 174–5, 177, 181–4, 186–9, 202–3, 206n; *see also* subject, of truth

universality, 7, 12, 21, 82, 89, 95–7, 103n, 105, 113–15, 122–3, 125, 130, 133n, 187, 196, 202–3
   singular, 95, 187, 203

Végső, Roland, 14n, 21, 23, 27, 29, 33–5, 37, 42, 45n, 48n, 118, 198–9
Villeneuve, Denis, 205
virtuality, 10, 61, 70–1, 73, 76, 78, 80, 82–3, 97–8, 144
void, 63, 72–3, 85–90

Wajcman, Gérard, 159n
Winckelmann, Johann Joachim, 153
Wittgenstein, Ludwig, 2
world(s)
   actual, 4, 6, 8–10, 12, 36, 39, 44, 59, 65, 66n, 69, 74, 80, 98, 137, 139–45, 147, 158, 168–9, 195–6, 206n
   belief in, 75, 81–2
   best of all possible, 4, 9, 51, 53–4, 59–61, 63–4, 77, 167
   bifurcation of, 6–8, 40, 43, 62–3, 82, 95–6, 118, 123, 125, 138, 143–4, 201, 204–5
   coexistence of, 3–4, 9, 17, 36, 40, 43, 79–82, 97–8, 106, 124, 127, 168, 184, 187–8, 195, 204–5
   common, 4–5, 7, 11–12, 30–3, 36, 41, 96, 106, 115–18, 131, 154, 199, 203
   conflict of, 13, 43, 96, 126, 128, 131, 188, 196, 204–5; *see also* politics, as conflict of
   fictional, 6, 12, 131, 139–47, 158, 181, 183–5, 195
   interference between, 6–8, 12–13, 96, 98, 138–9, 147, 187–8, 196–7, 201, 205–6
   life-world, 3, 5, 25–6, 32, 34
   lost, 2, 4–5, 8–9, 11, 17, 23–5, 37–8, 41–4, 45n, 81–3, 106, 115–17, 119–21, 195, 207n
   multiplicity of, 2–13, 14n, 17, 20, 23, 30, 32, 35–44, 50–65, 69–98, 106, 116, 120–3, 125, 127, 131, 137–9, 143–5, 152, 158, 164, 166, 168–9, 171, 176–7, 179, 183, 185, 187–9, 196–7, 200–5, 206n; cosmological, 2, 8–9, 42, 50–1, 65n, 186; logical, 3, 8; modal, 9, 50–2; perspectivist, 9, 52, 56–9; transcendental, 3, 8–12, 41, 74, 186, 196; *see also* multiplicity, transcendental
   obsolete, 1–2, 8–9, 17–23, 35, 42, 80, 195, 207n
   overlapping of, 3, 11, 22, 36, 94, 97, 138, 147, 187–8, 197, 202–3
   play of the, 40, 60, 62, 78–9, 83

plurality of, 12, 23, 36–9, 64, 94, 106, 120–2, 198
possible, 3–4, 6, 9–10, 12, 35–6, 40, 43, 50–4, 59–60, 62, 65–6n, 77, 80, 82, 95, 121, 138–45, 147, 166–7, 192n, 199, 206n
proliferation of, 7, 9, 69, 97, 106, 119, 121, 139, 143, 158, 169, 198, 204
prose of, 7, 12–13, 164–5, 197
shared, 5–6, 12, 24, 32, 44, 119–21
singular, 2, 7, 12, 23, 115–16, 121–23, 169, 187, 194n
surrounding, 12, 23–5, 105, 174, 178, 180
world alienation, 2, 30, 105, 116–19

worldlessness, 4, 7, 14n, 23, 27–9, 33–5, 37, 42, 45n, 103n, 106, 116–19, 121–2, 158, 169, 197–200, 202
worldliness, in Proust, 170–1, 174–5, 182
worldliness (related to the concept of world), 2, 12, 26–7, 29–30, 43, 106, 116–17, 119–20, 124, 145, 197–9, 201
  ideal of, 7, 11, 34–5, 41, 43–4, 106, 121–3, 195, 202
worldview, 5, 18–9, 25, 29, 42–3

Žižek, Slavoj, 8, 20, 90–1, 199, 201

EU representative:
Easy Access System Europe
Mustamäe tee 50, 10621 Tallinn, Estonia
Gpsr.requests@easproject.com

www.ingramcontent.com/pod-product-compliance
Lightning Source LLC
Chambersburg PA
CBHW051122160426
43195CB00014B/2299